REA

ACPL IT
DISCARD

ALLEN COUNTY PUBLIC LIBRARY
3 1833 05426 5

D0345445

MAR 1 3 2008

ONE HELLUVA RIDE

ONE
HELLUVA
RIDE

How NASCAR Swept the Nation

Liz Clarke

 VILLARD BOOKS · NEW YORK

Copyright © 2008 by Liz Clarke

All rights reserved.

Published in the United States by Villard Books,
an imprint of The Random House Publishing Group,
a division of Random House, Inc., New York.

VILLARD and "V" CIRCLED Design are registered
trademarks of Random House, Inc.

Clarke, Liz
One helluva ride: how NASCAR swept the nation/Liz Clarke
p.   cm.
Includes index.
ISBN 978-0-345-49988-2 (hardcover: alk. paper)
1. Stock car racing–United States—History.   2. NASCAR (Association)—
History.   3. Stock cars (Automobiles)—United States.   I. Title.
GV1029.9.S74C53 2008
769.72—dc22
2007043564

34, 34 Where next do you flee © Wendell Scott Jr. Used by permission.

Printed in the United States of America on acid-free paper

www.villard.com

1 2 3 4 5 6 7 8 9

First Edition

Book design by Mary A. Wirth

To the world's best parents, with love and gratitude

FOREWORD

Richard Petty, seven-time NASCAR champion

I've been going to stock-car races since I was eleven years old. First with my dad, Lee Petty, who won three championships in the 1950s, then as a driver myself, for thirty-five years. And since 1992, as a car owner. And the more I've watched, the more I see that every race is different. From the very first race they had to the very last race, the only thing that's the same is that they throw the green flag when it starts, and they throw the checkered flag when it's over.

The magic part of racing is that you get all the sports in one. And everyone can relate to it. You might not play football or baseball or basketball, or you might not golf—but everyone drives a car. And people are car nuts, even if they have just a plain old sedan. Another good thing about racing is you really don't have to understand the rules. A five-year-old can watch a race, and a 105-year-old can watch it. Even if they've never seen it before, they can understand what's going on: cars are passing cars, cars are crashing.

When NASCAR first got started, the cars were the drawing card. No one had ever heard tell of Lee Petty or Fireball Roberts or Junior Johnson. People came to watch the Fords and the Chevrolets and the

Chryslers run. But they got caught up in the excitement of the wrecks, the competition, and the strategy. And over a period of time, the drivers started bringing people in just because of their names—Junior Johnson, Lee Petty, Curtis Turner. It's sort of like if you're a Green Bay Packers fan, you want Green Bay to win the game. But you *go* to watch Brett Favre throw touchdown passes.

I think the majority of people can relate to NASCAR drivers better than they can to other pro athletes because most drivers made it happen for themselves. People can relate to some guy who started running on a quarter-mile track in Oshkosh, Wisconsin, and pulled himself up by his own bootstraps. Fans read about his life story and say, "I know somebody like him." To the general public, racecar drivers are more human—just plain old guys who just happen to drive racecars.

That's what I was, a twenty-one-year-old kid, when I ran in the first Daytona 500 in 1959. I'd never been to a track that big—two and a half miles around—or seen anything like that. It was very impressive. We didn't have any tests at the track before the drivers went down for the race. The first time we took the cars out for practice that week, the flag man told us to just run three or four laps on the flat part of the track. He didn't want us up on the high banks yet because no one was sure what would happen. I went out and ran through Turns 1 and 2 on the flat. I ran through 3 and 4 on the flat. It was no big deal. So I went up on the bank and got black-flagged, which made me the first guy to get black-flagged at Daytona. Nothing scares you when you're twenty-one!

Over the years I drove just about every kind of car, but they all had to perform. The car had to have a decent engine. It had to handle well. It had to have a decent pit crew. There's no *I* in racing, for sure. It's more of a team sport than the average fan thinks. The driver is just the quarterback. And the greatest quarterback in the world is nothing if he doesn't have someone to throw the ball to or hand-off to.

I never really realized the impact of the 1979 Daytona 500, my sixth win in the race, until much later because I was so caught up in running the race. But it was on national television, flag to flag, for the first time. They had a big snowstorm up and down the East Coast, so a lot of people that wouldn't normally tune in were watching. And it was a heck of a race. I was doing all I could to run for third, but then Donnie Allison and Cale Yarborough, who were leading, crashed on the last lap. Fate stepped in and took us from third to first without us doing anything.

NASCAR was a southern sport up until the late-1980s, even though we wandered up north and out to California from time to time. The sponsors are as responsible as anyone for taking us to new markets, like Indianapolis Motor Speedway. I wish I could have run the inaugural Brickyard 400 in 1994, but I had retired two years earlier. That was a big feather in NASCAR's cap. When we went to Indy, it made us legitimate. Television looked at us different. The sponsors looked at us different. And everyone said, "You finally made it."

I just loved racing so much that I never thought about *not* doing it. I guess that was the reason it was so hard for me to retire, even though I knew I needed to get out of the car for the business side of the deal. I knew I wasn't up to winning races and doing what I had done before. But I just loved to drive a racecar. I just loved being out there and trying to beat somebody.

It doesn't feel like that was fifteen years ago. But just by watching the races since then, I've learned so much.

When you're in the car, you can't see the forest for the trees because you're right in the middle of it. But if you stand back and look, you get a different perspective. Each driver has a trait you probably wouldn't have known if you had been out there racing with him. But after you watch race after race, you understand their philosophy. You understand how they lap cars, how they race cars, how they act and react under adverse circumstances, how they act when they're ahead, how they get through traffic. You can see their strategy and a bunch of different things I never thought about when I was driving.

If someone who has never been to a NASCAR race is going for the first time, I tell them to get the best seat in the house, right at the start–finish line, just as high up as they can get. The higher up you are, the more you can see. And if you've got someone to pull for, it always makes it easier to watch.

We used to have a lot of fans, kids mainly, just because the No. 43 car was so bright. They didn't know Richard Petty from Adam's housecat, but they could pick out the blue-and-red car anywhere. It was easy for them to follow, so they pulled for that bright car.

But if you just go to a race and don't know any drivers, just pick out a car and follow it and see how things develop. By the time you come back a second or third time, you'll have picked out your favorite place to sit. And you'll have picked out a favorite driver. And maybe you'll still be watching fifty years from now.

Back when I ran that first Daytona 500, I didn't even know what fifty years was. I was just thinking about next week. I never envisioned the world being this big. I never envisioned 300 million people living in the United States, either. Not in 1959! But fifty years from now, NASCAR just might still be racing. If there's still an automobile, I suspect it will.

CONTENTS

INTRODUCTION

My first mistake was wearing a dress. Dresses, I learned, weren't allowed in the NASCAR garage unless modeled by Miss Winston, Miss Mopar, Miss Mello-Yello, or whatever honorary beauty queen reigned that day, replete with tiara and satin sash across an ample bosom. But for women not born to ride atop floats, wearing a dress meant you didn't get in.

It was the first item on a long list of things I didn't know about stock-car racing when I was sent to cover my first NASCAR practice in 1991.

It was a geographical fluke that I drew the assignment, having landed in Charlotte, North Carolina, as a young sportswriter the previous fall. And it was a quirk of the era that it later became my beat—an era that saw major newspapers confront the reality that NASCAR, long derided as a fixation of a semiliterate southern fringe, had started commanding TV ratings that warranted broader coverage. The only thing I knew about NASCAR at the time was that Bruce Springsteen had once mentioned Junior Johnson in a song. I knew the lyrics to

"Cadillac Ranch" cold, but I wasn't sure if Johnson was real or fictional, dead or alive.

So I headed to Charlotte Motor Speedway steeled against the prospect of introducing myself to wild, crude, belching men whose only means of making a living, since they clearly lacked basic common sense and a job skill, was going around in circles at 200 miles an hour.

In the years that followed, I learned that NASCAR, which stands for the National Association for Stock Car Auto Racing, really *was* a mind-numbing series of left turns—unless, of course, you cared about the drivers strapped in the cars. And they proved far more interesting than I imagined—earnest, driven, self-made, and lacking the arrogance and entitlement that afflicted so many professional athletes. Once I came to know the driver, it was as if his car suddenly took on his characteristics. It was no longer simply 3,400 pounds of motor and sheet metal, but an extension of the personality inside.

The famed No. 43 driven by Richard Petty clearly lacked the muscle and grit to mix it up with the hellions up front in the early nineties, the waning years of the King's career, but it was determined to turn in an honest day's work, making one noncompetitive lap after another to keep the fans happy.

The No. 23 Ford driven by Jimmy Spencer, known mockingly as "Mr. Excitement," caromed around the track like a pinball in an arcade game, bouncing off walls and fenders before creaking over the finish line as crumpled as a discarded paper cup.

And Dale Earnhardt's black No. 3 was menacing and conniving, lurking back in the pack until it decided to charge to the front. And then, what a show it staged! It took 190-miles-per-hour shortcuts across the infield grass, knocked rivals out of its way, spun out cars by disrupting the air around them and never left a mark, its mastery of the aerodynamic draft was so supreme.

The essence of NASCAR's appeal resided in having an opinion

about the drivers. And no place was as opinionated as Charlotte Motor Speedway, the home track for most of the race teams, where sell-out crowds of 150,000 brandished their loyalties with abandon, cheering drivers they loved and flipping the bird at those they loved to hate, as if convinced drivers could *see* their middle finger from forty rows away while zooming past in a high-speed blur.

If it seems foolish, imagine a stock-car race that included Barry Bonds in a BALCO-sponsored car and Cal Ripken Jr. in a car with "Got Milk?" on its hood. Or imagine a last-lap duel between Al Gore in a blue Toyota and Dick Cheney in a red Chevrolet. Few would feel indifferent about the outcome. In its purest form, NASCAR was like that, tapping the core beliefs and passions of the audience. So I hardly blinked when the promoter at North Wilkesboro (North Carolina) Motor Speedway handed me a press release a few years later about a longtime fan from upstate New York who had just passed away. The fan asked in his will that he be cremated, and that his ashes be driven one lap around the track by Richard Petty before being scattered along the start–finish line, where they would be sent on to heaven by the forty-three-car field at the drop of the green flag.

Petty complied.

From the zeal of its fans to the carnival atmosphere of its venues, NASCAR's eccentricities drew me in. It was as grand a spectacle as you could imagine, starting from the first time I drove my rental car through the tunnel that burrows under the fourth turn of Daytona International Speedway and opens onto the infield, where mechanics, racers, and reporters spend their workday on one side of a chain-link fence while the fans hang on the other side, cameras and autograph pens in hand, hoping desperately for a glimpse of one of their heroes.

Steering your car into Daytona's infield tunnel is like entering a darkened hallway that leads into a movie theater. Daylight disappears for a few seconds. And suddenly you pop up into a sun-drenched in-field so massive you can't take it all in. You're transported into a new world smack in the middle of a hulking, banked oval that encircles you like the sides of a bowl. It's as if you're on an epic stage, surrounded by asphalt and grandstands twelve stories high, and nothing that happens on the outside matters.

And no matter how early you arrive, scores of mechanics are already at work, sipping steaming cups of coffee while debating whether the sun is going to come out, which would dictate subtle adjustments to the springs and shocks. The grandstands are empty. Trash skitters over the grounds, and flocks of seagulls scavenge for crumbs.

Soon the generators fire up. Then the engines—one rumble, then dozens. It's so loud that everyone starts talking in hand signals. But you don't really need ears to hear the roar; NASCAR engines spew so much noise that you can actually *feel* it rattle your insides.

Most sportswriters, of course, didn't know and didn't care. I'd see them at NFL games, Final Fours, and college bowl games, and they'd laugh or snort as if I'd just delivered a punch line when I'd tell them I was covering NASCAR, and then stare with a look of pity or disdain, as if I'd been exiled to sportswriting's most demeaning job. Fine enough. But who *wouldn't* want to write about this, I thought to myself—part circus; part county fair.

In 1992, arguably the sport's most riveting season, I covered the first night race held at Charlotte Motor Speedway. Fifteen years later I can still close my eyes and see the sparks that erupted on the thrilling last lap. That same year I covered Richard Petty's retirement and Jeff Gordon's first race. I once sipped moonshine made by the legendary Junior Johnson, who, I was thrilled to learn, was very much alive. It was called Cherry Bounce, and a Mason jar of the liquid fire was passed around at a party I attended. Years later I interviewed Johnson at his farm in the North Carolina foothills. As I was getting ready to leave, he offered me one of his 'coon dogs who kept rolling over at my feet. She wasn't good for anything, he said, except getting her belly rubbed. It was the only piece of journalistic graft I've ever regretted turning down.

In 1994 I got goose bumps walking into the garage at Indianapolis Motor Speedway for NASCAR's inaugural Brickyard. The sign read "Gasoline Alley," and for reasons I can't fully explain, when I walked through the speedway's gates I felt as if NASCAR and the whole stock-car racing press corps had been invited to an exclusive ball.

In 1998 I was among dozens of reporters who committed the journalistic sin of cheering in the press box, rising to give Earnhardt a standing ovation after he snapped a nineteen-year jinx to win his first (and only) Daytona 500. Three years later I was in that same press box when he died.

In the years I covered racing, I came to find there was no greater gulf between an athlete's private and public persona than there was with Earnhardt. If NASCAR's Intimidator wanted to come out from behind his mirrored sunglasses, he'd propose conducting an interview at his Iredell County farm. I got to know the landscape well, riding around in his truck and running my tape recorder as he fielded questions in between checking on his chicken houses, feeding the catfish in his pond, and showing off the new appliances in the rental house that he was fixing up for Dale Jr., who had just signed a $50 million sponsorship deal with Budweiser. On one of those rambles Earnhardt confided that his grandmother had taught him how to control a car that was on the brink of being out of control. Her house sat at the bottom of a gravel driveway, he explained, and she'd have to feather the throttle with just the right touch as she fishtailed her way onto the main road each day.

It helped my rapport with the Intimidator that I worked at the *Charlotte Observer*, his hometown newspaper and NASCAR's paper of record. It also helped, inadvertently, when I told him I gave myself three shots a day to manage my diabetes. His eyes widened. "I could *never* do that!" he said, as if my bravery eclipsed his. From then on, he was a persistent nag. "You don't need to be hanging around those other reporters and drinking!" he said more than once. "You've got the sugar."

It changes you, covering a sport in which death is among the possible outcomes. But no death changed me more than his.

Linda Vaughn, stock-car racing's longest-reigning beauty queen, once explained to me her system for packing her suitcase for race weekends. She put the big hair dryer on top to keep everything nice and pressed, with a black dress—"Just in case . . ."—folded at the bottom. It is something I have done ever since.

· · ·

This is the story of the NASCAR that roars on, more popular than ever, having buried its heroes, pulled up its small-town roots, and teamed with Madison Avenue and Hollywood to reinvent itself not simply as a sport but as a multimedia marketing platform. And of the drivers and promoters who engineered that implausible transformation:

The racing families that spanned generations—the Pettys of Level Cross, North Carolina; the Allisons of Hueytown, Alabama; and the Earnhardts of Kannapolis, North Carolina, stock-car dynasties led by stubborn, humble, hardworking men who were convinced there was no finer way to make a living and who sacrificed far too much for the privilege.

The Frances of Daytona Beach, Florida, the sport's founding family, who have ruled stock-car racing with an iron fist since NASCAR's inception in 1947, and become billionaires under third-generation CEO Brian France.

The sports marketing executives at Winston-Salem, North Carolina–based R.J. Reynolds, whose expertise taught the Frances how to package their sport and hook an audience after signing on as the title sponsor in 1971, when the federal government banned tobacco advertising on television.

And of NASCAR's uncommonly loyal fans, including those who couldn't afford tickets but set out lawn chairs by the side of the road leading out of the speedway at Rockingham, North Carolina, just to wave at the race teams' giant transporter rigs rumbling past.

It's the story of an era that spans the best of NASCAR's past and the dawn of its future, heralded by the arrival of California's Jeff Gordon, whose telegenic gifts redefined what a NASCAR driver looked and acted like, and whose driving talent recalibrated the paydays for the current generation of stock-car racers, millionaires all. And, on a much smaller scale, it's a personal story in which I discovered an affinity for the sport, developed an affection for its personalities, grieved over the deaths of a half-dozen drivers, came to resent the rationalizations that invariably followed, and, more recently, settled on an arm's-length admiration for the business success it has achieved. But most of all, it's the story of a once humble sport's remarkable coming of age.

ONE HELLUVA RIDE

Chapter 1

A HARDSCRABBLE PAST

A full moon rose over the backstretch of Charlotte Motor Speedway the night of NASCAR's 1992 all-star race, The Winston. It was the first time that a stock-car race would be run at night on a 1.5-mile superspeedway, and illuminating a venue massive enough to hold eight National Football League stadiums demanded a feat of engineering so monumental that the company that lit the movie *Dances with Wolves* was hired for the task.

Night racing on such a huge scale was the idea of the speedway's president, H. A. "Humpy" Wheeler, a master showman who had never run a competitive lap himself but was determined to give NASCAR ticket buyers—mostly shift workers who lived black-and-white lives by day—Technicolor entertainment once they walked through his gates. As an undistinguished member of the University of South Carolina's football team in the 1950s, Wheeler had watched in awe from the bench when the Gamecocks visited Louisiana State University for a Saturday-night game. LSU had its mascot, a live tiger, spitting at spectators and clawing the air from the sidelines, and the effect made Wheeler's hair stand on end. *That* was the feeling he wanted to replicate at his race.

Wheeler's second agenda was getting his track's biggest race, the Coca-Cola 600, out from under the shadow of the Indianapolis 500—its rival in the battle for TV viewers on the crowded Memorial Day weekend. If Wheeler could figure out a way to run his 600-miler at night, it could have its own niche in prime time and no longer have to compete head-to-head with Indy.

As Wheeler geared up for his bold experiment in NASCAR's future, an all-star cast of drivers strapped in for its heart-stopping present.

The hotshot Davey Allison, son of NASCAR's 1983 champion Bobby Allison, was on the pole, having run the fastest lap in qualifying. The legendary Richard Petty, stock-car racing's "King," was in the field, along with *his* son, Kyle. So was the man chasing Richard Petty's record seven NASCAR championships, Dale Earnhardt, the local hero from Kannapolis, North Carolina, considered the meanest cuss ever to wheel a stock car.

The Winston wasn't part of NASCAR's twenty-nine-race regular season, in which drivers collected points toward the championship. It was a novelty event, named for the flagship brand of series sponsor R.J. Reynolds Tobacco Company and scripted for sheer entertainment, with a $500,000 payout to the winner. In The Winston, all that mattered was winning, not salvaging points or even salvaging the car. The top drivers had a fleet of new racecars back at their shops. From their 700-horsepower engines to the sheet-metal skin that was hand-sanded to aerodynamic perfection, the cars on the starting grid had been built for one performance only.

It was as pure a form of racing as there was—a flat-out dash for cash—on as spectacular a stage as NASCAR had ever seen. Would Wheeler's lighting system work, turning night into day, as he promised? Or would it skew depth perception as drivers hurtled into the corners at 185 miles per hour?

From the moment the green flag dropped, magic filled the air. The brightly painted racecars shimmered like jewels under the lights, heightening the sense of insane speeds as the cars zoomed past. But NASCAR's most faithful audience hardly needed daylight or slow motion to pick out their favorite. Even at a high-octane blur they could spot Dale Earnhardt's black No. 3 from a mile away, and not only tell you it was a Chevrolet with "the Intimidator" slouched and smirking behind the wheel, but they could also identify every corporate sponsor on Earnhardt's driving suit, reel off his wife's name (plus the two ex-wives) and the names of his four children, and point out where he liked to pass on the track.

The black-and-red No. 28 was a Ford Thunderbird driven by Allison. At thirty-one, Davey was the most successful of a crop of second-generation racers who represented the sport's future, as well as the front-runner for the season's championship.

Piloting the black-and-yellow No. 42 Pontiac Grand Prix was Kyle Petty, stock-car racing royalty on the cusp of forging his own place in the sport. Petty was as affable as Earnhardt was ornery, with long hair and a pierced ear that clashed with stock-car racing's mores of the day. But he was a Petty, and that alone was reason to pay homage.

Petty's streaking Pontiac had surged to the front when the white flag signaled one lap to go, with Earnhardt closing fast as they barreled down the backstretch. Earnhardt always said that the only lap that mattered was the one that paid money, and he looked hell-bent on taking it. Fans had seen him do crazy things to win this race in the past, including ducking onto the infield grass to fend off a charge from Bill Elliott by taking a shortcut to the finish line in 1987—a move that sealed his reputation as the nerviest driver in the garage, considering it's as impossible to control a racecar on grass as it is on an ice-skating rink. And they were all on their feet, clamoring for another amazing feat of daring.

Petty had no idea what Earnhardt had in mind. He had looked

over at his nemesis when they dueled side by side earlier in the race, and all he saw was Earnhardt's bushy mustache grinning back at him. "What in the hell is he grinnin' about?" Petty thought to himself. "What does *he* know that I don't?"

They entered Turn 3 of the final lap locked side by side. Earnhardt had the outside lane and was pinching Petty low on the track, testing his nerve to force him to lift off the throttle. At that point, there was nothing left for Earnhardt's pit crew to do but watch.

"We were beat," crew chief Kirk Shelmerdine recalled, laughing at the memory. "We didn't have the fastest car, so we knew Dale was going to do some desperation thing that probably doesn't work. And it was gonna be cool!"

Petty kept it mashed to the floor, and suddenly the black No. 3 spun and smacked the wall. No sooner had Petty vanquished Earnhardt than Allison surged into view. His path now clear, Allison whipped alongside Petty entering Turn 4, and the two banged doors as they raced to the checkered flag. Allison nudged his Thunderbird's nose ahead for the victory, but his car bobbled the moment it crossed the finish line and slammed the wall, sending showers of fiery sparks in the air. When the screeching and crashing came to an end, both cars were torn to pieces, and Allison sat slumped and motionless in his seat, knocked unconscious by the blow.

Back in the garage, where the also-rans climbed out of their cars, Petty was swarmed by reporters clamoring for a firsthand account of the last-lap mayhem. He had barely launched in when Earnhardt stormed toward him, reared up to well over his six-foot height, raw emotion spewing from his pores like steam from a sweltering city street. Reporters froze, unsure whether they were about to witness NASCAR's Intimidator cuss the King's son or punch him in the nose. Instead Earnhardt broke into a huge grin, flung his arm around Petty's shoulders, and gushed, "Great racing, man! Great racing!"

Over in Victory Lane, an argument broke out between Robert

Yates, owner of Allison's team, and an ecstatic Wheeler over whether the mangled Thunderbird would be hauled in on a wrecker for the customary postrace photographs. Wheeler wanted to immortalize the slugfest, while Yates, distraught over his driver's condition, thought it was in poor taste and blocked the wrecker's path with his body. Meantime, Miss Winston, NASCAR's R.J. Reynolds–branded beauty queen, was stood up for the first time in her twenty-year reign. Puckered up to deliver the congratulatory kiss on the biggest night of the year for the series sponsor, Miss Winston suddenly had no purpose as Allison, still fluttering in and out of consciousness, was pulled from his car, strapped to a stretcher, and loaded onto a helicopter that whirred through the night sky to a local hospital.

It was, for me, the most thrilling night in racing. One of those nights that, even as it unfolded, you knew would never come again. "Remember this," my brain shouted as I frantically scribbled notes amid the chaos. "Remember everything about it, because it won't come again."

• • •

NASCAR wasn't as big that night as it is today. But it never filled a screen any bigger. Its personalities were never in more sharp relief. The point was never so clear.

In the decade that followed, Wheeler proved prescient beyond measure. Night racing opened new worlds for Charlotte Motor Speedway and the sport. The Coca-Cola 600 eventually moved its starting time to dusk. NASCAR eclipsed Indy cars as the dominant form of motorsports in America. And NASCAR, fueled by its first national TV deal, became the fastest-growing sport in the country.

• • •

From stock-car racing's beginning, there was something illicit about it—like early rock 'n' roll—that suggested a certain depravity, as if nothing but trouble could come from the raw noise and unbridled lo-comotion of a V-8 engine. It was a sport at the fringe of the rules. So much so that rules barely existed.

Stock-car racing began as an outlet for automotive-obsessed scofflaws and moonshine runners and mushroomed in the postwar years, fueled by World War II veterans back from the war and hungry for a comparable adrenaline fix. In some parts of the country, like southern California, the postwar fixation with the automobile mani-fested itself in drag racing. Teenagers would pair off in their hot rods on a back road at midnight and race in a straight line—one man's nerve and engine against another's in a furious burst from Point A to Point B. Picture Natalie Wood dropping the flag, then spinning on her heels and running to see if James Dean were alive or dead in *Rebel Without a Cause.*

But in the South, with its Faulknerian flair for drama, no one was in such a hurry to see this crowd-pleasing duel of horsepower and guts end. There wasn't much else to do in the isolated South, passed over by major-league sports of the day, so the car races were drawn-out affairs, staged on oval tracks at county fairgrounds or on half-mile circuits bulldozed out of red clay that was too poor to farm. Grand-stands were a rare amenity. In most cases paying fans would drive right up to the edge of the track and perch on the hoods of their cars or congregate on hillsides, climb onto concrete blocks, or set up lawn chairs and spend the day watching the wild show, as cars crashed into flimsy guardrails, engines expired, and, eventually, somebody won the race of attrition.

The best cars were built by the mechanics who retooled the 1938 and '39 Fords for bootleggers. Schooled in taking junkyard heaps and boring out the cylinders and fitting them with dual manifolds, rein-forcing the wheels and suspension, adding bigger springs and extra carburetors, they created deceptively fast getaway cars that doubled as nearly indestructible delivery trucks, thanks to their oversized trunks and the extra room after you tore out the back seat.

Naturally, the best stock-car racers were ex-bootleggers, skilled in the art of outrunning the law. When failing at your livelihood meant spending a year and a day in jail (the standard penalty for running liquor), you learned to be fearless and inventive behind the wheel. Compared to the threat of getting arrested after a wild chase on a mountain back road in the wee hours of dawn, racing for sheer fun in front of a cheering crowd, with a chance to win $500 if you outran everybody else, was a joyride.

There are so many dueling versions of NASCAR's history that it's preposterous. Some of the sport's veterans, still rankled by stock-car racing's stepchild status, all but deny its bootlegging roots. Others wear it like a badge of honor and will argue till death about whether the mountains of north Georgia or the western North Carolina hills gave rise to the best there ever was. Regardless of who's spinning the tale, a few common ingredients led to this combustible brew: migration patterns, cultural history, isolation, poverty, and necessity.

The Scots-Irish who immigrated to the United States generally arrived in the port of Philadelphia and migrated down the great Philadelphia Wagon Road that took them through the mountain foothills and hollows of western Virginia, North Carolina, South Carolina, and Georgia. They brought with them the tradition of making their own liquor and a profound resentment, expressed most forcefully in the Whiskey Rebellion of 1794, of the federal government's claim that such liquor should be taxed.

Whiskey wasn't just the drink of choice among the immigrants who settled the frontier. It was a form of liquid currency in a bartering-based economy. And nearly fifteen thousand western Pennsylvania farmers, most of Scots-Irish descent, rioted against what they viewed as discriminatory overreaching as the eighteenth century drew to a close. Their basic distrust of federal authority was handed down to the generations that followed, along with the labor-intensive process of distilling liquor out of sugar and surplus corn.

Writing about the defining traits of Scots-Irish immigrants in general, author James Webb characterized them as "openly unafraid of higher authority, intent on personal honor, quick to defend itself against attack of any sort, and deeply patriotic. . . . The measure of a man was not how much money he made or how much land he held, but whether he was bold—often to the point of recklessness— whether he would fight, and whether he could lead."

For the moonshiners among them (the name derived from the fact that they tended their stills and delivered their brew in the dead of night, by the light of the moon), the repeal of Prohibition in 1933 had no more effect than its enactment. The South remained full of "dry" counties. And with no means of scratching out a living on the stingy red clay, particularly in the hard years of the Depression, they went into the business of selling their home-brewed corn mash to meet demand. By necessity, they needed fast cars and brave delivery boys to elude the tax man, who hounded them with even more zeal in the post-Prohibition era. And more often than not, the moonshine runner won, blessed with a strain of courage and self-determination more virulent than the average revenue agent.

I missed this era and the wild racing it spawned. But it lives on in faded newspaper clippings, grainy photographs, scrapbooks, and the proud memory of those who lived it. To find it, all you need to do is head down North Carolina's Highway 421, which gets renamed Junior Johnson Highway once it crosses into Wilkes County. Just past a handful of modest brick homes is a 278-acre ranch bordered by a black fence. Turn up the gated driveway that leads to the 14,000-square-foot Georgian mansion looming in the distance, past the Santa Gertrudis cattle grazing on either side, and the sign that reads "Slow Down Please, Children Are At Play." But rather than drive up to the grand circular drive, veer left, to the nondescript white garage at the edge of the woods. At least one dog will run up to greet you—maybe a wiry 'coon dog or, on this day, a muscular Rhodesian ridgeback, intent on sniffing out every crumb of food ever dropped between your car seats.

3 1833 05426 5340

Inside, meet Robert Glenn Johnson Jr., white-haired and seventy-five, who still answers to "Junior," reading the morning paper while keeping an eye on the breakfast he cooks every weekday morning—sausage, bacon, and hot dogs—still warming in the oven. He's a multi-millionaire, owner of all the eye can see, plus real estate holdings and a ham-producing company. But a day rarely dawns without Junior putting on a faded pair of overalls, convinced man never invented a more sensible item of clothing. And today is no exception.

As a moonshine runner for his daddy, the biggest producer of white lightning in Wilkes County, Junior was never outrun by the law, which is no small point of pride more than a half-century later. He was arrested on foot, nabbed during a stakeout of the family liquor still when he went to stoke the fire one night. As a NASCAR driver, he was the hell-raising sort, determined to win or crash trying. And he retired in his prime, at age thirty-five, with fifty victories. Later, as a NASCAR team owner, he was as wily as they came—a masterful mechanic despite an eighth-grade education, and a keen judge of racing talent. He won six championships with drivers Cale Yarborough and Darrell Waltrip.

True to his Scots-Irish heritage, Junior Johnson will tell you he has never bent a knee to any man—not the judge who sentenced him to two years in the federal penitentiary in Chillicothe, Ohio; the president of General Motors; or NASCAR's founding France family. And he'll proudly lay it all out for you, the battles he won and those he lost, in his own brand of English, with rough-hewn common sense and a master storyteller's flair.

And though he served time for his moonshining (pardoned by President Ronald Reagan in 1985) and was busted repeatedly by NASCAR officials for running oversized engines in his racecars, Johnson had a fierce personal ethic of right and wrong. When he finally got fed up with NASCAR's politics and the heavy-handed tactics of Bill France Jr. in 1995, Junior sold his entire racing operation to driver Brett Bodine—every racecar, wrench, nut, and bolt—and turned his back on the sport. Bodine carted away what he needed to launch his new team and held an auction a few weeks later to get rid of what was left, including the property. Who showed up but Junior, who started bidding on stuff.

Bodine went up to him and asked, "*Junior!* What are you *doing?*"

"Gaw," Junior replied. "I gotta have some tools around the house and around the shop. I needed some nuts and bolts."

Bodine just shook his head. "All you had to do was *ask!*"

Junior Johnson was born within twenty miles of his present-day mansion, in Ingle Hollow. You could argue that NASCAR was, too, when Enoch Staley took a bulldozer to his farm and carved out a half-mile dirt track known as North Wilkesboro Speedway in 1947.

There wasn't much money in racing—Junior made more hauling liquor—but the thrill of outrunning another boy's Chevrolet was even better than outrunning the tax man.

Conditions in the car were crude. With no seat belts, most drivers lashed themselves to the seat with a rope to keep from flopping out if the car flipped. The intrepid salvaged safety belts from old surplus fighter planes and bolted them in their cars. Some used dog collars to keep the car doors fastened. Others used chains. Eventually, they welded the doors shut.

It got brutally hot as the races wore on, so Junior wore white pants and a white T-shirt to keep as cool as possible. Few cars were re-inforced with roll bars, so they'd crumple easily in a crash. For helmets, early drivers wore little caps with a bill that would crack to pieces on impact. Asked if he carried a fire extinguisher in the car, as NASCAR drivers do today, Junior guffaws. "I didn't even know they *made* fire extinguishers!"

Most drivers, like Junior, worked on their cars themselves. Having rebuilt its engine, reinforced its suspension, and swapped out its springs and hubs, Junior raced it with total abandon, commanding it to do what he wanted it to do—no different from those days when he drove the stubborn old mule that plowed the family farm.

"I *did* try to run it wide open all the time," Junior says. "When everybody else thought I was crazy, my car was doing what I asked it to do. And I had it fixed to where I *knowed* what it would do. And when I got it like it was 'sposed to be, ain't *nobody* that could run with it."

And that's what the fans in the South came to see: just how fast a rum-runner's car could go. It was a rough bunch in the stands, three-quarters men, if not more, from small towns all around Virginia, the Carolinas, and Georgia, who'd pile into cars and caravan to the races in Martinsville, Virginia; North Wilkesboro, North Carolina; and Darlington, South Carolina. They bet on the cars, and they brawled over the finish. And nearly all went home with a snout-full of dirt. The cars kicked up so much red clay during the races, according to one early promoter's account, that the sign advertising "lemonade" at the concession stands got replaced by a sign advertising "pink lemonade" by day's end.

The racers were even tougher than the fans. Virginia's Curtis Turner and the Flock brothers out of Georgia, for example, brought the same credentials as Junior—bootlegging expertise, a daredevil's thirst for thrills, and the need to put food on the table.

The late Smokey Yunick, self-taught mechanic extraordinaire, set the scene: "Stock-car racing was a format whereby everyone started even: next to no education and no money. A racer was a special outcast—no chance for credit, no insurance, not wanted in hotels, social status just a little better than an ex-con. . . ."

Being short on the privilege that education and money afforded, the racers formed a close-knit fraternity of their own, traveling the racing circuit like gypsies, butting heads on the racetrack, trading blows afterward, and taking care of one another in times of crisis.

"They was a wild bunch back then," said the late Tim Flock in a

1991 interview at his Charlotte home. "All they did was party, and there was a lot of fights in the pits. The old ones were ex-bootleggers who raced in overalls and drank liquor. I can name you two or three guys who kept liquor in gallon containers behind their seat. They had a big tube they put over their roll bar so they could suck on it down the straightaways. One time a NASCAR official stuck his head in a car and said, 'Son! Don't you know you can't drink in the car?' And the driver said, 'I don't mind driving this m-f'er down the straightaways. But I'm going to let Lord Calvert [whiskey] help me through the turns!' "

It took a firm hand to rein in the circus atmosphere of stock-car racing's early days. And it arrived in the form of the iron fist of Bill France.

• • •

The very acronym NASCAR suggests that an impartial body governs the sport, composed perhaps of representative track owners, car owners, drivers, and promoters. Nothing could be further from the truth. NASCAR is owned by one family, the Frances of Daytona Beach, Florida, who also control most of the sport's major venues through their track-owning company, International Speedway Corporation. The result has made present-day billionaires of the heirs of the late Bill France, NASCAR's founding president and driving force, whose imposing physique (six feet five and 220 pounds) and manner earned him the moniker "Big Bill."

Big Bill didn't invent stock-car racing any more than he invented the automobile. His genius was in seeing the need to govern it and package it for mass consumption in the postwar era, while deftly creating a corporate structure that gave him total control and, in due time, total ownership. NASCAR's patriarch built his monument to automotive daring, Daytona International Speedway, along the central Florida coast, less than an hour from Disney World. And until he handed the reins to his elder son, Bill Jr., Big Bill ruled his kingdom with the authority of a Mafia don and the imagination of Walt Disney himself.

France was a tireless worker, and he was utterly committed to building stock-car racing into a populist phenomenon. To that end he channeled a gift for oratory, keen political instincts, and a willingness to act, employing whatever means it took, including threats and intimidation, to push NASCAR forward. France made heroes out of some racers and quashed the careers of others. But even his detractors will tell you that no other man, and no other methods, could have gotten the same results. "I give him all the credit in the world," said Flock, among those who tangled with France and lost. "I don't think nobody can tell you what he went through."

He was a Depression-era migrant from Washington, D.C., heading down the Florida coast with his wife and first child when he decided that Daytona Beach was as good a place to settle as any. The city had called itself "the Birthplace of Speed" since the turn of the century, when daredevils used its hard-packed sand as runways in their attempts to set land-speed records, and that was part of its allure.

An auto mechanic by trade, France opened a gas station on Main Street and soon got involved in the local racing scene. He was unremarkable as a racecar driver. His calling, it turned out, was in putting on shows. France helped design and build the city's first oval track— a preposterous circuit with one straightaway that ran down the hard-packed beach and the other on a portion of state highway A1A. It made for wild events, in which fields of more than fifty jalopies hurtled down the asphalt road, veered left onto the sand, charged back up the beach, then onto the highway again. Few cars finished. Engines expired. Drivers roared into the surf or crashed into one another. But thousands came to cheer the mayhem.

Stock-car racing stood poised for a popularity surge in the postwar years, and not just in the Southeast. But the rules and the very definition of a "stock" car varied as wildly as the skills of the drivers and the ethics of the promoters. After sizing up both the looming potential and pitfalls, France invited the key players in racing to a four-day summit at Daytona's Streamline Hotel. His agenda was to bring order to the mayhem—creating a points system to give each season a narrative arc that would hook fans and the media, standardizing the rules to create competitive balance and guaranteeing payouts to attract the top drivers. His vision was a sport for Everyman.

Two dozen of the sport's top mechanics, racers, and track owners from as far away as Massachusetts and Ohio gathered in the hotel's smoke-filled cocktail lounge, where France explained that stock-car racing had arrived at a crossroads. To progress further, he argued, it needed a governing body and consistent rules. In his book *Driving with the Devil: Southern Moonshine, Detroit Wheels, and the Birth of NASCAR,* Neal Thompson details the politicking that followed. France's oratory was persuasive and powerful. And he set his audience in a conciliatory frame of mind, Thompson writes, by providing free liquor and hiring swimsuit-clad models from a local charm school to mingle with his guests. Four days later the group voted to create NASCAR and made France its president.

France hired a lawyer to draw up the incorporation papers and create 100 shares of NASCAR stock, which was divided three ways, according to Thompson. A 10 percent share went to the lawyer, 40 percent to fellow promoter Bill Tuthill of New York, and 50 percent to France. In time, France controlled all the shares.

France wasn't unerring. NASCAR had a few early misadventures, such as its division for convertibles. And not every revolutionary development sprang from him. But he knew when to scuttle a bad idea and when to seize a good one. Take Darlington (South Carolina) Raceway—the brainchild of an equally ambitious promoter named Harold Brasington, who dreamed of building a southern stock-car track to rival the famed Indianapolis Motor Speedway. The result was an egg-shaped asphalt oval (oddly shaped because Brasington's farmland abutted a neighbor's fishpond) that ended up only half as big as Indianapolis. But at 1.25 miles around, Darlington was NASCAR's first behemoth when it opened in 1950, dwarfing the half-mile dirt tracks that dominated the circuit. And it immediately developed a reputation as a treacherous, if not downright possessed, venue that tested drivers' nerve and skill like none other. In time, France would own Darlington, too.

France had limitless ambition for NASCAR. And he passed that on to his elder son, Bill France Jr., who took the reins in 1975 and accelerated its improbable growth with an even more audacious vision.

"Bill France [Jr.] has the future of the sport in mind," said Gary Nelson, then NASCAR's director of competition, when asked about the sport's second-generation president in a 1993 interview. "He has the ability to see ten, twenty years down the road when we're thinking about having to pick up our laundry today."

But the very fact that Bill France Jr. had the latitude to *have* such vision was because, as NASCAR's patriarch, his father had established and institutionalized supreme authority over the sport.

"NASCAR basically is a dictatorship," seven-time champion Richard Petty explained shortly before retiring as a driver in 1992. "A man owns it. It's his business. He runs it. I got no problem with that. If I want to play in his ballpark, I play by his rules. If I don't want to play, I go home. That's the way it is. It's always been that way."

The source of France's power was NASCAR's rulebook, which he could both wield like a club and ignore or rewrite at will. While it laid out the specifications for racecars and the procedures for race day in detail, every rule in it was governed by the NASCAR principle of "EIRI"—shorthand, in garage parlance, for "except in rare instances."

In NASCAR's formative years, France's biggest challenge was

taming the hooligans who raced the cars, and securing their loyalty to his series, particularly if they drew a ticket-buying crowd.

Tim Flock was among the first to challenge France's authority, driving against his wishes in a stock-car race staged by a rival promoter named Bruton Smith in 1950. At the time, Flock led NASCAR's points standings and was a cinch to win its biggest crown: the Grand National championship. But after racing for Smith, Flock found that NASCAR had deducted 488 points from his total. That dumped him out of the top ten and cost him the title. (He went on to win championships in 1952 and '55.)

The decade that followed saw France twice break up drivers' attempts to unionize. Curtis Turner, among the era's more popular drivers, had teamed with Smith, the rival promoter, to build a giant speedway in Charlotte. After Turner ran into financial trouble in 1961, he got a loan from the pension fund of Jimmy Hoffa's Teamsters Union in exchange for a promise to unionize the stock-car drivers. Arguing that it was time drivers forced NASCAR to pay bigger purses—Turner estimated competitors were getting just 5 to 12 percent of gate receipts—Turner got Flock, Buck Baker, and Fireball Roberts to join the fight to create the Federation of Professional Athletes and signed up just about every driver in the garage.

"You could understand his motive," recalls two-time NASCAR champion Ned Jarrett. "There was certainly concern among the drivers and the car owners in those days, about the way things were going, and that they were not having any say about what was going on. There were issues to be met, no question about that. And Curtis painted a pretty picture. He had been educated to believe, I guess, that it could be a tremendous boost for the sport and for the drivers in particular."

Among those abstaining was Junior Johnson, wary of organized labor and mindful of the alarms it set off in the South. Johnson was one of the few drivers with a deep-pocketed sponsor, North Carolina–based Holly Farms, which was waging its own war against union activity in its chicken-packing plants, and he didn't want to lose its backing. "If I joined against NASCAR," Johnson recalled, "then *I'm* out of racing."

France responded at NASCAR's next event, summoning all the drivers to a prerace meeting in the football players' locker room at Bowman Gray Stadium in Winston-Salem, North Carolina. Few on hand ever forgot what followed. France told the drivers he had a form for them to sign, releasing them from the union. If they refused, he added, don't bother getting back in the racecar.

Recalls Jarrett: "He said, 'I *know* what's going on as far as a union is concerned. And we will *not* have a union in NASCAR! You are independent contractors [rather than employees]. And I'll plow up every racetrack that I have anything to do with and plant corn! We will *not* have a union!' "

Other accounts say that France wielded a pistol as he spoke. Jarrett never saw it. "I don't doubt that for a moment, though," he added. "He could have had one. He certainly put the fear of God in me!"

Every driver signed the form except Turner, Roberts, and Flock. Roberts eventually relented, but the other two pressed the matter in a Daytona court. As Flock recalled, the judge read comic books during the drivers' testimony. They lost the case, and France banned both from NASCAR for life.

France also had more subtle means of enforcing order. The mandatory prerace inspection of racecars gave NASCAR officials total control over which drivers and cars could compete. And over the years, most competitors came to regard the process as a potentially punitive tool: get out of line, fail inspection. At the other extreme, France could help favored drivers by steering potential corporate sponsors their way. But France knew when to loosen his grip on competitors, too.

Hard times had a way of bringing out France's charitable streak, and 1965 was one of those times. Ford was dominating the races, and France had banned Chrysler from competing because he didn't approve of its new Hemi engine, which relied on larger valves in the engine's combustion chamber, creating what France deemed an unfair advantage. The ban sidelined NASCAR's biggest drawing card at the time, Richard Petty. The result left France in need of someone to spice up NASCAR's show. So he reinstated Turner and Flock, deciding that his point had been made. Turner made a limited return; Flock didn't bother.

As a young reporter I had wondered about Flock's characterization of the comic book–reading Daytona judge who apparently was so beholden to NASCAR's interests that he hadn't given Flock a fair hearing at trial. Forty years had passed. Had Flock's memory embellished an understandably painful episode? Had the legal system really been so unfair?

About a month after Bill France died in June 1992, following his wife, Anne, who had passed away earlier that year, I phoned the probate division in Volusia County, Florida, to ask about getting a copy of France's will. Perhaps that would shed light on his succession plans for NASCAR—a topic of great interest to readers of the *Charlotte Observer.* I was told that indeed the will was a matter of public record: File #92-11186 PRDL, to be precise. The clerk looked it up for me. It was nineteen pages long. At one dollar per page, plus a two-dollar fee, I could get a certified copy if I mailed a check payable to the Clerk of Circuit Court and included a stamped, self-addressed envelope.

After nearly a week had passed and nothing arrived, I phoned the clerk's office again. "I can't provide any documents in that file anymore," I was told. "The entire contents of that file are confidential."

I pressed for an explanation. A judge's order sealing the file indefinitely had arrived the day after I made the initial request.

• • •

Bill France's vision of a sport for Everyman was rooted in two fundamental myths: that NASCAR's "stock cars" were no different from the Fords and Chevrolets in the typical family garage, and that the drivers were no different from the average American. Those principles guided development of the rule book, which, in the interest of safety and durability, initially allowed only minimal modifications to showroom-model cars. Catastrophic injury and fatalities hastened the cars' departure from "strictly stock" status. A rash of deaths from fire (including the 1964 death of Fireball Roberts, nicknamed for his blistering pitching arm as a high school baseball player) led to the development of the fuel cell, which greatly reduced the likelihood of an explosion on impact. The installation of steel roll cages reinforced the cars' bodies and encased the drivers in a protective cocoon. Neither feature could be found on a showroom-model sedan.

Meanwhile, what had begun as a love affair with the American automobile morphed into a love affair with the drivers, who loomed larger than life on the racetrack yet were as regular as the guy next door. NASCAR reaped the benefits of its quirky cast of characters, who became folk heroes for their daring, showmanship, and plain ways.

Fireball Roberts was NASCAR's first hero. Author Tom Wolfe, writing in *Esquire* in 1965, declared Junior Johnson America's last. But in truth, the sport churned out heroes in droves well before and long after Roberts and Johnson dominated the high banks of Daytona and Darlington. One clan of daredevils simply followed another. First came a mess of Flocks (three racing brothers and a racing sister, named Ethel, according to historian Larry Fielden, in honor of the gasoline their father used in his taxicab business), then generations of Bakers, Pettys, Jarretts, Allisons, and Earnhardts.

The youngest and most successful Flock, Tim, ran nine NASCAR races in 1953 with a rhesus monkey named Jocko Flocko, who was outfitted in a tiny racing uniform and helmet and sat in a special seat installed next to the passenger door so he could wave to fans. Flock's racecar wasn't simply a Hudson. He gave it a name and painted it on the side in spectacular script, drawing cheers each time "The Fabulous Hudson Hornet" pulled onto the starting grid.

Ned Jarrett's father cast his son's lot by taking him to the races at North Wilkesboro and Charlotte when Ned was just twelve. "It didn't take but one time," Jarrett says today. But the last thing his father had wanted was a stock-car racer in the family. He forbade it, in fact. A devout Christian, he had worked hard to build his sawmill and lumber business, H.K. Jarrett and Sons, in Hickory, North Carolina. An elder son worked in the family mill, and Ned, more adept with numbers, had kept the business's books since he was thirteen.

After Ned drove his first race at a nearby dirt track without his father's permission, he was summoned for a parental talk. "He pointed out that he needed me in the business, and the fact that the majority of the drivers were bootleggers," Jarrett recalled. "He was concerned about the image that it would project because he had worked so hard to try to build respect and a good image for the family."

The son agreed to quit racing and satisfy his yen by sharing ownership of the racecar, which his partner would drive from then on. But after a few months behind the wheel it was clear Ned was the better driver. So he started competing under his partner's name, John Lentz. Word got back to his father after Ned won his first race, and he was summoned for another talk. The message: if you're so determined to drive one of those cars, use your own name and get credit for your accomplishments. Jarrett went on to win two NASCAR championships in a thirteen-year career. And he did so without compromising the family name, earning the nickname "Gentleman Ned."

NASCAR was as southern as kudzu in its early days, but its reputation as a sport in which nerve and speed were rewarded began luring a few speed-obsessed Yankees and midwesterners below the Mason-Dixon line. Fred Lorenzen of Elmhurst, Illinois, was among them. He was a promoter's dream in the early 1960s: fearless enough to whup Curtis Turner, Junior Johnson, and Fireball Roberts, and handsome enough, radiating matinee-idol good looks, to coax female fans to the grandstands.

Drivers weren't paid until after each race, lining up at the track office to collect their cash. No matter how long the line was, Fireball would barge to the front, and the other drivers would let him through as a gesture of respect for the reigning superstar. Just to raise a little hell on his way out, Roberts would walk back through the line and tell the drivers behind him, "He gave me an extra hundred!" and laugh as the shouting broke out.

And then came Richard Petty, son of three-time champion Lee Petty, the biggest attraction of all. Wherever NASCAR raced, Petty would tow his No. 43 Plymouth, whip out his black pen, and sign autographs until it was time to strap into the racecar and put on a show. Then he'd climb back out, perch on the pit wall, and sign autographs until there wasn't anybody left. "If you didn't have Richard Petty in your race, you didn't sell tickets," said Jim Hunter, the longtime president of Darlington Raceway and current NASCAR spokesman.

As shrewd a businessman as he was a driver, Petty also set the standard for appearance money in the 1960s—a bonus that only the sport's top names could command. It was typically a few hundred dollars in addition to whatever prize money the driver won. But promoters had to come up with it, striking the deal in advance to make sure they'd have enough star-wattage in their race to attract a paying audience.

"If you wanted [David] Pearson to run your race, then you had to pay Pearson the same thing you gave Petty," Hunter recalled. "He'd say, 'Whatever you're giving Richard, that's *fine* with me.' Pearson didn't want any less. And if he ever found out that somebody was paying less, he wouldn't come."

Pearson, a native of Spartanburg, South Carolina, was the ideal foil for Petty, who won a staggering twenty-seven races in 1967. In that era it seemed as if Pearson, dubbed the Silver Fox in his Holman-Moody

Ford, was the only driver capable of beating Petty—particularly on the giant superspeedways. Throngs of fans descended on the track each time they squared off. But the Pearson-Petty rivalry was more a high-speed artistic duel than a simmering blood feud, such as the one that developed later between Petty and Bobby Allison.

If Petty was stock-car racing royalty with the common man's comportment, Allison was the scrappy underdog. He had clawed his way into the sport in chronically underfunded equipment, working on the racecars himself and competing in NASCAR's top division on the weekends and short-track races throughout the Midwest during the week. In many ways Allison was Dale Earnhardt, stock-car racing's original hardworking man, before Earnhardt—a wage earner determined to beat the odds while holding down two jobs and rearing four children.

Still, stick-and-ball sports reigned supreme throughout most of the country at the time. If anything other than football, basketball, or baseball made its way onto the nation's airwaves or sports pages, it was generally a singular, spectacular event—such as Secretariat's 1973 run to the Triple Crown, Arthur Ashe's Wimbledon triumph in 1975, or Nadia Comaneci's seven perfect 10.0 marks at the 1976 Olympics.

France was determined to carve out turf for NASCAR, too. And he got his biggest boost from two serendipitous events: the federal government's 1971 ban of tobacco ads on TV, which resulted in R.J. Reynolds redirecting its marketing war chest and expertise to NASCAR, whose trackside billboards served the brilliant surreptitious purpose of getting its Winston brand back in the public's view; and the brawl that erupted in the aftermath of the 1979 Daytona 500—NASCAR's first 500-mile race televised live from start to finish on national TV.

Cale Yarborough was the driver to beat in the race—hardheaded, fearless, and strapped inside an Oldsmobile fielded by the cagey Junior Johnson. The duo had won the last three championships together, but on this day Yarborough had been dogged from the start by the Allison brothers, Donnie and Bobby. The three had tangled just thirty-two laps into the race, forcing all of their cars in for repairs. But with one lap to go, Donnie was leading, and Yarborough was close behind with no other contenders in his rearview mirror. All Yarborough had to do was pull off a slingshot pass—a maneuver that had been perfected decades earlier by Johnson, in which a driver deliberately lags behind the car ahead and then whips around it in a flash—and roar to victory.

But Donnie ducked low on the track to block, and Yarborough refused to be cowed. Instead he plowed forward, ramming Allison hard enough to send both cars in a smoking, spinning heap on the infield grass. Running a distant third was Petty, who sailed to his sixth Daytona 500 victory amid the carnage, hardly believing his good fortune.

The melee was witnessed by a rapt CBS audience, hundreds of thousands of whom had been shut in by a snowstorm that blanketed the East Coast. And the drama wasn't over yet. Bobby Allison jumped out of his car to see if his brother was okay, and the rumble erupted as punches, helmets, and dirt flew. The next day, NASCAR was splashed on the front page of the *New York Times* sports section.

"We got fortunate to win the race, but we still won," Petty says with no small measure of pride today. "When you read the record books, it says '1979 Daytona 500: Richard Petty won the race.' It don't say that the guys that was two miles ahead of him run into each other! It was a heck of a race—even if one of those guys had won it. It was a heck of a race! But then the fight was just the icing on the cake!"

The unmistakable lesson was that controversy was good for NASCAR. And the decades that followed brought plenty—much of it courtesy of a scruffy, second-generation racer making his rookie debut in that 1979 Daytona 500, Dale Earnhardt, whose eighth-place finish hardly drew notice.

The race marked the beginning of a remarkable growth surge that would see NASCAR transform itself, shuttering some of its more storied racetracks, such as North Wilkesboro Speedway, and glossing over its hardscrabble past. Asked if it didn't make him a bit sad, the sixty-nine-year-old Petty flashed his famous smile.

"In a small way," he conceded. "But I like the expansion part of it. It's gonna sound greedy . . .. but the bigger NASCAR is, the bigger Richard Petty *was*."

Chapter 2

THE FANS ANOINT A KING

Even before he ran his first race, Richard Petty was thinking about how to do something special for race fans. At eighteen and fresh out of Randleman High School, he was pretty sure that life couldn't get better. The year before, he and his younger brother, Maurice, had helped their father, Lee Petty, win NASCAR's 1954 championship. Now, diploma in hand, Richard had a full-time job working on the family racecar and the best seat in the house, a mechanic's perch on pit road, for studying just what made one racecar driver better than the next.

Lee Petty, a hard-edged son of the Depression, never raced with the abandon of Junior Johnson or Fireball Roberts. He was deliberate behind the wheel, taking care of the only racecar in the family stable by easing off the pace with calculated precision so he could mount a challenge at the end, often outfoxing the hard chargers who had an edge in horsepower. Lee wasn't what you'd call a nurturer. He didn't talk much, and he took pains to explain even less. So lap after lap, Richard studied his father's tactics and guile until one day, at eighteen, he felt ready to try racing himself.

"I want to start driving," Richard announced. "I mean, I want to *see* if I want to drive. I don't *know* that I want to drive, but I'd like to try to see if I want to do that."

"No," snapped Lee, not one to waste two words when one would do.

"Well, Buddy Baker's driving," Richard countered, pointing to NASCAR driver Buck Baker's son, who was only sixteen at the time.

"I don't care *who's* driving!" Lee growled. "*You're* not driving. Not for *me*! Come back when you're twenty-one."

Richard knew better than to press the point. But his dream hardly idled. At his father's insistence he enrolled as a part-time student at King's Business College in Greensboro, North Carolina, about fifteen miles from the family's home in Level Cross, to learn the basics of balancing books. Penmanship was among the required courses, deemed essential to keeping orderly ledgers. And Richard liked the class so much that he signed up for an elective, Oriental penmanship. If he couldn't race just yet, he figured, he might as well start working on his autograph.

Seven NASCAR championships, two hundred victories, and a half-century later, it's hard to say where Richard Petty ranks among NASCAR's bookkeepers. But he has no peer when it comes to autographs. Petty's signature is the most distinctive, most requested, and most generously given in the history of motorsports, if not all sports. And he still fashions his autograph as if adorning a canvas, replete with all the loops and flourishes of a ceiling fresco at Versailles.

"One of the first things my dad always told me was, 'Anything worth doing, is worth doing right,'" Petty explains. "So if you're going to sign your name, it should be so that the people that get your name know who you are."

• • •

The man who became stock-car racing's King came from humble roots—Randolph County, North Carolina, located near the center of the state, with little to commend itself but the clay underfoot. The dairy farmers who called it home took that clay and cultivated fields for grazing cattle. Other farmers planted tobacco. In the tiny crossroads of Seagrove, clans of Coles and Owens scooped it up by handfuls, picked out the sticks and stones, and fired it into jugs and crocks, spawning a pottery colony that came to be known as Jugtown. In the town of Level Cross, the Pettys built racecars.

The Petty racing compound isn't far from the state road that connects Greensboro to Asheboro, just a few miles west of a stretch now known as Richard Petty Highway. It sits behind a white picket fence—part homeplace and part garage, which is fitting because for four generations of Pettys, family and vocation have been indistinguishable. The white frame house set back from the road is where Richard was born in 1937. The series of white garages next to it sprouted up in the decades that followed. An old toolshed served as Lee's first garage, and he carried his wrenches to the racetrack in a breadbox. When he outgrew the one-car garage, he built a second. Then a third to store parts and pieces. And so on, until the sheds worked their way down the hillside.

There's no barbed wire encircling the compound. Just a fence with a sign next to the gate at the parking lot asking visitors to check in at the office. When you walk through that gate, you're stepping into NASCAR's history. Lee Petty raced in the first NASCAR race, and the Pettys have been there ever since.

A lifelong tinkerer with cars, Lee Petty had worked as a salesman for a biscuit company as a young man. With a family to support, he started a trucking business and would deny all his life that moonshine was ever part of his freight. Richard is less sure.

"He was on the outskirts of that deal," Petty says with a chuckle. Kyle Petty, Lee's grandson, has no doubt. A few of his great-uncles did time in jail for having counterfeit sugar stamps during World War II (sugar, of course, being a key ingredient in moonshine). Either way, no one went hungry in the Petty household, but putting meals on the table demanded creativity on Elizabeth Petty's part. And Lee had his turn to improvise when the family's house burned down after a kerosene stove exploded. He fashioned a makeshift home from an abandoned construction trailer in the woods, with three rooms and a ceiling not quite high enough for his lanky frame.

Richard, who was six years old at the time, recalled for biographer Bill Libby: "I remember standing outside it and watching it burn and not believing and wonderin' what was gonna happen to us. I remember goin' back that evenin' and looking at the smoulderin' embers and wonderin' what had happened to my clothes and toys. Maybe it was lucky that we didn't have much, because we didn't have much to replace."

Rural North Carolina, by extension, didn't have much in the way of entertainment for those not privileged enough to attend college and revel in the sports culture that teemed around it. For most everyone else, messing with cars became the obsession of choice in the post–World War II era—the workingman's Tar Heel basketball.

"They raced up and down the highways in Randolph and Guilford County," Richard recalls of the men of his father's era. "They went to Daytona and Atlanta and raced people on the road. It wasn't really a circuit; it wasn't organized. Somebody in Daytona would find out that there was a guy in North Carolina who had a fast car and had some money that he would bet. So they would hook up and go to someplace and run each other, like at two or three o'clock at night. They had a starting line and a finish line that was two miles down the road or ten miles down the road. And whoever got there first won."

For Lee Petty, stock-car racing ended up being no different from what it was for Bill France: a passion that became a family business, with the modest proceeds dumped back into the operation and the most trusted jobs filled by relatives, nearly all of whom lived within shouting distance.

Richard was made an apprentice mechanic at twelve; allowed to sweep the garage floor and wash his father's high-powered sedan. In time, he learned to pack the wheel bearings and change the oil and tires. NASCAR was just getting started, and Bill France's rulebook demanded that the racecars be "strictly stock," with no juiced-up engines or fancy modifications. That left little for drivers to do except tape up the headlights and strap themselves in. But as the notion of "strictly stock" fell by the wayside, mainly because the typical sedan couldn't take the pounding of NASCAR's long races, the Petty brothers took on more challenging tasks. Richard turned his focus to building his father a sturdier chassis; Maurice, a stronger engine.

And when he turned twenty-one on July 2, 1958, Richard reminded his father about the promise to let him try racing. He had never run any kind of race before. His experience behind the wheel consisted of moving the car from one spot to another and making a few laps around a dirt track to help dry the surface before a race. But he had no idea how the car handled at top speed.

"There's a car over in the corner," Lee said flatly. "Get the thing ready and take it down to Columbia."

Columbia, South Carolina, held its stock-car races on Thursday nights, because that's the day the servicemen at the local army base got paid. Lee didn't accompany his son on his racing debut; he was racing elsewhere that weekend. Nor did he send him off with any pointers or much encouragement. So Richard grabbed his second cousin, Dale Inman (the two were closer than brothers), and headed to Columbia. He knew enough to fasten his helmet and seat belt before the green flag flew. Everything after that was instinct. He immediately steered the car up close to the wall amid the mayhem on the first lap—so close, in fact, that his sedan's right side scraped the wall all the way down the straightaways. At least that way, Richard figured, he'd have to spend less time hurtling out of control before he crashed. He was scared to death as faster cars and famous names roared past. Somehow he finished sixth. And in the process, he fell in love.

"I come home and I told Dad, 'You know, I'm liable to *like* this!'" Richard says, laughing.

It was as pure a love as he had known. And when he proposed to the pretty high school girl he had been dating, Richard laid his emotions bare. "I told her, 'Racing is Number One. If you try *real* hard, you could be Number Two.'"

The following year Richard won his first race at the same track in Columbia. That night, the first fan asked for his autograph. "That tickled the *fire* out of me!" Petty recalls. "I'd been working on the cars for years, and nobody ever knew. The second race I won, I probably had two people come ask. And when the third person came, I said, 'This is great! They know I'm here!'"

As a NASCAR rookie, Richard played a secondary role to his father in 1958, not really a factor in the races they both competed in. Even then you'd hardly know they were kin. Lee did his son no favors on the track. In fact, he protested Richard's first victory, arguing that NASCAR's official scorer had erred in counting the laps during a 1959 race at Atlanta's Lakewood Speedway. While Richard drove to Victory Lane, Lee circled the track one more time, lodged a protest, and prevailed, convincing race officials to strip the trophy from his son and give it to him.

Lee Petty was hardly NASCAR's most charismatic or most skilled driver in the sport's early years. But he might have been its most stubborn, reared in a world in which men had to earn what they got and fight for what they earned. It served him well in the inaugural Daytona 500.

• • •

The construction of Daytona International Speedway in 1958 was Bill France's crowning achievement to that point. At 2.5 miles around, the giant oval was precisely the same size as the country's most famous track, Indianapolis Motor Speedway, which represented everything France aspired to as he struggled to upgrade stock-car racing's image. Built in 1909, the Indianapolis track hosted only one event each year, the Indianapolis 500, which was restricted to the fenderless, low-slung, open-wheel racecars that represented the height of automotive technology.

France decided to build his own speedway in his adoptive hometown of Daytona Beach, where the old oval track that spanned the beach and beachfront highway was getting squeezed out by development. France mapped out a speedway every bit as big as the Indianapolis behemoth. But France's idea mimicked a carnival's Tilt-a-Whirl; as long as the track's surface was banked high enough, and speeds were fast enough, the stock cars could hurtle around it without slipping. The result was an act of sheer engineering hubris, fueled, in part, according to veteran motorsports journalist Ed Hinton, by the rude reception France and his wife had received when they made a goodwill visit to the hallowed Indiana speedway in the early 1950s.

France's masterwork still elicits awe today, whether from children who have only raced toy cars on their living room carpets or from sportswriters who, until they entered Daytona's gates, presumed the biggest spectacle in sports was the Super Bowl.

Robin Pemberton, who would rise from the ranks of NASCAR mechanics to become the sport's vice president of competition, was a smart-mouthed high school kid from upstate New York when he attended his first race at Daytona in 1974. He still remembers the feeling when he entered the enormous infield. "You pull down in the tunnel, and you pull up into the infield, and you look around, and that's Turn 3. That's the thing kids dream of!" says Pemberton. "I just wanted to pass out. It was the coolest thing ever. It just made my hair stand up. It does today."

France couldn't have scripted a more riveting finish for his inaugural Daytona 500. Three racecars crossed the finish line in a virtual dead heat: the Oldsmobile of three-time NASCAR champion Lee Petty, Johnny Beauchamp's Ford Thunderbird, and a lapped car that obscured the view from the scoring stand. France declared Beauchamp the winner, but Petty pulled into Victory Lane, confident he had won. It took three days to resolve the dispute, with France reversing course and awarding the trophy to Petty after reviewing newsreel footage to clarify the mess.

The controversy proved a public-relations boon, stretching what should have been a one-day sports story into three days. The lesson wouldn't be lost on Bill France. In his book *Daytona,* Hinton wrote of Daytona's controversial debut: "That was the moment when Bill France and Lee Petty transformed automobile racing's national image from that of an engineering exercise into entertainment. That was the moment at which NASCAR began to stalk every other form of motor racing for the heart and mind of Everyman."

· · ·

Richard, it turned out, had inherited Lee's resolve behind the wheel, as well as his knack for keeping his car's nose out of trouble until the money-paying lap. He also seemed to have a preternatural understanding of the car, able to figure out what adjustments it needed to go faster and explain them to his crew chief, Dale Inman, and engine-building brother, Maurice.

"My edge always felt like it was not my ability to drive the car, but my ability to work on the car and understand the car and make it feel like what I wanted it to," Richard said. "Dale was doing the work, but he didn't do anything I didn't tell him to do or we didn't discuss. So I was a mechanical driver, more or less. My expertise was knowin' a little bit about the car. And then I just went out and tried to get what I knew was *in* the car out."

The results showed themselves quickly. NASCAR's Rookie of the Year in 1959, Richard went on to win two races in 1961, eight in 1962, and fourteen (twice as many as the famed Junior Johnson) in 1963. His rivals groused privately that they could have achieved as much with the same equipment. In their view, Lee had handed his elder son a championship-caliber car and championship-caliber crew, and Richard was simply making the most of it. But they couldn't speak harshly about Richard, because he was so decent—generous with parts and pieces if he had them to share, and generous with advice.

To the delight of promoters, fans responded to Richard's personality as they had no other driver. Until Richard Petty started dominating, the cars themselves had been NASCAR's chief draw. Fans came to see Junior Johnson's Chevrolet face off against the Fords built by the famous Holman-Moody race shop. But after Petty seized the spotlight with his toothy smile, folksy manner, and never-met-a-stranger attitude of a man running for office, NASCAR fans started branding themselves as Petty fans every bit as much as their predecessors had declared themselves Ford fans or Chevy fans. Almost overnight, it seemed, Petty became NASCAR's cultural ambassador.

In the small, southeastern towns that populated the NASCAR circuit in the mid-1960s, movie stars and sports stars existed only on magazine covers and in newsreel footage. So when Richard Petty towed his light-blue No. 43 Plymouth to shopping centers in Macon, Georgia; Greenville, South Carolina; Weaverville, North Carolina; or South Boston, Virginia, and signed autographs before a race, that was bigger than the circus coming to town. And the race that followed? Well, that beat all! The roaring engines, screeching tires, and banging sheet metal were things folks didn't get to see every day. And Petty delivered: he was a spectacular circus elephant, charismatic carnival barker, and daring trapeze artist all in one. And when his act was over, he had all the time in the world for the fans.

"He would sit there on that old fence at Darlington after a race and sign autographs until there wasn't anybody asking," recalls Jim Hunter, a sportswriter for the Columbia, South Carolina, newspaper at the time. As his victories mounted and fame grew, Petty made more time for NASCAR fans, not less.

Kyle Petty, Richard's eldest child, remembers the routine well, having ridden with his mother and sisters to hundreds of his father's races as a youngster. "We would park in the infield and sit while the race would go on," Kyle says. "And when the race was over with, we'd wait until everybody came out of the garage area, and the King would come out. If they had won the race, we'd have been to Victory Lane, and we had a trophy, and then we'd head home. Or we sat and waited until everybody left. We were always some of the last people to leave the racetrack because he was doing the thing [signing autographs]."

Petty won his first Daytona 500 in 1964 in a Plymouth powered by a revolutionary Hemi engine, its pistons arranged in a hemisphere, rather than the conventional straight line, to maximize horsepower. He won the first of his seven NASCAR championships that year, too. The outclassed Ford teams lobbied Bill France so hard to rein in Chrysler's Hemi that NASCAR's CEO took the draconian step of banning the engine for the 1965 season. Chrysler executives refused to run anything else; the Hemi was what their dealers were selling in the showrooms. So they boycotted NASCAR's 1965 season. Petty, under contract to drive Chrysler products, had no choice but to follow suit.

Ford won the 1965 championship with driver Ned Jarrett, but the crowds dropped off without Petty in the field. Meanwhile, NASCAR's King dabbled in drag-racing to fulfill his contract with Chrysler. After his dragster lost a wheel, flew out of control, and struck and killed an eight-year-old boy watching from the other side of a fence during a race in Georgia, Petty had no heart to continue. And France lost his resolve to uphold the Hemi ban, having seen his sport sputter without its newfound meal ticket. With roughly two-thirds of the 1965 season over, Petty returned to NASCAR's fold and won four of the fifteen races he entered.

There simply was no NASCAR story line other than Richard Petty in 1967. Of the season's fifty races, Petty won twenty-seven. Bobby Allison, the second-most successful driver, won six. But to the reporters who covered stock-car racing, nearly all of whom worked for southern newspapers, it hardly mattered who won if Petty fell short. The lead of their stories, as well as the headlines atop them, invariably focused on Petty's fortunes, much as modern-day golf coverage focuses on the performance of Tiger Woods. It was as if NASCAR had a single heartbeat—Richard Petty's—and everything else was white noise.

. . .

Stock-car racing was growing as the 1960s came to a close. New tracks had opened. Crowds were picking up. But the drivers didn't see their lot improving. Many felt the purses weren't keeping pace with the promoters' income. Conditions at several tracks were cause for concern. Flimsy metal guardrails that separated the fans from the race-cars often caused more injury than they prevented when drivers crashed into them. And basic amenities were lacking, like bathrooms and half-decent grandstands that drivers considered safe enough for their wives and children.

In hopes of prodding NASCAR to make changes, drivers tried a second time in the decade to organize. They steered clear of the word *union,* mindful of France's no-tolerance policy toward unions, and dubbed their group the Professional Drivers Association (PDA). And they asked Petty to lead it.

But the PDA's first showdown with France was its last.

France's track-owning and operating company, International Speedway Corporation, was set to unveil its biggest racetrack yet, the 2.66-mile Alabama International Motor Speedway (later renamed Talladega Superspeedway), in September 1969. Problems surfaced from the start. With the 33-degree banks and nearly mile-long straightaways, speeds were faster than anyone anticipated, nearing 200 miles per hour. And the racecar tires shredded under the strain during practice.

"The tires would just come apart," recalled veteran racer Dave Marcis. "We had never run anywhere with those speeds constant, 198, 199 miles an hour."

The PDA asked France to postpone the inaugural race until the problems could be fixed. France was irate. He strapped on a helmet, hopped in a Ford, and drove around the track at 176 miles per hour himself to prove it was safe. The drivers weren't convinced, and all but Bobby Isaac loaded up their cars and headed home.

France filled the race-day field with replacement drivers who didn't stage much of a show in their rickety equipment. Only fifteen cars were still running at the end. And of those, only three completed the full distance. Richard Brickhouse, an unknown from Rocky Point, North Carolina, claimed the only victory of his career that day. And Isaac, the only "name" driver in the field, was rewarded with a gold Rolex watch as a gesture of thanks from Bill France. France also gave every fan who attended a free pass to any race at his other show-place, Daytona International Speedway.

The drivers may have spoiled Talladega's coming-out party, but France's message was unmistakable, even in the face of financial calamity. NASCAR drivers could protest all they wanted, but France owned the major racetracks. And he was going to stage his races, with or without them. There would always be another driver, if not an-other hundred, just waiting for the chance to strap into a racecar. The next week the PDA disbanded, and the drivers returned to work.

While France had made examples of drivers who crossed him in the past, Petty says he never felt any repercussions for his part in lead-ing the PDA. "I was probably not looked at in favor," he says, "but I was still their lead man. I was their Earnhardt at the time. So if NASCAR had said, 'Richard started this deal, so we're going to black-ball him for a year or kick him out,' that would not have went over. I was valuable to myself, but I was valuable to them, too. Not that they couldn't have run races and everything. But they would have got a bad image at the time, so they were smart enough to sort of suck it up and keep quiet."

From the outset, NASCAR's rulebook made clear that drivers as-sumed all liability once they strapped into a racecar. So it was their choice how reckless they wanted to be. If they wanted to reinforce their cars' frames with steel roll bars, that was fine with NASCAR. If they didn't, that was fine, too. The same went for helmets, protective gloves, and the practice of carrying a fire extinguisher in the cars. For the most part, NASCAR steered clear of issues related to drivers' personal safety.

And conditions were brutal in the cars even when they didn't crash or catch fire. Temperatures soared well over 130 degrees, with heat from the engine torrid enough to cook a driver's feet through the floorboards. Some drivers taped Styrofoam cups to their shoes as protection. Petty drove in cowboy boots to keep his feet from burning up. He had a scarecrow's physique to start with, but he'd still sweat off ten pounds during a three-hour race. He'd guzzle Cokes and Pepsis and any kind of soda he could get his hands on during pit stops to try to keep cool. But he switched to milk after his ulcers got so bad he had to have nearly half his stomach removed.

NASCAR's laissez-faire attitude toward safety changed after the 1964 death of Fireball Roberts, who died of pneumonia that set in after he suffered third-degree burns when his car's fuel tank ruptured during a crash at Charlotte. Spurred by Roberts's death, as well as that of several open-wheel drivers in fiery crashes that year, Firestone developed a fuel cell that encased the gasoline in a protective bladder, decreasing the chance of gas-fueled fires on impact. NASCAR made the fuel cell mandatory equipment the following year.

Petty's 1970 crash at Darlington, the most savage wreck of his career, prompted another safety innovation. As his Plymouth exited Turn 4, it slammed into the track's concrete retaining wall, spun sideways, and took flight, flipping twelve times as his spindly frame flopped around in the car. To the horror of fans, Petty's left arm dangled out the driver's-side window, sure to get sheared off if the car landed just so. The King was still in one piece when the battered heap finally came to rest, but he was passed out cold. The following year,

NASCAR required that driver's-side windows (which were open to the air, rather than fitted with glass) be covered with a seat belt–tough netting to keep drivers' extremities inside.

Petty returned to racing in less than a month. By the time he retired, nearly every bone in his body had been broken, set, and reknitted at least once, including his neck, both shoulders, sternum, so many ribs he lost count, legs, feet, multiple fingers, and nose.

"Pain don't hurt me like it hurts the average guy," he explained years later. "A lot of that is the mind. I'm a strong believer in mind over matter. As far as the bones and stuff, it never crosses my mind that any of it hurts. The good Lord built me for what I'm doing."

So he kept on racing.

. . .

While dozens of race teams dabbled in NASCAR in the early 1970s, only a handful consistently won: Petty Enterprises; Junior Johnson's boys; the Wood Brothers of Stuart, Virginia; and Bud Moore's bunch from Spartanburg, South Carolina. And of those, only Petty Enterprises had what marketing executives considered "the whole package"—a peak-performing car, a durable engine, and a charismatic driver. So it was no surprise that STP wanted to hitch its product to Petty's star in 1972.

Few race teams had sponsors at the time. Those who did were typically aligned with a local tire store, restaurant, or towing service that helped defray their expenses. STP was the first national company to sponsor a NASCAR team, and the deal was worth an unprecedented $250,000 a year, which the Pettys poured into better equipment and a bigger shop. Richard also rewarded his family with a bigger home just down the road from the brick ranch he and Lynda had started out in. But he didn't get swept up by the trappings of financial success, and he was wary of those who did. Petty Enterprises remained a lean operation. Elizabeth Petty continued keeping the books for the family business. And Lee, long retired as a driver, looked in on the balance sheet from time to time. Being a good steward of a dollar was a bedrock Petty value.

So was humility. The Pettys were so adamant about preaching the virtue to their children "not get above their raising" that Kyle didn't even tell his elementary school classmates about his father being invited to the White House to meet President Nixon for fear it would sound too proud. His teacher, who had read about it in the newspaper, told the class instead.

"Where we came from, we just went to school and were part of the community," Kyle explained years later. "It was a little pretentious to have your father go to the White House. We just didn't talk about it at the time. But for our family, it was huge. It would have to be for any family. To think I knew somebody who actually went to the White House! It put what he had done, and the sport, in a totally different perspective."

When it was time to go racing, Petty would slip a cover with an STP logo over his sleek No. 43 Plymouth and tow it to the track on a trailer. Whenever possible, he'd load Lynda and the children in a Dodge van and take them, too. Whether Kyle, Sharon, Lisa, and Rebecca ended up liking stock-car racing didn't matter. Richard and Lynda Petty believed their children could learn a lot from seeing other parts of the world, whether it was the Grand Ole Opry, the Smithsonian, the Henry Ford Museum, or a rowdy NASCAR infield.

"There's things they learn on the road that I could never teach them at home," Petty once said. "Just looking at some of those drunk fans tells them a lot about drinking, for instance."

Wherever he went, Petty sold himself, STP motor oil, and NASCAR. He was stock-car racing's Pied Piper, wooing fans up and down the East Coast. Decades later, you can wander through NASCAR's garage and ask any of the mechanics in their forties or fifties why they got into racing. More likely than not, it had something to do with Richard Petty.

The Pettys ran two NASCAR teams out of the Level Cross shop, building the cars and engines with only eighteen people. Everyone from Richard on down drove to the racetracks; no one took commercial flights. The King typically rode in the van's backseat, where he slept in between spitting tobacco juice into a cup and critiquing whoever was driving. They doubled up in hotel rooms, never staying anywhere fancy, and kept all their receipts.

All the top teams were run that way. And no one bothered to calculate their hourly wage or conduct a cost-benefit analysis of their livelihood. Nothing could beat the thrill of making a living by turning a wrench on a championship racecar. A similar passion drew the fans. As one decade slipped to the next, Petty hopped from a Dodge to a Ford and then back to Chrysler, and briefly drove an Oldsmobile before switching to Plymouth. Petty fans stayed with him no matter what. Once you were a Petty fan, you didn't switch. And you usually passed that allegiance on to your children.

It unfolded much the same in the Petty household, as Kyle, who had played football, basketball, baseball, and golf at Randleman High, found his calling the same place his father and grandfather had found theirs.

"I knew I was going to like it," Kyle says. "It's the same thing if you grow up on the farm. You know by the time you're nine or ten whether you want to be a farmer or not. You either like the land— you like getting up at four in the morning milking; you like priming tobacco; you like being on a tractor—or you don't. A lot of people choose to leave the farm, but just as many people choose to stay on the farm because they love the land. There's no magic moment. There's no lightbulb that comes on. It's just all the sudden you wake up one day and you're fifteen or sixteen and it's like, 'Dang! I know a lot about that!' Whether I studied it or not, I know a lot about that through osmosis—just from being around it, I absorb stuff. . . . Little by little you just realize: this is what you knew. This is what you did. And I knew this is what I wanted to do."

While an eighteen-year-old Kyle Petty set about carving his

niche in the sport, Richard ruled the day. Over the course of a career that spanned five decades, Petty would see challengers come and go, from gentlemanly Ned Jarrett, who won NASCAR's title in 1961 and '65, to Tim Richmond, a dazzling talent who won thirteen races in six quick seasons before disappearing from the circuit and dying of an AIDS-related illness in 1989. South Carolina's David Pearson was Petty's most worthy opponent on the giant superspeedways. Bobby Allison and Cale Yarborough were his most dogged competitors. And his mouthiest, by far, was a brash upstart from Owensboro, Kentucky, named Darrell Waltrip. But Petty met them all with unshakable confidence in his car and his command behind the wheel.

Robin Pemberton, a young mechanic on the team, marveled at Petty's savvy behind the wheel as he listened to the King talking strategy with his crew chief over the radio during races. Modern-day NASCAR drivers can get by with virtually no understanding of strategy, relying on their crew chiefs to tell them when to pit for tires and gas, how many laps remain in a race, and how many seconds faster the lead car is running. All relevant data are tracked on laptop computers, and crew chiefs spit out the essential statistics as drivers whiz by, lap after lap. In Petty's prime, all that data resided in the driver's head.

"He could strategize the whole race in his mind," Pemberton recalls. "He knew where he was on the racetrack, what lap he was on, who he had lapped, how many laps till the next pit stop. There were times Richard would come over the radio and ask a question, and it was amazing the things that he knew were going on."

Petty embodied everything a fan or a corporation wanted in an athlete in his day. He was equal parts Andy Griffith and Elvis Presley, instinctively modulating between the two depending on the circumstance. He was the folksy, friendly, paternal Griffith when dealing with fans. But the moment he climbed in his racecar, he was Elvis—the iconic figure who took a quintessentially American art form and remade it in his image. If, for a time, rock 'n' roll was indistinguishable from Elvis Presley, so too was NASCAR indistinguishable from

Richard Petty. Other drivers knew they'd be fools to copy Petty's style, but all took note of the way he treated fans. It set a garage standard. Petty, in effect, taught NASCAR drivers how to behave.

"The biggest lesson he taught me was 'We work for the fans,'" Kyle Petty says. "It came from my father saying, 'I work for the guy who pays fifteen bucks for a Saturday-night ticket to come watch me race, because *that's* the money that goes into the purse and pays me to race.' It was all about that—and putting yourself in the other person's shoes."

• • •

The King's performance began to decline in the 1980s, as younger, more aggressive drivers ramped up the competition. Waltrip's pairing with car owner Junior Johnson produced three championships in the decade, the audacity of Waltrip's arrogant mouth eclipsed only by the audacity of Johnson's refusal to be constrained by NASCAR's rulebook. The north Georgia mountains produced a redheaded driver named Bill Elliott, who had a southern accent strong enough to bend sheet metal and a smooth way of racing that evoked the King's style. The midwestern stock-car circuit spawned upstarts Mark Martin and Rusty Wallace. In Charlotte, North Carolina, an ambitious car dealer named Rick Hendrick was determined to prove that it made better business sense to own multiple race teams than just one.

And in the textile mill town of nearby Kannapolis, the scruffy, ill-mannered son of the late Ralph Earnhardt, a Carolina dirt-track legend who never made a mark in NASCAR's top ranks, was raising hell. Dale Earnhardt had little more than his father's last name when he finally got the chance to prove his bloodline on the track. But even in shoddy racecars his raw talent screamed out. And he had more nerve than talent. There didn't seem to be anything Ralph's boy was scared of behind the wheel, and there wasn't anything or anyone he wouldn't hit to run up front.

Still, Petty wasn't interested in retiring, even after his fiftieth birthday came and went. He was hardly the first to stave off the day when he'd quit racing. Indeed, NASCAR had produced few role models for a graceful exit from the sport. Ned Jarrett was the rare competitor to retire on top, bowing out as a two-time defending NASCAR champion to enter the less risky profession of racetrack management. But for too many champions, the decision was made for them. Bobby Allison's career was cut short by a catastrophic injury, as was Lee Petty's. Bobby Isaac heard a voice that told him to get out of the car during a race at Talladega, and he was so spooked he obeyed. Curtis Turner, Joe Weatherly, and others with less famous names died doing what they loved.

For the King, there were still glorious moments ahead. They just were fewer and farther between.

His last NASCAR victory—the 1984 Pepsi 400 at Daytona International Speedway—brought his career wins to two hundred, a mark that has never been equaled. Even better for NASCAR's purposes, President Ronald Reagan became the first commander in chief to attend a NASCAR race, bestowing the national stamp of approval that France had coveted for so long. Reagan gave the famous command, "Gentleman, start your engines," from Air Force One en route to the Daytona Beach airport. And he was ensconced in a luxury suite overlooking the mammoth oval as Petty and Yarborough battled door-to-door over the furious last laps. With three laps to go, a wreck brought out the caution flag, signaling that the running order would be frozen once the cars passed the scoring stand. Petty surged past Yarborough to claim the victory by a car-length.

Petty would call the achievement "the pinnacle of my career," coming on the Fourth of July, replete with drama and the president in attendance. Skeptics would question whether NASCAR hadn't helped the King to the historic mark by letting an oversized engine slip past its prerace inspectors—a charge Petty dismisses as nonsense. Reagan joined the King in Victory Lane and followed up with a second invitation to the White House. This time, the whole family was included. So was Petty's No. 43 racecar, which was displayed on the White House lawn.

Kyle, twenty-four at the time, was humbled by the honor. "We grew up in Level Cross, and obviously we spent our time at race-tracks, so you were just in awe to walk through the White House and to come out in the Rose Garden," he said. "To have sat home and watched so much go on at the Rose Garden, you were awed by the history of the place."

He was also struck by how gracious the president was—and how soft-spoken. "To have him call you by name, to have him call my sisters by name and call my mother by name . . . I'm sure he was briefed like crazy," Kyle said. "But to think of everything going on in the world at that time—and he had fifteen or twenty minutes, and he remembered your name—it was incredible."

•   •   •

Richard Petty would race another eight seasons in pursuit of a 201st victory, but he wasn't a competitive threat. Still, fans clamored to see him. And with NASCAR now a regular presence on television, Petty was earning as much for simply competing in races as he had for winning them years earlier. But more than anything, Petty found it hard to give up the only calling he had known.

"It ain't the money nor the glory," Petty once explained. "I just like to drive. It's that simple. Some cats, they like to watch cows eat grass. That's their thing. Me, I like to drive. It's my thing. I like the feel of metal around me, the feel of tires under me."

When he finally accepted the inevitability of retirement, he set the plans in motion a year in advance. It wouldn't come down to one last race. Instead, he'd devote the entire 1992 NASCAR season to bidding farewell to the fans who had supported him for thirty-five years. The result was the Richard Petty Fan Appreciation Tour—a ten-month celebration of the love affair between NASCAR's most successful driver and his fans. It was organized like a modern-day concert tour, with corporate sponsors, commemorative merchandise, and sold-out venues in nearly every town. Virtually every entity associated with NASCAR benefited, from series sponsor R.J. Reynolds down to little memorabilia shops like Charlotte Sports Collectibles.

Eleven companies paid $225,000 apiece to sponsor the tour, which gave them the right to emblazon their products with the official tour logo and use Petty in their advertising campaigns. R.J. Reynolds hired the band Alabama to write a song in Petty's honor, titled "The Fan." The song was then set to a ten-minute music video, augmented by archival footage and available only with the purchase of a carton of Winston cigarettes.

Until 1992, NASCAR souvenirs generally consisted of T-shirts, caps, and trading cards. Petty's farewell changed that, proving that once a fan claimed a driver as his own, there was almost nothing he wouldn't buy to proclaim his allegiance. Fans gobbled up wood-grain clocks shaped like Petty's racecar, telephones shaped like his car, Petty-edition pistols, and Petty-edition Pepsi bottles. Just about anything big enough to feature Petty's name, picture, or car number was branded as a commemorative, and the souvenirs flew off the shelves as soon as they were displayed. A series of Match Box–size die-cast cars, one for each of his final thirty races, was the centerpiece of the merchandising blitz, generating more than $15 million alone.

Business boomed at every stop on the circuit. Track owners built new grandstands to accommodate the hordes who wanted to witness the King's last ride. And every race was preceded by a tribute: two hundred parachutists leaped from helicopters to honor his two hundred victories at one track; a menagerie of circus animals was paraded about at another.

And from the first race of 1992 to the last, no driver worked harder to please the fans and satisfy their need to touch a piece of

NASCAR history. At a rail-thin six feet two, Petty *was* that relic of stock-car racing history—NASCAR's living, breathing Shroud of Turin—who let fans shake his hand and huddle next to him for photographs with unfailing geniality, never betraying a trace of irritation or impatience.

Midway through the season Petty invited fans to an open house at the family's racing compound. An estimated thirty thousand showed up, many of them camping overnight in the Level Cross Ball Park. It was a sweltering weekend in the middle of July, and the Pettys' front lawn teemed with visitors who wanted to say thank you, get an autograph, take a picture, and tour the shop where the Petty clan had turned hunks of metal into lightning bolts.

Nearly all brought a photograph, a trading card, or a toy car to be signed. And three generations of Pettys obliged. Lee, the patriarch, sat in a chair on the front porch to receive guests, taking a break at midday to go inside and eat a hot dog. Richard, wearing snakeskin boots, blue jeans, a white short-sleeved shirt, black sunglasses, and feathered cowboy hat, sat on a custom-made sofa fashioned after the tail end of his No. 43 blue-and-red Pontiac. A white canopy shielded him from the sun, and a seven-foot wrought-iron fan blew cool air over his shoulder. To his right sat three boxes of black felt-tip markers, twelve to a box. Petty grabbed one, and set to work.

Moms plopped babies in the King's lap. Grown men flung their arms around his shoulders. A few women pecked his cheek. One little boy, paralyzed with awe, could only stare at Petty's knee. Another child was so entranced he pushed his face within an inch or so of the King's to peer into his black glasses. Petty just smiled and kept signing: hats, die-cast cars, newspapers, calendars, T-shirts, trading cards, life-size cardboard Petty stand-ups—even someone's leg.

"They say he's signed more autographs than anyone in the world," said Vance Gibson of Oak Ridge, North Carolina. "More than anyone. Even Elvis Presley."

He still gave the same fancy autograph, but with a technique he had refined over the years, no different from Tom Seaver's pitching motion or Pete Sampras's serve. Petty didn't write with his fingers anymore; his fingers simply clasped the pen like a drill grips a drill bit. His wrist never flexed. All the motion came from the elbow. That way his fingers never cramped, and his wrist didn't tire no matter how many autographs he signed.

"As long as you fed him, gave him a Pepsi to drink, and let him have his potty break, he was a like a wind-up doll," said Chuck Spicer, then STP's public-relations man. "The best I'd ever seen."

Kyle Petty, who was in the thick of a battle for the 1992 championship with Davey Allison, Bill Elliott, and Alan Kulwicki, signed his share of autographs, too. And dozens of Petty children, grandchildren, cousins, and second cousins ran and played amid the giant carnival in the yard. There were food booths with hamburgers, catfish, popcorn, peanuts, homemade ice cream, and baked goods. There were corporate booths, too, hawking Petty-endorsed hot dogs, car wax, antifreeze, and tools. And there were souvenirs: everything from $1 decals to a $4,000 engraved Richard Petty Colt .45, including Petty cross-stitch kits, gift wrap, barbecue sauce, truck-bed liners, lithographs, pocketknives, and toolboxes.

The hours ticked away, but the autograph line, which by eight a.m. snaked three miles through the scrubby pines, never seemed to get shorter. For most Petty fans, it was a day when wishes came true. All but Darrell Britt, who longed to see Petty win one more race at the season finale in Atlanta, which was four months away. "That's where my federal income-tax return went, my truck payment— everything I've saved up over the last year," Britt said. "I got my plane ticket, race ticket, rental car reserved and everything. He's never forgot what got him to the top. His fans."

• • •

By the time he flipped the ignition on his 1,185th and final NASCAR race, Richard Petty was "just wore slap-dead out," as he put it.

Ten months of hullabaloo had finally come to an end, capped by a party at Atlanta's new indoor football stadium, the Georgia Dome, the night before. Nearly fifty thousand attended, and relief was about the only emotion Petty had left on race day. He hadn't had a top-ten finish all season, but NASCAR fans showered him with louder cheers than ever. It didn't matter where he started a race or finished it. He had their respect. Richard Petty had been NASCAR's backbone for as long as many could remember. And it wasn't clear what would become of the sport without him.

Sure, there were other personalities. Five of them still had a shot at winning the 1992 title, the standings were so knotted entering the Atlanta finale—including second-generation racer Davey Allison and Petty's own son, Kyle. A twenty-one-year-old Californian named Jeff Gordon was making his debut in NASCAR's top division the following day. If the baby-faced Gordon were half as gifted as touted, insiders said, he might amount to something one day. And who knew what the future held for NASCAR's Intimidator, five-time champion Dale Earnhardt, who had pouted his way through a lousy year?

Petty's last ride would have no storybook finish. His No. 43 Pontiac was snared in a six-car pileup before the race reached the halfway point. With flames erupting from under his hood and no safety workers en route, Petty steered his barbecued heap toward a fire truck parked on the infield, climbed out, and waved to the fans to signal he was okay. Then he walked to his team's transporter truck, where his wife and daughters were waiting, all of them crying.

Petty wept, too, utterly spent and relieved the day was over. His team had other ideas, determined that the King's chariot would still be running at the finish of the race. So while Petty sat with his family, his crew ripped away the car's mangled sheet metal, wrapped what was left in black electrical tape, and got it ready to drive. With only a few laps remaining, Petty surveyed the battered car, which didn't even have a hood anymore, turned to his public-relations man, and asked for an STP decal. He slipped on his helmet and slapped the decal smack on the car's radiator—right where its hood should have been. And he steered the Pontiac back onto the track to thunderous applause.

• • •

As a sportswriter you become inured to athletes who behave one way when TV cameras are on and another when they're off. The list of frauds and phonies in college and professional sports is long, and no sport is immune. But with Petty, the warmth with strangers and ease in his own skin wasn't an act. It is simply his way, as if imprinted in his very DNA. In the South, it's known as "not getting above your raising." And it's almost unknown in the overpaid, overhyped, oversexed playpen of big-time sports, which oozes a toxic air of arrogance and entitlement.

As eager as fans were to put the King on a pedestal, Petty refused to acknowledge that anything about what he did for a living made him any better a person or any more deserving of recognition than a farmer, a schoolteacher, or the neighbors he prayed alongside in church. He viewed God as having given him a gift for stock-car racing and the constitution to suffer its blows. And he viewed fans as the boss who signed his paycheck each week, convinced he owed them a bigger debt than he owed NASCAR's founding France family; his sponsor, STP; or racetrack owners, promoters, and reporters combined.

"One of the very first lessons I learned from my dad was, 'Be yourself,'" Petty said in a recent interview. "In other words, 'You're a country boy; don't try to be a city boy. Just be yourself.' Sometimes it hurts, because you're in a situation where you'd be better off if you was looked at a little different. People might think, 'He don't talk right.' Or, 'He don't dress right.' Know what I mean? But it's hard to play a role all the time. I play *my* role all the time because what you see is what you get. It's easy. . . . I don't know that if I came in today, that my personality would fit the norm. I look back at my career and say, the good Lord put me on earth at the right time, in the right place, under the right circumstances with the right people."

Chapter 3

RACING'S MOUNTAINTOPS AND VALLEYS

Bobby Allison remembers having dinner with a big crowd at his favorite Daytona Beach restaurant, Parks Seafood, on February 14, 1988. He remembers that he liked the frog legs. And he remembers they were celebrating something. Everything else about what happened that day is gone, stripped from his memory by the massive brain injury he suffered five months later in a near-fatal crash at Pennsylvania's Pocono Raceway.

February 14 had been the sort of day a racecar driver dreams about since childhood: the day he wins the Daytona 500. In Allison's case, it was the day he won the Daytona 500 a third time and, at fifty, became the oldest winner on record of NASCAR's grand spectacle. Better still, his son Davey finished second, trailing his father across the line just two car lengths back.

It was as if God were embarrassing the Allison family with riches. And after the champagne-drenched celebration in Victory Lane, Bobby's wife of twenty-eight years looked on with joyful disbelief as Bobby, who was joined by twenty-six-year-old Davey, fielded reporters' questions in the press box.

"My husband and my son!" Judy Allison said. "My husband and my son! My husband and my son!"

Bobby beamed. "It was a great feeling to look back and see somebody you think is the best coming up and know it is your own son," he said. "It is a very special feeling, and it is hard to put in words."

But after the Pocono crash those words were as alien to Bobby as the videotaped footage of the father-son Daytona finish. From hearing others describe it, Bobby felt sure it had been the best day of his life. But it might as well have happened to a stranger, or to his rival Richard Petty.

"I would put the tape in, and it would begin to annoy me very quickly because I couldn't relate to anything," Bobby recalled years later. "Nothing would come. It was like I was watching a movie somebody else had made. It is a great disappointment: having something that had to be the ultimate, be so totally missing. There are no words that would let you understand what I'm talking about."

The sport of auto racing loves its photo-finishes and Victory Lane celebrations. But it has a capacity for grief that is unparalleled in sports. No family experienced its extremes more than the Allisons of Hueytown, Alabama. Yet Bobby has refused to put the sport on some abstract scale of justice and weigh what it has given him against what it has taken away. A devout Catholic, he views life as a series of mountaintops and valleys. And sees no reason why he deserved to have been spared the valleys, though he admits wishing that they had not been quite so low.

"What I do is this: I say, 'I cannot redo yesterday. I don't have to like it, but I have to accept it,'" Allison explains. "So I accept it. And I don't like it."

• • •

Bobby Allison bulldozed his way into NASCAR in 1961 as an undersized, unapologetic workingman who raced on guile and determination. "In many ways he was Earnhardt before there was Earnhardt," says Eddie Gossage, Allison's former public-relations man and now president of Texas Motor Speedway.

Too small to play high school sports, the five-foot-four, 110-pound Allison wore a No. 41 football jersey around his south Florida school. It was a gift from the team's manager, who felt sorry there wasn't a place on the squad for such a tiny guy. So that was the number, 41, Bobby painted on the door of his first racecar, a 1938 Chevy Coupe that he drove to school when he launched his short-track racing career under the name "Bob Sunderman" because his parents wouldn't sign a permission slip.

But Mom and Pop Allison didn't object a few years later when Bobby, now utterly consumed with racing, announced he was moving to Alabama, where he'd heard there were short tracks all over the state run by promoters who paid thick wads of cash. All his parents asked is that he take his younger brother Donnie with him. So the boys loaded a pickup truck and headed off, like Depression-era migrants, looking for a better life.

In the years that followed, Bobby drove that pickup to tracks all over Alabama, towing his racecar behind. His young wife rode up front with him, holding their little baby on her lap. They were all the fan club Bobby needed. Judy was his biggest cheerleader; Davey, his best buddy. Bobby loved the fact that Davey's first words were engine sounds—"Vroom! Vroom! Hhood-un! Hhood-un!"—rather than "Mom" or "Dad." To Bobby's ears it was the most incredible first noise a baby ever made.

The smallest boy in a family of ten children (three other siblings had died in infancy), Bobby Allison had been cast as the underdog from birth. And he never shook that identity even after he won NASCAR's championship in 1983. For the most part, that Daytona-size chip on his shoulder is what drove him to beat the meager expectations that surrounded him.

As a mechanic, Bobby had a bit of the mad scientist about him, always tinkering with different components of the racecar that might help it go faster, like trick suspensions and reinforced engine parts. He also pioneered front-end steering in stock-car racing, moving the linkages, which made the car turn, from the rear to the front. The result was better control. As a driver, he wasn't polished. And he pissed off a lot of people battling for position. So be it. To Bobby, taking the checkered flag with grit was every bit as sweet as winning with finesse.

But at times, his obsession with being the world's underdog was a self-defeating liability.

Never satisfied with his equipment, he bounced from team to team in search of something better. In twenty-five NASCAR seasons, Allison drove for twenty-three different car owners. Whether he finished second or thirty-second, he told himself that every driver who finished ahead of him had cheated. Consumed by all forms of racing, he ran himself ragged jumping from one circuit to another. He got a pilot's license to make his exhausting weekend commutes possible, hopping from a Friday-night short-track race in one town to a Saturday-night feature in another and making it back for NASCAR's green flag on Sunday. He even competed in the Indianapolis 500 in 1973 and '76, showing a versatility that was unheard of among stock-car racers. He led one lap at Indy but finished thirty-second and twenty-fifth, respectively, in his two starts.

But no matter how many NASCAR victories he compiled (and to this day, he claims one more, for a total of eighty-five, than NASCAR credits him), Bobby Allison felt he was stock-car racing's redheaded stepchild. And he couldn't hide his particular jealousy of Richard Petty, the sport's favored son. Petty always had the best equipment. Petty had the best pit crew. Petty had the best sponsor. A natural politician, Petty enjoyed a good relationship with NASCAR founder Bill France, and he had an easy rapport with NASCAR's inspectors and racecar officials—all of whom, it seemed to Bobby, smiled too generously on the No. 43 STP car.

While fans flocked to NASCAR's speedways in the late 1960s to watch Petty duel with South Carolina's David Pearson, the rivalry between Petty and Allison generated more heat, with most of the enmity supplied by Allison. Allison even viewed signing autographs as a competition. Sure, Petty's signature was more elaborate, with its fancy loops and curlicues. But Allison's scribble was more efficient.

"For every one of those things Richard does, I can sign two!" Allison once bragged to Gossage. "So I can get to more fans."

Allison's best year, 1972, saw him rout all his rivals. He won nearly a third of the races—ten of thirty-one—in a Chevrolet built by the legendary Junior Johnson. Despite their success together, Allison grew increasingly annoyed by Johnson's high-handed management style and quit at season's end, thinking he had a better ride lined up with Holman-Moody. But the deal fell through, and he went back to driving a racecar he owned himself in 1973.

It's not in Allison's vocabulary to admit mistakes. But that one decision still weighs on him more than thirty years later. "If I could have kept Junior Johnson as a car owner," Allison says, "*we* would have won two hundred races, and Richard Petty wouldn't have."

Yet even in that brilliant 1972 season, when no driver could keep up with Allison, NASCAR's spotlight shone just a little brighter on stock-car racing's King. Petty won eight races to Allison's ten but still managed to edge him for the championship. And that goes a long way toward explaining how extraordinary it was, in 1983, when Bobby Allison was finally crowned NASCAR's champion. After twenty-two years of racing in Petty's shadow, Allison finally shook the miserable mantle of being second best. For a man as proud as Bobby Allison, it had been a gut-wrenching role to play.

The 1988 wreck at Pocono changed everything. In an instant, everything stopped.

The terrible chain of events started when Bobby's Buick blew a tire on the first lap of the race. As he tried making his way back to the pits, the car's rear end whipped around and smacked the wall. The caution flag flew, but in those days NASCAR didn't freeze the running order the moment the yellow flag signaled trouble. Instead, drivers raced back to the start–finish line, where the caution technically took effect, dicing for position all the way. In the frenzy that followed, Allison's lame Buick, which had spun sideways and come to a standstill near Turn 2, was T-boned at top speed in the driver's-side door. The impact was horrifying, and track workers labored to extricate Allison's unconscious, mangled body from the wreckage.

After his injuries were quickly diagnosed at the infield care center, he was loaded onto a helicopter and airlifted to Lehigh Valley Medical Center in Allentown. He had suffered a broken right shoulder blade; several broken ribs; a broken left leg, which was fractured in three places; and, most gravely, profound trauma to the brain. The moment Judy granted consent, doctors drilled a hole in Bobby's skull to relieve the pressure on his brain. If they couldn't ease that, there was no point in treating anything else.

He stayed in that Pennsylvania hospital for two months, receiving such well-wishers as actor Paul Newman, though Hollywood's most famous racing enthusiast may as well have been a vagrant off the street in Bobby's morphine-induced haze. He then spent another two months in a rehabilitation facility in Alabama. The recovery was excruciating. He was slow to walk again, and his gait was halting, unsure, and unsteady. Even slower was his recovery from the head injury, which left him with huge gaps in his memory and more emotional than before—alternately frustrated, impatient, and disinterested.

Doctors suggested he watch TV, hoping that a random image or a particular program would stimulate his mind. But only racing sparked his interest. It had been the same when Davey was a cantankerous second-grader until Judy stepped in and suggested to his teacher, Miss Purdy, that she use pictures of racecars to get her son's attention instead of pictures of apples and oranges. In both cases, racecars went a long way toward fixing what ailed the Allisons.

Still, nearly three years passed before Bobby could make sense out of basic conversation. Until then, he figured out that he could fool people into thinking he was okay if he just smiled and nodded when they spoke. So that's what he did—smile and nod—because he wanted everyone to think he was fine.

Davey, meanwhile, was progressing up NASCAR's ranks. There hadn't been a day in his childhood that he didn't want to spend helping his dad, whether that meant sweeping the garage floor or sorting bolts in the shop. And that old-fashioned schooling, learning racecars from the inside out, was paying off as a young racer.

"What made Davey so good," said fellow racer Rusty Wallace, "was he knew every shock and every spring on the car. He knew tire pressures. He was absolutely, one hundred percent, a chip off the old block of his dad."

In addition, Davey had a natural charm that Bobby lacked, or at least refused to show around the racetracks. And Davey's future looked even more promising after his race team, owned by Harry Ranier, was bought by the sport's most creative engine builder, Robert Yates, the son of a North Carolina minister who found his calling underneath the hoods of racecars. Yates had supplied the horsepower as a member of Bobby's championship team in 1983. Now, as a fledgling NASCAR team owner, he was mentoring Bobby's firstborn.

Davey's success in Yates's No. 28 Ford seemed to awaken something in his younger brother, Clifford, who had been the wilder, less dutiful son growing up. Clifford had dabbled in stock-car racing but hadn't thrown himself into the sport with the zeal of his dad and brother. But with Davey doing so well, and his dad slowly progressing, Clifford took a new interest in racing. It was as if he sensed it would be good therapy for his dad—or at least as good as anything the doctors had come up with. So Clifford found a ride in NASCAR's Grand National ranks, one rung down from the elite Winston Cup circuit, and gently prodded his dad to help him.

"C'mon, Dad," he'd say. "Show me what to do here! Help me with this."

For Bobby, finding his footing in racing again through Clifford had a way of killing the pain.

They were together at Michigan International Speedway on August 13, 1992, when Clifford went out to practice for that weekend's 200-mile Grand National race. The 2-mile tri-oval was so huge it was impossible to see what was happening on the track while standing in the garage, as Bobby was. To monitor a particular car, you had to be standing on the roof of one of the team's transporter trucks, or be hooked up to the driver by two-way radio.

"He just crashed," Clifford's crew chief announced in disgust just a few laps into the session.

Bobby asked if Clifford was talking to him on the radio. The crew chief didn't answer. Then the ambulance drove against traffic down pit road—a sign that something serious had happened. So Bobby walked out of the garage and headed toward the car—not running, but walking as quickly as he could.

When he got within a few yards he was stopped by a NASCAR inspector.

"They don't want you to go up there," the inspector said.

Bobby was adamant. "I'm going to go," he replied. "I will not get in anybody's way."

When he got closer he could see Clifford's helmet and the front of his racing suit through the window. Clifford was slumped to the right, and a NASCAR official was leaning in the car through the left side window, trying to unhook his safety belt.

Bobby went around to the front of the car, which had spun and hit the wall hard on the driver's side. He knew at once that his son was dead.

Bobby turned just in time to grab Clifford's wife, Elisa, who had jumped two chain-link fences in a dash to reach the car.

"Is he talking?" she asked.

"No."

"Is he breathing?" she asked.

"I don't know."

Clifford Allison wasn't well-known among most NASCAR fans. But his death, at age twenty-seven, brought strong men to tears in the steel-mill town of Hueytown, Alabama, where the Allisons had made their home since 1959.

Brothers Bobby and Donnie, and their racing buddy Red Farmer, all of whom had migrated from Florida, formed the nucleus of the stock-car racing bunch known as "the Alabama Gang." In time Neil Bonnett joined the fold, as did young Davey. And in the town of 15,280, it was a big point of pride that Bobby always said he was from Hueytown, rather than the big city of Birmingham less than ten miles away—even after he became a NASCAR champion. U.S. Steel kept Hueytown in business, but racing gave the town its identity. And the city fathers redesigned the official seal in acknowledgment, including a checkered flag alongside the American flag, a dogwood blossom, a cross, a baseball, and a football.

Hueytown called itself "The City of Pride, Progress and Patriotism." The deepest vein of that pride sprang from the Allisons' achievements.

So when Mayor Lillian P. Howard got the telephone call informing her that Clifford Allison had been killed, she ordered the flag in front of the town hall lowered to half staff.

It had been a hard few years for the town's first family. Bobby and Donnie had seen their racing careers cut short by head injuries. (Donnie bowed out in 1988, the same year Bobby was forced out, never having fully recovered from a 1981 wreck at Charlotte.) The family's patriarch, Pop Allison, had died that spring. Davey had been in four major wrecks that season alone. The latest, triggered by a tap from Darrell Waltrip at the same Pennsylvania track where Bobby was nearly killed, sent Davey's car flipping eleven times and left him with a broken forearm, wrist, and collarbone.

"Anything that happens to the Allisons hits this community deep," said Lieutenant Joe Williams of the town's police department. "The Allisons—starting with Bobby and Donnie and Pop Allison— put Hueytown on the map. Between them and Little League baseball, it's just about that simple."

. . .

When the phone rang in the *Charlotte Observer*'s sports department one afternoon in July 1993, we all muttered about it being another crazy call from a NASCAR fan who didn't have anything better to do than spread stupid rumors. This caller had heard that Davey Allison was in a helicopter crash. Was it true?

Ridiculous, we said. There wasn't any story on the wire service about a crash. And fate simply couldn't be that cruel.

The phone rang again. Different caller, same rumor.

A few seconds later Eddie Gossage, a longtime Allison family friend, phoned from the Charlotte speedway to let us know. David Poole's face turned ashen. And Poole, the most boisterous editor in the department, never blanched at anything.

Finally the Associated Press issued a story from Birmingham, Alabama, labeled "URGENT," filled with details too impossible to grasp: a helicopter that Davey Allison was piloting had crashed as it attempted to land at Talladega Superspeedway. Red Farmer, Davey's only passenger, managed to crawl from the wreckage. But Davey was unconscious and had to be cut from his safety belt after the descending helicopter abruptly lifted, then tilted after snagging a fence topped with barbed wire and slammed to the ground on the pilot's side.

I don't recall packing a suitcase, but within an hour Mark Sluder, an *Observer* photographer, and I were on a plane to Birmingham, where Davey lay in a coma.

TV satellite trucks ringed Carraway Methodist Medical Center, where Allison and Farmer had been flown on an emergency medical helicopter at 4:45 p.m. The lobby was packed, and the switchboard was flooded with calls. Dozens of reporters milled around, and Allison relatives huddled on couches and spilled over the all-night snack bar at one end of the lobby. Davey's wife, Liz, and his parents were keeping vigil in the fifth-floor neurointensive care unit.

At midnight a hospital spokesman gave the final status report of the day: "Very critical." There was nothing to do but come back in the morning. Slowly the crowd trickled out. But leaving didn't feel right.

Brian VanDercook, who handled Davey's public relations, couldn't quit thinking about the night Davey had been rushed to the hospital following his savage wreck at Pocono the year before. Clifford hadn't left his bedside. He sat with his older brother all through the night. VanDercook had seen what he called "the Allison fate" at work over the years. Its cruelty knew no limits, delivering all the success anyone dared wish for—and then following up with a sucker punch of tragedy. And he feared the worst again.

Still, there were reasons to be optimistic. Davey was undersized like his dad, but he was every bit the fighter. "He would fit in your watch pocket," Davey's high school football coach used to say, "but you couldn't fit his guts into a dump truck."

Shortly after midnight the mood shifted. Someone swore they'd seen Davey's eyes twinkle in response to a doctor's probing flashlight. And his eyelids seemed to flutter when Liz ran her finger along his brow. "Honey, I'm here," she said, gently lifting his eyelids.

Liz noticed doctors had put a clip on Davey's toe to monitor his pulse. "My husband doesn't like things on his feet," she told them. And Davey's foot moved, she said, as if in silent affirmation.

By 2:10 a.m. things seemed so positive that Liz and Judy came down to the lobby to tell their closest friends and relatives. Judy fingered her rosary as Liz recounted Davey's responsiveness. She was so animated, and her optimism was contagious. Davey's uncle joked that since Liz was having such a positive effect, the doctors ought to just get Davey to scoot over and let Liz move into the hospital room. *She'd fix him up!*

At 7:30 a.m., a woman's voice paged a doctor in an urgent tone. Moments later, she paged Bobby Allison.

The morning's first media briefing followed at nine-thirty. Red Farmer, the hospital spokesman explained, rested comfortably and was in stable condition, although he remained in the intensive care unit.

Then he added: "Regarding Mr. Davey Allison, many of you have heard some news about him. Mr. Allison, thirty-two, of Hueytown, Alabama, injured in a private helicopter crash yesterday at Talladega Superspeedway, died this morning. . . ."

Throughout the country NASCAR fans grieved his loss and prayed for the Allisons. Many congregated at Robert Yates's race shop in Charlotte, including one fan who drove eight hundred miles from his home in New London, Connecticut, to pay his respects.

In Hueytown, it was as if part of the community's soul had died. Neighbors tied yellow ribbons to the oak trees that lined Bobby and Judy's street. The National Bank of Commerce, where Davey opened his first checking account at age ten, tied black ribbons around its columns. And signs sprouted up in front of nearly every auto-parts store, every fast-food restaurant, and every place of worship.

"Davey's in Racing Heaven" proclaimed the local Hardee's.

"We Pray God's Peace to the Allisons in Their Loss" read the sign in front of Anderson Cleaners.

At Young Land Day Care: "We Loved Him, Too."

And on a scrubby patch of dirt at the intersection of Hueytown Road and Warrior River Road, a sign declared, "God Is Making a Beautiful Bouquet."

Seven months later, that mysterious bouquet added another stem, plucked once again from Hueytown.

Neil Bonnett had been determined to make a comeback in NASCAR despite idling three years after a 1990 crash at Darlington, South Carolina. His wife begged him not to. But doctors cleared him to race again; there was no evidence of lingering brain damage, even though he'd suffered amnesia for several days after the wreck. While practicing for the 1994 Daytona 500, Bonnett crashed again. He was killed instantly.

The news tore Elisa Allison apart. She hadn't wanted Bonnett, a longtime family friend, to race again, either. But as a racecar driver's wife, she knew how futile that wish had been.

"You have to know them," said Elisa, left to rear three children after Clifford's death. "You just have to know how they are and what racing means to them. It's an addiction. It's the worst kind of addiction. It's in their blood. They're not completely happy unless they're doing it. When you love somebody, their happiness is everything to you. And racecar drivers are not completely happy unless they're behind the wheel."

•   •   •

Death tends to come in clusters in racing, interspersed by long stretches without any fatalities. Each time a driver walks away from the mangled remains of a Ford that has flipped a dozen times or hops out of a Chevrolet that's spewing flames, fans erupt in raucous cheers, thrilled by the bravery and reassured once again that nothing bad can happen to the superstars inside.

But a five-year span saw a generation of talent in NASCAR's top ranks lost in accidents both on and off the track. Rob Moroso, the reigning Grand National champion, was killed in a 1990 car wreck driving home from North Wilkesboro Speedway after stopping for a few beers. Defending Winston Cup champion Alan Kulwicki died in a plane crash en route to Bristol Motor Speedway in April 1993. Clifford Allison had been killed at Michigan eight months earlier; Davey would follow three months later. And Neil Bonnett's death set a grim stage for the 1994 Daytona 500.

Still, most NASCAR drivers say that death isn't something they think about.

On every lap, racecar drivers make countless split-second calculations of risk versus reward. Do I go high to miss the wreck ahead? Do I dart low? Do I try to pass now, or will I wreck us both? But rarely do they step back and calculate the risk versus reward of the sport as a whole, weighing the danger it represents against the thrill. For most drivers, racing is a compulsion—something they can't imagine living without.

Many of the best argue that stock-car racing is no more perilous than driving down the street. "Everything is dangerous," Mark Martin said after a fellow driver's death. "You have to weigh the risk about going to the grocery store. Do you go at night? Or do you go during the day?"

Others respond with rationalizations. A driver dies, and his peers dismiss it as "a freak deal." The wreck proved fatal only because of some bizarre sequence of events: the angle the car hit, for example, combined with the fact that the driver's steering failed; the on-rushing car blew a tire; and the track's guardrail shattered. Because it was a freak deal, the thinking goes, it won't happen again. One fatality, while tragic, is no cause for alarm.

Conversely, some drivers insist there was an obvious *reason* for the fatality. The driver was a rookie. The driver was too old. His racecar was a piece of junk. Again, no reason to worry, they tell themselves, because *I* know what I'm doing. *I'm* at the peak of my game. *My* racecar is a state-of-the-art steel tank.

From the day NASCAR's first rulebook was written, the sport's posture toward drivers' safety was to leave it up to the competitors. Drivers were classified as independent contractors rather than NASCAR employees. They raced at their own risk, then as they do now, and signed liability waivers before taking part in the sport (as do journalists).

For many drivers, safety measures boiled down to a matter of cost or personal preference. Dale Earnhardt raced without fireproof gloves in his early years because he couldn't afford them. Even after he was a millionaire he refused to wear a full-faced helmet because he felt it restricted his vision. Many drivers from NASCAR's early days honored superstitions, believing they'd be safe as long as they never raced in a green car, never set their helmet upside down, and never let peanuts near their racecar. All three—green cars, upside-down helmets, and peanuts—were said to have been associated with fatal wrecks in the past.

When drivers are involved in violent wrecks, they seldom remember the impact itself. They typically remember the sequence of events leading up to it. But then the memory goes blank, as if a benevolent angel had swooped down to erase the part they wouldn't want to relive anyway.

Geoff Bodine was an exception. He underwent what's called a "crossover experience" during a horrific wreck in NASCAR's inaugural truck race at Daytona in 2000. Bodine's 700-horsepower pickup slammed into the frontstretch fence, burst into flames, and cartwheeled down the track, spewing fiery debris as it disintegrated before anguished spectators. In that murky state between life and death, Bodine remembers seeing a vision of his late father. He is convinced that at that moment, God's hand reached down to spare him.

"We all know that this can be a deadly sport, but it isn't a death sport," Bodine said later, his love of racing undeterred. "We don't go out there with the idea in our head that we're going to get killed today. Nothing like that! It's just the opposite. We go out there with the idea that we're going to win. And if we don't, we're going to try next week."

Most drivers lose all orientation during crashes that send them flipping, unclear whether they're right-side up or upside-down or spinning. But they can tell they're airborne by the silence—that means the car's wheels have left the asphalt. And if huge chunks of dirt start flying in a window, it's a sure bet the car has landed on its roof. If they're able to extricate themselves when the wreck is over, most NASCAR drivers will check their car over before checking on themselves, staggering around the mangled heap, holding an arm or a shoulder blade in place while trying to figure out if their car is still drivable.

After Bobby Allison's terrible crash at Talladega in 1987, in which his Buick took flight and tore down 150 feet of safety fencing along the main grandstands, he was sick with worry when he saw the gaping hole his car had punched in the fence. How many had been slaughtered, he asked. Remarkably, none. Two steel cables had held, keeping the flying car from plowing into hundreds of fans.

The prospect of killing spectators has consistently been the one intolerable scenario for NASCAR. The sport reacted immediately following that near disaster at Talladega, vowing that its stock cars would never again top 200 miles per hour—the speed at which they were apt to get airborne. And carburetor restrictor plates, which limit horsepower, were required at NASCAR's two biggest tracks from then on to achieve the goal.

But NASCAR was slower to react to driver deaths, often waiting for a common cause or pattern to emerge before taking action. To its credit, when the sport's top minds *were* marshaled to address a problem, the result was a major leap forward in safety, whether it was the development of fuel cells in the 1960s to limit fires or the invention of roof flaps in the 1990s to prevent cars from taking flight and flipping.

Technological advances aren't the only source of comfort for racecar drivers. Faith is another.

The day of a NASCAR race, most drivers will bow their heads at least four times. There is a joint prayer to conclude the mandatory prerace drivers' meeting; prayer during the chapel service that follows in the garage; and a private prayer beside each driver's car, if he likes, led by a chaplain for the sport's traveling ministry, Motor Racing Outreach. Finally, for the benefit of the 100,000 or so fans in the stands, there is a prayer over the public-address system before the command to start engines.

No driver asks God to put him in Victory Lane. But each acknowledges, with his head bowed, that he is putting his life in God's hands. He prays for peace of mind for his family, wisdom for himself, and, finally, His blessing in keeping everyone safe.

NASCAR's southern roots partly explain why evangelical Christianity is so embedded in its culture. The sport's inherent danger is also a factor. Says two-time champion NASCAR team owner Joe Gibbs, a devout Christian: "It's like that old statement, 'There are no atheists in a foxhole.' When those bombs start going off, few of us say, 'Well, I don't know about God. . . .'"

• • •

Richard Petty once said that auto racing began the moment the second automobile rolled out of the factory. Something similar can be said of auto-racing deaths.

Indianapolis Motor Speedway opened in 1909, and two men were killed on the first day of racing. William Bourque was running second in the inaugural race, a 250-miler, when his car hit a hole, plowed through two fences and hit a tree, killing him and his on-board mechanic. Two days later, three more died when a racecar shredded a tire, sailed over the wall, and killed a mechanic and two spectators. Three days of racing: five dead.

In the 1980s, the International Council for Motorsports Science, a group of doctors and engineers affiliated with racing, tried to collect data about auto-racing fatalities from leading racing organizations. Most groups declined to participate, explaining they lacked the staff. Others worried about lawsuits. NASCAR president Bill France Jr. called the proposed data bank "a fishpond for plaintiff's attorneys," the *Orlando Sentinel* reported.

Nearly two decades later, the *Charlotte Observer* undertook a similar initiative, setting out to compile statistics on the number of racing fatalities in the country from 1990 to 2001. Its reporters looked for commonalities among the deaths. Then they asked experts whether basic preventive measures could be taken to reduce the rate of fatalities in the future.

What they found shocked even veterans of the sport. In the twelve-year period, there were 260 deaths (roughly 22 each year): 204 drivers, 29 spectators, 14 track staff, 10 crew members, and 3 journalists in stock-car racing, sprint-car racing, and drag racing in the United States.

More than half the deaths (150) occurred at small, oval tracks; most of those on circuits several rungs below NASCAR's top divisions.

Humpy Wheeler, who had spent a career promoting auto races, guessed the total would be half that and said the industry had a moral obligation to make racing safer. Indy car champion Mario Andretti agreed, telling the paper: "We know how to make the cars go fast. Now, maybe we should spend even more time and energy in making the cars safer."

The reason the newspaper's figures shocked so many was that no organization kept track of how many people died in racing, analogous to the way the Federal Aviation Administration monitors air safety or the National Transportation Safety Board monitors the nation's highways.

Deaths at short tracks in small markets receive little publicity. And deaths at more prominent venues are frequently deemed freak occurrences, calling for little or no follow-up, unlike the crash of a commercial airplane or a community's school bus.

Three drivers were killed at Charlotte Motor Speedway during the six years the track hosted NASCAR's short-lived Sportsman Division. The goal of the amateur division was to give part-time racers with big-time dreams a chance to test their mettle as the next Dale Earnhardt on a high-banked, high-speed oval that was roughly three times bigger and 50 miles per hour faster than any track they had driven before.

The novice drivers had limited experience, if any, on tracks bigger than a half-mile. While nearly all could summon the nerve to race as fast as their cars would carry them on Charlotte's huge straightaways, not everyone had the track-smarts and lightning reflexes to dodge trouble if a car wrecked in front of them. Closing speed at 150 miles per hour is much faster than it is at 100 miles per hour. Moreover, their racecars were generally hand-me-downs, salvaged and rebuilt after having been wrecked numerous times.

After the first fatality, in 1990, track officials introduced new safety measures. Drivers lined up for the start and restarts in single file to reduce the dense packs that often led to trouble. Drivers were required to use "spotters" (crew members with binoculars who are connected by two-way radio) to guide them through difficult situations. And drivers were required to document their racing experience and supply references.

But none of those measures prevented the second "freak deal," in which a Sportsman driver burned to death. Or the third, in which a Chevrolet driven by a Sportsman driver and part-time firefighter from Charlotte got slammed roof-first into the concrete retaining wall in a scramble to avoid two spinning cars. The Chevy skidded upside-down before dropping back onto the track, its roof sheared away. The driver was beheaded.

The next morning the Sportsman hopefuls returned to the track with badges of the fallen driver's car number, 57, on their jumpsuits. A minister offered a memorial service. "He was a Christian," he said.

"He was saved." Then he reminded them that they needed to prepare for the worst when they went out on the track.

"Every time you go out, you may not be coming back," he said. "You need to be ready. You need to be prepared to die."

And another day of racing began, with the spot on the wall where the Chevy had hit covered by a fresh coat of white paint.

In 1966, Pulitzer Prize–winning sports columnist Jim Murray, who wrote for the *Los Angeles Times,* drew praise and epithets alike for his reaction to the carnage associated with the Indianapolis 500 after three competitors were killed on the track in less than twelve months. Murray replied with a gruesomely satirical account of an Indy 500 that was staged by promoters for maximum horror. Wrote Murray: "Gentlemen, start your coffins."

Most motorsports journalists, by contrast, preferred to cloak death in soft, oblique language in an effort to spare readers, as well as racers' families, the horror. It is an unspoken tradition in the profession, similar to the way Hollywood directors depicted murder scenes in a gentler era, including only the sound of a gunshot followed by the victim falling over but never bleeding.

Journalist Ed Hinton remembers being scolded by a veteran NASCAR writer with a tender heart as Hinton dictated his story in the press box following yet another racer's death. "*Don't* write that he was killed, Ed!" the writer snapped. "Write that he lost his life."

But death ceases being an abstraction when you see it enough. It is a reality that sets auto racing apart from other sports. It's hardly an everyday occurrence, or even monthly or annually. But in one eleven-year span covering motorsports, I wrote about the deaths of fourteen drivers—stock-car racers and open-wheel racers alike—and attended services for five.

Sportswriters pick up arcane bits of knowledge covering different beats—knowledge they probably never wanted to have, but knowledge that's essential to understanding a given sport. In football, it's the hazards of meniscus tears, the scourge of NFL linemen. In baseball, it's the ramifications of the luxury tax in the collective-bargaining agreement. In track and field, it's the normally occurring testosterone-to-epitestosterone ratios in the human body. In auto racing, it's the ability to recognize potential tragedy in seemingly innocuous events.

If a racecar's window net is not lowered immediately after a crash, for example, the driver is badly injured or unconscious.

But if a safety worker at the scene of a crash pats his head, the injury is life-threatening.

If a racecar flips multiple times and shreds to bits in spectacular fashion, the driver is actually safer than he would likely be if his car suddenly veered into the wall.

And silence is the most frightening sound on a racetrack. When the roar of engines stops, someone has crashed.

• • •

In time, NASCAR changed its fundamental approach toward drivers' safety and began pouring resources into preventing fatal crashes rather than reacting to them. Meanwhile, those drivers who managed to survive wrecks that nearly killed them—Bobby Allison, Ernie Irvan, and Jerry Nadeau, among them—slowly rebuilt their lives.

For the Allisons, the hardships continued after Davey's death in 1993. Bobby's insurance company refused to pay the bills for his lengthy rehabilitation from his 1988 Pocono crash, which wiped out his savings. His marriage of thirty-six years ended. And he was forced to auction off the contents of the family's ranch-style home in Hueytown to cover expenses. Judy Allison watched from her mother-in-law's driveway as more than three hundred people showed up to comb through the family's belongings and cart away Bobby's pool table, his golf clubs, his custom-made ostrich boots, and her doll collection.

But four years later, the Allisons reconciled, remarried, and found happiness again.

Now in their late sixties, they have faced hardships as a couple, with only slight interruption, for forty-seven years. They live in a ranch-style home on Lake Norman, just north of Charlotte, where many of their old racing friends are neighbors. Their living room is filled with family photographs—of children, grandchildren, and, now, a great-grandchild. Large picture windows look out on a backyard dotted with bird feeders, each tailored to a different species, and a tranquil cove beyond. A paddle boat and small fishing boat sit at the end of the dock.

Bobby's eyes sparkle when Judy enters the room. She pours him an iced tea, and they sit and reminisce. Bobby believes in starting stories at the beginning. In this case, that means an elaborate description of his 1938 Chevy Coupe—the one he drove to high school and ran in his first race.

Judy chides him for talking about himself too much. She smiles at me and turns to her husband.

"She wants to hear about the *family*," she says, patting his leg.

They finish each other's sentences. They quibble over which son was more trouble.

Bobby says it was Clifford.

"You're *way* off the deal here!" she says, cutting her eyes at Bobby. "How many times did you go to the school that Davey needed a whipping? And how many times did you go that Clifford needed a whipping?"

She turns and smiles. "There are a lot of things that Bobby has a tendency to want to forget."

Chapter 4

DALE EARNHARDT: WORKING-CLASS HERO

S ports physiologists have tried to pinpoint what makes a great racecar driver, searching for the defining characteristics with the zeal of a geneticist trying to unravel a strand of DNA. They have measured drivers' peripheral vision and pulse rates, hand–eye coordination and reflexes, lung capacity and adrenaline levels, ability to stay calm in the face of enormous pressure and ability to remain focused for hours despite withering heat.

All of those qualities play a part. But Kirk Shelmerdine, a former champion NASCAR crew chief with a knack for reducing complexities to their essence, has his own definition.

Selfishness.

"You have to have an insatiable desire to be in front of the other car," he says. "It's such a childish, selfish thing. But a racecar driver is the most selfish thing there is. Otherwise, he's not a good racecar driver because there has to be something inside you that craves that."

On this point—the insatiable hunger to be first—Dale Earnhardt had no peer. Yet Earnhardt was never driven by a sense of entitlement. He was fueled by its opposite: desperation.

He dropped out of school after failing eighth grade. At seventeen he got a girl pregnant. At eighteen he was a husband and father, pumping gas and wiping windshields at a service station while watching the world pass him by. And by the time he finally got the chance to prove himself in NASCAR's big leagues, his life's accomplishments consisted of two broken marriages, three children, and roughly $16,000 of debt for spare parts and tires loaned by men who had faith that he might amount to something on a racetrack one day.

The stakes were obvious. If Earnhardt didn't make it in NASCAR, he'd be left with his choice of dead-end jobs and a life not so much lived as served out like a sentence for some undefined crime.

None of this was stated. But it was palpable in the way Earnhardt drove, from the first time he muscled a 3,400-pound stock car around a racetrack to the last. Sportswriters could denigrate his fans all they wanted for being the coarsest of a coarse lot, but you didn't need a diploma to understand what Earnhardt was saying when he slipped behind the wheel of his skulking black No. 3 Chevrolet. Even the way he sat in the car bucked the rules, slumped in his seat like a panther crouched low, sizing up its prey and preparing to pounce. That irked Richard Petty no end as Earnhardt was crashing his way to the front in his furious attempt to carve out a place in the sport in the early 1980s.

"That's why he hits everything," Petty groused at the time. "He can't see over the damn steering wheel!"

Petty may have been the people's King during the era that Earnhardt bullied his way into NASCAR, but Earnhardt would come to represent the people. The hardest-working people. With every pass for position, Earnhardt fulfilled the fantasy of every wage earner who dreamed of telling his boss where he could shove it. With every lap he led, Earnhardt evened the score for the guy who was invisible to society—the guy who cleans the gutters, jackhammers the pavement, and services the air conditioner without ever making eye contact.

And with every race he won, he thrust a fist to the heavens. Earn-hardt's fans didn't need him to win for Dale's sake, but for theirs.

And though Earnhardt would become the only driver to match Petty's mark of seven NASCAR championships, his hunger for shov-ing his car's snout in front of the next guy's wouldn't be dulled by fame or riches or any other measure of having "made it."

Says Shelmerdine, Earnhardt's crew chief for four of those cham-pionships: "The way his life came up—from working in the cotton mill to what he became—he knew racing was his thing, and he didn't have any other choices. It was a do-or-die thing for him for a while. And he was able to capture that fight-or-flight feeling and transform it into doing what he did. For him, it was survival. For him, it was like life or death."

·   ·   ·

Kannapolis, North Carolina, was founded in 1887 for a single pur-pose, and everything about it was laid out to that end. At its center stood the giant smokestacks of Cannon Mills Plant No. 1, which at its peak produced most of the sheets and towels used in American homes. Radiating outward was a network of streets on which textile baron James William Cannon, the town's founder, built homes for the mill's workers and later added stores, schools, churches, and a YMCA. Implicit in the planning of Kannapolis, and that of so many other company towns throughout the South, was that no matter how much education the workers' children got by day and no matter what dreams they dreamed at night, their lives would always revolve around the mill. And for a time, there was nothing to suggest that the middle child of Ralph and Martha Earnhardt would escape that fate.

Ralph, one of eight children, had worked at the mill, as had nearly everyone in town. But he was a full-time mechanic by the time his first son came along. Soon afterward he moved the family from a rental unit on Coach Street to one of those bungalows on Sedan Avenue, not far from the mill's smokestacks, with a garage out back where he worked on the racecar that he competed in every chance he got. Ralph Earnhardt never won a race in NASCAR's top division, but he earned a formidable reputation on the short tracks closer to home. He also earned the nickname Iron Heart for his grit behind the wheel and his ability to do more with less than just about anybody. Between races he worked on cars for other people. Stock-car racing was a break-even proposition at best, though his five children— Martha Kaye, Cathy Lee, Ralph Dale, Randy Eugene, and Danny Ray—never sensed times were lean.

When Dale was eight, Ralph built him a go-kart. And the boy, who answered to "Buster" as a child, drove it around in circles in the front yard. When his dad let him, he rode with him to the races in the 1959 Ford truck that towed the car from one track to another. And Dale would climb up on a stack of tires in the infield and watch, imagining he was taking every left turn with him.

"He was a pretty calculating guy," Earnhardt said of his dad's style behind the wheel. "I'd see him run second to people he thought he could get by, maybe, if he roughed 'em up and tore up his racecar. But he'd run second and say, 'I needed the money worse than I needed to spend all week working on the racecar.' "

Ralph wasn't much of a talker, but Dale studied every bolt he turned on the car and hung on his every word—except the part about staying in school. Spelling and math were okay, but he couldn't see the point of all that reading. All he wanted to do was race cars, like his dad. But his father had even less to say to him after he dropped out. "He said his piece, I'll tell you what," Earnhardt recalled. "That was it, and I never heard another word about it. In fact, I never heard another word for about a year."

There never was a need for Ralph to say "I told you so." Life in Kannapolis had its own way of harping on Dale's mistake.

He came of age in the early 1960s, when teenagers with pocket change for gas spent the weekends cruising the downtown circuit known as Idiot's Circle. The mill's whistle marked the passage of time. And every family's ambition was displayed on the street signs in town, among them, Buick Street, Cadillac Street, Chrysler Street, Desoto Avenue, and V8 Street. But with an eighth-grade education, the closest Dale could get to a fancy new sedan was servicing them at the gas station. His dream of becoming a racecar driver was as dead as an old battery. Racecars cost money. Racecars needed tires and parts he couldn't afford. And children, he found out, had needs of their own.

"I worked seventy, eighty hours a week—just about ran the station," Earnhardt said years later. "I found out what the real world was about. *This* is what you wanted? It was, 'Clean the windshield, check the oil, and pump me twenty-five cents worth of gas.' I learned a long time ago you can't please the public."

In the years to come, few would accuse him of trying.

• • •

Charm didn't come naturally, but Dale finally persuaded a local businessman who owned a racecar to let him fill in for a few events, and he consistently finished among the top five. By then he was working at a cotton mill in Denton, North Carolina, installing insulation while getting car parts made on the sly and smuggled out in lunch pails. By night he worked on racecars. The chilly relationship with his father had started to thaw. And Ralph, who had never expressed any enthusiasm over his son's racing ambitions, started helping Dale as best he could, steering him to men who were looking for part-time drivers and rebuilding his engines so his cars would run faster.

"He really didn't tell me how to drive or what to do, but he showed me what happened when I did get into trouble," Earnhardt recalled. "I had a ball. I was in fat city, running Metrolina Speedway and old Concord Speedway. Didn't have no money—just old junkyard stuff. I bent ball joints and tore up something on it, and I'd go to the junkyard and get new ball joints out and put 'em in that car. I had a big time! I had more damn fun. I mean, I didn't know no better."

After Ralph died of a heart attack at forty-five, Dale learned how hard life could get. The racing bug had caught hold of all five Earnhardt children, and they pulled together to turn what little their dad had left them into a chance for Dale, who was then twenty-two.

"Randy, Danny, and I kept working on the car," Earnhardt said. "Cathy helped us. And Kaye worried us to death about money. We'd argue about that racecar all week, and everybody thought we were mad at each other all the time till we'd get to the racetrack and we'd band together and argue against everybody else. People think you had a tough time, but you did what you had to do, you loved racing so much. We'd work on that car all night. Wake up holding on to a wrench under the bottom of the car and never knew I went to sleep. Wake up, keep on working."

The more Earnhardt raced, the deeper in debt he sank. But his talent was undeniable. At Myrtle Beach, South Carolina, where the track's wall was covered in ivy, the promoter bragged that Earnhardt hugged the wall so tightly on his laps that his car rustled the leaves without ever touching the concrete.

Two-time NASCAR champion Ned Jarrett, then a race promoter in nearby Hickory, felt at times as if he was watching his old rival Ralph when Dale took to the track. "If anyone ever had God-given talent as a race driver, he was it. And if there ever was a chip off the old block, that was Dale," said Jarrett, among the benefactors who funneled Earnhardt money after he wrecked yet another car and couldn't afford parts to fix it. "He was one of those that *had* to build his own cars. He worked very hard at it. He put everything into it. That was his life, that's what he wanted to do. And if he won a race, he didn't go out and blow the money and have a big party. He put the money back in the car and tried to build his career."

Earnhardt's big break came in 1979 when a businessman named Rod Osterland gave him a chance to compete for NASCAR's Rookie of the Year in the elite Winston Cup series. He won his first race that year at Bristol Motor Speedway, a half-mile track that resembled the small bullrings where he had apprenticed. But before he could climb out of debt, he saw his golden opportunity slip away. A wreck at Pocono broke both collarbones and sidelined him for four races. Osterland tapped veteran David Pearson to fill in, and Earnhardt felt as if his soul had been wrenched from his body. "I was on top of the world, and then, just like that, I was back listening to the races on the radio," he later told biographer Frank Vehorn.

The forced layoff from racing only fueled his drive to make it in NASCAR.

• • •

The best racecar drivers understand the limits of the car and can summon the nerve to push it to the ragged edge, extracting every bit of horsepower without losing control. Earnhardt could sense those limits like a hound dog sniffing out a buried bone. But time and again he ignored them, pushing the car too hard and wrecking whoever got in his way. When horsepower failed him, he resorted to intimidation.

He became an even bigger bully after winning NASCAR's 1980 championship, a stunning achievement for a driver just one year removed from his rookie campaign. And his tactics wore on veteran racers. Coo Coo Marlin accused him of having set NASCAR back twenty years by roughhousing his way through races. Groused Buddy Baker: "Dale Earnhardt would give an aspirin a headache."

Earnhardt's balls-out style served him poorly during a two-year stint with car owner Bud Moore in 1982–83. Moore's Fords were fast, all right, but their engines were ill suited to Earnhardt's punishment. In sixty races with the team, Earnhardt failed to finish twenty-six races. Sometimes he crashed; more often something failed on the car—typically the engine, brakes, or clutch. So when car owner Richard Childress, a former racer whose hard-luck childhood eclipsed Earnhardt's own, came calling, Earnhardt jumped.

Childress had hired Earnhardt to drive his No. 3 Chevrolet for the last eleven races of 1981, after Osterland abruptly sold his championship team. But they parted ways at the end of the season, with Earnhardt leaving at Childress's prodding for Moore's better-funded team. By 1984, Childress was on firmer financial ground. He had hired a precocious young crew chief, Kirk Shelmerdine, who had turned his back on a Penn State education to chase a dream of racing southern stock cars. And together they set to work crafting racecars that could stand up to Earnhardt's rough driving style.

For starters, they reinforced the bumpers, keenly aware that Earnhardt liked to use his bumper to clear cars out of his path. Then, to keep him from breaking carburetors (the result of stomping on the gas pedal too hard), they invented a throttle stop that would blunt the pressure from Earnhardt's right foot. They built engines that were more durable than powerful. Every aspect of the racecar was tailored to Earnhardt's demands.

Said Shelmerdine: "The way I looked at it was: He's going to try and put the car in front of the other ones whether it belongs there or not, whether it can stand it or not. So we had to do gearing differently. We had to do durability stuff on the suspension. If the car blows up, or if it crashes, or if it won't stick to the ground going at the speeds that the leaders are going, he's going to do it anyway. So you better damn well make the car suitable to that kind of thing."

In his first season with Childress, Earnhardt failed to finish only two races out of thirty (both engine failures). He hadn't changed his driving style overnight. He was simply racing cars built to stand the heat he put on them.

"Sometimes that was a little counterproductive as far as speed goes," Shelmerdine noted. "You had to make choices about what's fastest and what's strongest. So we didn't sit on a lot of poles; we didn't qualify good. He wasn't the greatest qualifier, anyway, so why did we want to build cars that would qualify fast? I mean, it's not what we were about."

Winning was. And if that meant putting the bumper to someone, so be it.

But Earnhardt's ability involved more than being a bully. He had uncanny peripheral vision—a huge asset in the cramped quarters of NASCAR's short tracks. On superspeedways, where aerodynamics came into play, his rivals swore Earnhardt could "see the air" and use its invisible slipstream to suck his car through traffic. He knew the racecar's inner workings so well that when he wrecked, he'd start barking over the radio while the car was still crashing to tell his pit crew what parts and pieces they'd need to fix the damage so they wouldn't lose time scrambling for tools after he pulled in for repairs. During practice sessions he could make three or four laps in a racecar and tell whether it was capable of winning or not. And on days when the car wasn't fast, he still wrung more out of it than it deserved.

He knew how to wring speed out of a racetrack, too. Most drivers tend to follow the same path (or "run the same line") around a track. Take a helicopter over one after a race, and you'll see a band about twelve feet wide where the cars' tires have laid down rubber all day. Earnhardt could poke his car outside that band if a different line was faster—sticking it deep into the corners or even scooting across the grass, if need be—and bring it back intact.

"He orchestrates a racecar like you would a fiddle or a guitar," Junior Johnson once mused. "You want a guy that's determined, that has the skills and don't give up. One of 'em's always missing. But if you drive hard enough and are brave enough, sooner or later you'll figure it out. And then you're Dale Earnhardt."

That persona meshed perfectly with his first major sponsor—Wrangler jeans, whose advertising campaign branded Earnhardt "One Tough Customer."

After back-to-back championships with Childress in 1986 and '87, GM Goodwrench replaced Wrangler as the team's sponsor and gave Earnhardt's yellow-and-blue Chevy a menacing makeover. The result was the black No. 3 Chevrolet. And Earnhardt's gritty image was recast to match, as NASCAR's Man in Black.

The black car suited him perfectly. So did his new nickname. Martha Earnhardt couldn't have done better had she written "Intimidator" on her middle child's birth certificate instead of "Ralph Dale." The moment his blue eyes opened to the world it was as if the little baby knew that his life would depend on sizing up his enemies.

Earnhardt reveled in provoking the short-fused and antagonizing the edgy. He took special delight in needling Geoff Bodine, a native of Chemung, New York, who had earned his reputation in so-called modified racecars popular in the Northeast, labeling him "a little peabrain, no good Yankee." When Bodine whined, Earnhardt told reporters, "You guys have gotta wrap a gas rag around that guy's ankles so the piss-ants won't crawl up and bite his candy ass!"

Few can recall Earnhardt laying a hand on another driver or flinging a helmet at another car in anger. Yet he was regarded as the toughest guy in the garage. Slumped in his black car with his cold, blue eyes peering out from behind goggles, he preyed on weakness and hesitation. And he cultivated the perception that he would cross any line to get his car to the front. Even his own crew members weren't sure what he would do behind the wheel. That implied threat—that Earnhardt didn't obey the rules of normal men—proved a powerful weapon that he exploited to the hilt.

"Maybe you sped up, maybe you eased off, maybe you blocked," 1988 NASCAR champion Bill Elliott wrote about seeing Earnhardt in his rearview mirror. "But that bit of concern, that hint of indecision played right into Dale's game plan."

Elliott still chafes over Earnhardt's victory in the 1987 all-star race, known as The Winston, which concluded with a ten-lap dash for the spoils between the two. Earnhardt had the lead rounding Turn 3 when he shoved Elliott up into the wall, cutting a tire. The contact got Earnhardt's car sideways, and he roared through the grass—never surrendering the lead and somehow not losing control of the car—and bounced back on the track just in time to take the checkered flag.

"If that's what it takes to be the Winston Cup champion, I don't want it," Elliott said later, still steaming. "This aggressiveness has gotten out of hand. This is not Saturday-night wrestling."

Increasingly fans went crazy when the black No. 3 was rolled onto the starting grid. The sight alone guaranteed a show worth watching. Earnhardt had a way of making every driver in the race more important because of the way each man responded to him. Some shrank in his presence, others fought like they'd never fought before. He was still fully capable of putting another driver in the wall for a trophy. But he could just as easily wreck a car by disrupting the air around it and never leaving a mark, like a cop who beats a confession out of the accused by bashing him over the head with a phone book. Damage done, no fingerprints left behind.

"He had great car control," said Childress, his longtime car owner. "He could do things with that car that would just leave you standing there, shaking your head."

Yet he was an entirely different person out of the car. Moody, mischievous, insecure, and tenderhearted. That side of the Intimidator didn't win him any races, and it certainly didn't make him any money. So that side stayed tucked behind the mirrored sunglasses.

"He wanted to come off as the tough, tough guy from Kannapolis who made good, which he was," recalls fellow racer Ken Schrader. "But he had a heart of gold. I'd call him up and say, 'I'm gonna bring by a real good friend and introduce him, so now don't be a dickhead!' And he'd say, 'I can't even believe you'd *say* that!' And he'd be super—taking 'im all around and showing 'im everything. He had a heart about yea big, but he didn't want anybody to know it."

Says NASCAR's 1989 champion Rusty Wallace: "He would take you to dinner and then spin you out on Sunday and then take you on vacation with him the following week to make up."

Unlike Bodine, Wallace treasured his on-track battles with Earnhardt. A St. Louis native schooled on the midwestern stock-car circuit, Wallace was even more knowledgeable about racecars than
Earnhardt when he arrived in NASCAR's top ranks in 1980. But he
longed to have the swagger Earnhardt had.

"I always wanted to be like him because he was always so popular with the fans and such a tough guy," Wallace said. "It always
seemed like he hung out with the coolest people. He always had the
coolest boots, the coolest shirts. He'd show up with the trickest jack-
ets. He was six feet one, and I was six feet one. He wore ten-and-a-
half shoes, and I wore ten-and-a-half shoes. We wrecked a lot of
people together . . ."

Their battles were legendary. The most memorable came at
North Wilkesboro (North Carolina) Speedway one year when each
had a lightning-fast car. They had been joking around before the race,
and Wallace cracked, "You know, if you and I ever got to banging side
by side, we'd sell a pile of T-shirts!"

"We gotta do that," Earnhardt replied.

So at the drop of the green flag they took off, putting a hefty distance between their cars and the rest of the field. Wallace led, and
Earnhardt was on his bumper. "I glanced at him in the mirror, and I
could see his teeth!" Wallace recalled. "He was smiling."

And around they went, locked door-to-door for ten straight laps
around the tiny oval. Wallace let Earnhardt lead; Earnhardt returned
the favor. The fans went wild. And NASCAR president Bill France
Jr. chewed both out afterward for being idiots.

"They were the two baddest guys in the industry, and they knew
what it took to put people in the stands," said Robin Pemberton,
Wallace's crew chief from 1995 to 2001. "Those were the good times.
You played hard, you raced hard."

But for Earnhardt, there would always be something lacking no
matter how many T-shirts he sold, no matter how many races he
won, and no matter how many championships he amassed. With

Martha Earnhardt in the audience, Earnhardt accepted his fourth Winston Cup trophy at the 1990 season-ending awards banquet at New York's Waldorf-Astoria ballroom. "My dad has always had a place in my heart through all of my racing years," he said from the podium. "I grew up idolizing him. I stood up on the back of a truck on a tire, and every turn he took, I took. And it burned right into me what I wanted to do. I never dreamed I would be four-time champion of NASCAR. I have had help from people who were friends of my daddy and people he raced against. He is still in my heart. I remember him, and I miss him dearly."

• • •

I first met Earnhardt while covering a practice session at Charlotte Motor Speedway in 1992, and the gamesmanship started that day. All the teams' cars were parked in the main garage except the black No. 3. It sat at the far end of a secondary garage, isolated from the rest as if sent to the corner for bad behavior. Earnhardt was perched beside it in a director's chair, sulking while his crew worked under its hood. He hadn't won a race in nearly eight months, which accounted for his surly attitude. And when I extended my hand and introduced myself as a reporter from the *Charlotte Observer* sent to help motorsports writer Tom Higgins, he obliged with a firm handshake but wouldn't let go for an awkward amount of time. NASCAR's alpha wolf established control at the outset.

Interviewing Earnhardt, I came to learn, wasn't so much a conversation as a contest—something to be won or lost. He tested reporters just like he tested other drivers. He would quibble, evade, play dumb, offend, pretend he didn't hear you, or stretch out on the couch in his transporter truck and take a nap midsentence. His aim was to figure out more about you than you did about him. "What are you made of?" "What makes you flinch?" "How can I establish the upper hand?"

His fortunes had improved by the time I set out to write my first major story about him. He had opened the 1993 season with a new crew chief in Andy Petree and a near victory in the Daytona 500, the only major title to elude him. Earnhardt led more than half the race but got passed on the last lap by Dale Jarrett, whose father, two-time NASCAR champion Ned Jarrett, wept with pride while calling the race from the CBS broadcast booth. Ned's colleagues wisely fell silent during the frantic final turns, allowing the father to coach his son home.

"It's the Dale-and-Dale show as we come off Turn 4!" Ned said into the microphone, his voice trembling with emotion. "*You* know who I'm pulling for—it's Dale Jarrett! Bring her to the inside, Dale. Don't let him get down there. . . . He's going to make it! Dale Jarrett is going to win the Daytona 500!"

Still, Earnhardt's second-place finish set a promising tone. By fall, Earnhardt's old foe Rusty Wallace had scored more victories than the Intimidator, but Earnhardt held the lead in the battle for the championship because his car had still been running at the finish more often. He was closing on a sixth NASCAR title, and that was reason enough for the *Charlotte Observer* to weigh in on the local hero deemed stock-car racing's greatest driver. I drew the assignment and arranged to spend a full day with him, qualifying day at North Wilkesboro Speedway.

As instructed, I met him at 7:45 a.m. at the shop on his 370-acre Iredell County farm, home base for the racecar he occasionally ran in NASCAR's developmental Grand National series. Earnhardt was holding court with the team's crew when I walked in, and twenty-three pairs of dead eyes stared down at me from the mounted heads of the big game he had killed. He gave me a tour of the shop and his office, dominated by a framed photograph of his father wearing a bowl-shaped helmet with leather flaps and standing in Victory Lane with Miss Hickory Motor Speedway. He offered me a Sundrop soda and sausage biscuit. And he made a point of telling me he had worked a full day already, up since five a.m. to check on his farm and talk shop with his guys. He didn't announce the score, but clearly it was Earn-hardt 1, Bleary-Eyed Reporter, 0.

Four of us were making the trip to North Wilkesboro. Earnhardt pulled the shotgun from its rack in his big burgundy truck. "Won't be needing this," he said, and told everyone where to sit. Me up front. Kevin Triplett, the GM Goodwrench public-relations man, and Don Hawk, Earnhardt's business manager, in the backseat. He buckled his seat belt, glared until I buckled mine, plugged in the radar detector, slapped his Atlanta Braves baseball cap over it, and we took off down Coddle Creek Road.

The drive didn't take as long as it should have, and Earnhardt chatted nonstop. He was going to one of his favorite tracks, a devilish half-mile oval as old as the sport itself. And aside from his farm, a race-track was his favorite place to be. Either place, there was no question who was in charge.

As rural farmland opened onto the interstate that climbed to Wilkes County, Earnhardt talked about his father, his love of racing, and the interest his three older children—Kerry, then twenty-three; Kelley, twenty-one; and Dale Jr., eighteen—were showing in the sport. A millionaire many times over by then, he could have bought them anything they wanted to jump-start their careers. But he refused.

"They need to work harder at it—try to do it more themselves, instead of expecting me to help 'em," he said. "I'll help 'em. But they've got a long way to go to become racers. Real racers work hard. They don't sit around the house waiting for somebody to give 'em what they need. They don't sit around the garage. If they ain't got it, they figure out a way to get it."

When he wasn't yapping to me, he yapped at the cars on the road. "Move it over! Move it over!" he muttered, slumped against the driver's-side window, sizing up his opportunity to pass.

Once at the track, we wheeled around to find Dale Jr., who was preparing to qualify his own stock car in the entry-level late-model division, and dropped off a gear he had left back at the shop. Then

Earnhardt launched into his day, which started with checking on his racecar. I stood as far away as I could without getting out of earshot. He talked to his crew chief, Andy Petree; I scribbled in my notebook. He leaned against a stack of tires and studied the car; I scribbled in my notebook. He snuck up behind Ken Schrader and grabbed his neck like a giant bear; I scribbled in my notebook. Everywhere he went, I followed and scribbled in my notebook.

After about three hours, he finally erupted. "Don't you want to ask me any *questions*!?" he barked.

I shook my head. "I thought I might learn more by watching," I said.

His bushy mustache turned up in a smile. From then on, he called me by name. Not mine, but one he made up: "Little Higgins," a nod to the *Observer*'s veteran NASCAR writer.

It had been a mediocre qualifying run, notable only for being one spot ahead of Wallace. But he scored a decisive victory in the day's other contest: beating traffic out of the track. Earnhardt had devoted years to mastering his exit. He had parked the pickup truck outside the track, its nose pointed down a back road out. And by the time track workers opened the gate to let drivers out of the infield (there was no tunnel, so you were trapped inside until qualifying ended), he had changed into street clothes and torn across the track in his cowboy boots, first guy out, yelling at me to hurry up.

A little boy begged for an autograph. "Run along with me," Earnhardt shouted, and he signed with one hand while fishing his keys out of his pocket with the other. We hopped in as he screeched the tires, kicking up clouds of gravel and dirt, and roared off. Once back on the interstate, his radar detector started beeping hard and urgent as we closed on a state trooper dead ahead. The trooper stared hard in his rearview mirror. Earnhardt pulled close to his bumper, grinning out his windshield. The trooper slowed, looked in his mirrors again, first rearview, then side. And Earnhardt didn't flinch.

"Now, is he intimidating me?" he asked, delighted with this game. "Or am I intimidating him?"

In a moment the highway split. The trooper veered left; Earnhardt exited right. And somewhere in his mind, he notched another victory.

• • •

Earnhardt held off Rusty Wallace to win his sixth NASCAR title that year. And he made a mockery of the competition the next, winning NASCAR's 1994 championship by a 444-point margin. In doing so, he also equaled Richard Petty's seemingly unreachable mark of seven titles.

With Petty retired and three-time champion Darrell Waltrip's career on the wane, no NASCAR star was bigger. Earnhardt was a godlike figure to half the fans, who thrust three fingers in the air in tribute each time he zoomed past. And he was the devil incarnate to the other half, who thrust just one.

His following was particularly fervent at Bristol Motor Speedway, perched on the hills of eastern Tennessee, and at Talladega Superspeedway in central Alabama—tracks tucked in places that time seemed to have passed by. Each venue showcased one extreme of his ability: the half-mile bullring in Bristol, his short-track roughhousing; the 2.66-mile superspeedway in Talladega, his command of the aerodynamic draft. And twice each year when the NASCAR races came to town, the Bristol campgrounds and Talladega infield teemed with Earnhardt fans cut of the same cloth. A far cry from the white-collar demographic the sport's promoters so fervently courted, they were people who saw themselves in him. They sported "3" tattoos, drove black Monte Carlos that brandished Intimidator license plates, and collected Earnhardt trading cards and die-cast cars. They set up campgrounds days before the race, unfurling "3" flags as an oath of allegiance, and packed up the moment he crashed out. To legions of

NASCAR fans, the sun rose and set on how the No. 3 fared each Sunday.

Like most NASCAR racers, Earnhardt competed in the Winston Cup series as a hired hand. He didn't own his racecar but drove it for an annual salary and a percentage of his winnings for team owner Richard Childress from 1984 on. What proved far more lucrative was the fact that Earnhardt controlled the rights to his name, likeness, and the "Intimidator" persona, which turned out to be as effective at printing money as the U.S. Mint.

Earnhardt's third wife, the former Teresa Houston (whose uncle, Tommy Houston, raced in NASCAR's Grand National division), was quick to see her husband's marketing potential. And with a community college degree in interior design, she turned him into a powerful commodity, approving all of his contracts and earning a reputation as shrewd and tough-nosed in the boardroom. In 1985, Earnhardt was the first driver to park a souvenir trailer on the grounds of a racetrack, at Martinsville Speedway in southwest Virginia. Within a few years every NASCAR track was ringed with acres of souvenir rigs hawking T-shirts, caps, shot glasses, baby bibs, and every product imaginable bearing a driver's name, car number, and likeness.

His personal fortune ballooned along with his fan base, particularly after he hired Don Hawk, who had served as business manager for NASCAR's 1992 champion Alan Kulwicki, to handle his racing-related business affairs following Kulwicki's death in 1993. At Hawk's urging, Earnhardt bought the NASCAR-related marketing company Sports Image in 1994, and sales of Earnhardt-licensed merchandise jumped to $40 million annually. An Earnhardt appearance on the QVC Home Shopping network resulted in $1 million in sales in two hours, with more than a thousand callers still on hold when he left the studio. By the mid-1990s, Earnhardt's fleet of aircraft included three King Airs, a helicopter, and a $4 million Lear jet. *Forbes* magazine estimated his 1997 income at $19 million, of which $15.5 million came from endorsements, third-highest among professional athletes behind Michael Jordan and Tiger Woods.

After all those decades of doubt, Earnhardt wasn't worried about making it in racing anymore. He wasn't worried about making it in business, either, confident he could make his way in the world and provide for his family if his racing career came to an end. By every outward measure Earnhardt was comfortable. If he had a worry in the world, it was about time catching up to the frantic pace he had been running for so many years. As he approached his mid-forties, he heard its footsteps in the startling coming-of-age of a boyish Californian named Jeff Gordon.

Gordon would soon bring Earnhardt's supremacy to a halt, edging the seven-time champion for the 1995 NASCAR Winston Cup championship by 34 points. But Earnhardt wouldn't go gently.

.   .   .

The 1996 season dawned with promise. For the third time in four years, Earnhardt finished second in the season-opening Daytona 500. He won two of the first four races, at Richmond and Atlanta. And as summer wound down, he was solidly in the hunt for the eighth NASCAR title that would move him past the tie with Petty, trailing leader Terry Labonte by just 12 points as the circuit headed to the treacherous high-banks of Talladega.

A rainy, miserable morning delayed the start of the Diehard 500 for nearly three hours. But shortly after the green flag flew, Earnhardt whipped his No. 3 Chevy to the front of the furious pack and led much of the first half. He was still out front when Ernie Irvan and Sterling Marlin tangled just behind him. The contact snared Earnhardt, and the No. 3 jerked to the right and slammed the wall as it rounded the frontstretch tri-oval. It went tumbling across the start–finish line only to get battered anew by on-rushing cars once it came to rest.

Fans fell silent, while inside the mangled heap Earnhardt hollered at the safety workers who had rushed to the scene, ordering them not to cut the roof off the car and telling them how to pull him from the wreckage. Once out, he refused to be strapped onto a stretcher and hobbled toward the waiting ambulance, holding his breastbone with one hand and flashing a thumbs-up with the other. X-rays revealed a broken sternum and left collarbone.

It was the worst injury he had suffered since his rookie season in 1979, and the memory of having to surrender his racecar to a backup driver was as vivid and even less tolerable than before.

In six days NASCAR would race at Indianapolis Motor Speedway, where Earnhardt was the defending champion. He had dropped to third in the standings after failing to finish the Talladega race, and the only way he could earn points at Indianapolis was by starting the race and completing at least one lap. So, less than seventy-two hours after his savage Talladega crash, he strapped himself in his Chevrolet for the opening practice at Indy. The team had labored over the car during testing and Earnhardt could tell right away that it was good enough to win the race. That made his injury even tougher to bear.

The pain was more severe than he let on. Doctors had told Childress and Earnhardt both that if he sustained another major hit so soon, he'd likely be out for the season. He qualified the car twelfth fastest, and he agreed to yield to a relief driver once the race got under way. Childress tapped Mike Skinner, driver of his No. 3 truck in NASCAR's fledgling truck-racing series, to take over as soon as Earnhardt pulled the black Chevy into the pits—ideally at the first caution flag, if he could stand the pain that long.

It came on Lap 6. There were tears in Earnhardt's eyes when he climbed out. "This is my life here," he said.

Skinner rejoined the race, went on to collect five bonus points for leading a lap, and finished fifteenth, which was good enough to inch Earnhardt back to second in the standings. But what Skinner recalls most vividly about the experience was the pain in Earnhardt's eyes when he climbed out, and the leash he felt around his own neck after slipping into the most famous car in racing and trying not to screw it up.

"I was on pins and needles all day just being careful with that car," Skinner said. "We did exactly what we were asked to do, but the car was much better than it finished. I felt like I had a bit in my mouth the whole day."

Earnhardt ignored doctors' advice the next week on the road course of Watkins Glen, New York, where drivers' upper bodies are wrenched in all directions as they fling their racecars around the twisting right and left turns. He set a track record in winning the pole, explaining later that he hurt so bad that he couldn't tolerate the jolt of the car going over the curbs so he just focused on running a smooth, fluid lap. And though another relief driver was standing by during the race, Earnhardt refused to get out of the car. Chomping on Darvocets and wearing a clavicle strap that pulled his shoulders back, he led fifty-four of the ninety laps and finished sixth. Not bad for a guy who could only steer with his left hand.

"Now I know why all them women burned their bras!" he cracked later about the clavicle strap. "I couldn't stand that!"

Months later he acknowledged that he'd been foolish to race with such serious injuries. "It was a stupid mistake on my part," he said. "It was the hero thing to do when I was driving it, but it probably set me back two or three races—or a lot more than that, really."

Earnhardt was humbled by the Talladega crash in a way no defeat had ever humbled him. Getting injured wasn't the sort of thing he dwelled on. Like most racecar drivers, he pushed the thought out of his mind. He had been so desperate to claw his way into big-time stock-car racing that he never contemplated how or when to bow out. But the hard truth was that Earnhardt had been at the top of NASCAR for so long, that by the mid-1990s there was nowhere to go but down. The challenge now seemed to be doing so with dignity.

When NASCAR's 1997 season got under way, Earnhardt was

forty-five. He was graying around the temples and a grandfather twice over. He hadn't won a race in eleven months. Childress, his longtime car owner, had hired veteran crew chief Larry McReynolds in hopes of jump-starting the No. 3 team's fortunes. Childress had also started a second NASCAR team for Mike Skinner in hopes of staying competitive with the multicar operation of Hendrick Motorsports, which had just won its second consecutive championship, with Labonte's title coming on the heels of Jeff Gordon's.

Earnhardt didn't bother hiding his hostility toward having a teammate. Skinner was from the West Coast rather than East, but he had a similar hard-knocks pedigree that should have earned the Intimidator's respect. Like Earnhardt, he was a high school dropout who had earned a place in stock-car racing the hard way, moving south to take a job in the engine shop at Petty Enterprises for $205 a week. He later was a tire changer on Rusty Wallace's pit crew his rookie season. Skinner did body work and painted racecars. And every chance he got he raced local short tracks on the side. Childress gave him his first big break, hiring him to drive his No. 3 Chevy truck. But once Childress formed a second Winston Cup team and named Skinner to drive the No. 31 Chevy, Earnhardt treated him "like a butthole," to borrow Skinner's phrase.

The verdict wasn't in yet on the merits of adding a second or third car to an already successful race team, although Hendrick Motorsports was obviously making it work. The way Earnhardt saw it, he and Childress had won six NASCAR championships by focusing exclusively on the No. 3 Chevy. He didn't want any of that focus taken away. Plus, he felt that he and his crew had busted their tails developing racecars capable of winning. Why should they be expected to share that expertise with Skinner?

"I could understand that," Skinner says today. "He was like, 'Screw 'em! Let 'em get it on their own.' And *no one* could tell Dale what to do. It was, '*This* is how we're going to do this! You're not going to tell *me* how we're going to do this; I'm going to tell *you* how we're going to do it, because *you* work for *me!*' "

Earnhardt was only slightly more gracious about Skinner's addition to the fold in his public remarks. "I don't really look on him as a teammate," Earnhardt said. "If we can help each other in a race as far as the drafting goes, it'll be great. If it comes down to winning, I'm probably going to bend the fenders on the 31 just like I would on any other car to get to the front."

• • •

Despite the brash talk, Earnhardt was still winless when I returned to his Iredell County farm for an interview in May 1997—this time to talk about his rough start to the season and his plans to start his own NASCAR Winston Cup team, presumably with the future of his second son and namesake, Dale Earnhardt Jr., in mind. I found him, as usual, crowing about how much he had accomplished that morning and the previous day, a Monday, which he called a "honeydew day."

"A *what?*" I asked.

He was struck dumb by the question.

"Ain't you never had a honey?" he asked. "It's a 'Honey, do this! Honey, do that!' "

"Yes I *have* had a honey!" I sassed back. "But I never told him what to *do!*"

He found this hilarious, as well as hard to believe. Among the items the Intimidator had checked off his honey-do list: hanging wind chimes, putting in hitching posts for the horses, moving the doghouse, and staking stobs for a horseshoe pit.

We climbed in the pickup for a ride around the property. He wore a walkie-talkie to stay connected with whatever was going on in the office, the race shop, or on the farm, and he was determined to supervise them all no matter what else he was doing. In the middle of answering a question he'd stop to bark an order into the walkie-talkie, like, "Those horses need to be separated!" or "That engine has a skip in it! Can't you hear it? Fix it before it breaks!" or "It's too wet to be bailing hay!" Then he'd pick up where he left off, only to stop again a minute later to tell a neighbor's collie what to do. "That's Rocky Culp's collie," he said to me. Then he turned to the dog: "You need to go on home!"

In between he'd point out deer lurking in the woods that I wasn't quick or keen enough to spot; stop at his lake to feed his catfish and bream, which churned up the water like mad when the food pellets landed; and demonstrate the conveyor belt that transported the eggs laid that morning by his eight thousand hens.

Then we toured the race shop, stopping by the engine room so I could see just what a restrictor plate looked like. He pointed out the break room where his employees were having a 401(k) meeting, clearly proud that so many people depended on him for their livelihood. At each stop he'd introduce me around. By then I had earned my own name, no longer "Little Higgins." "This is Liz. *She* writes for *USA Today!*" he'd say. Or, on a later visit, "*She* works for the *Washington Post!*"

Each time I visited he had expanded the compound—built a new building, added another layer of security, and hired another forty or fifty employees. The burgeoning racing empire, Dale Earnhardt Incorporated, was intended as his legacy and livelihood after he retired from racing the No. 3 Chevy, which he envisioned being at least five years away. He and Teresa had founded the company years earlier and shared its ownership equally. At the time it consisted of a NASCAR Grand National team and a NASCAR Truck team. Within the next four years it would include three Winston Cup teams—including the No. 8 Chevrolet driven by Dale Earnhardt Jr., who proved the most skilled racer of the three elder Earnhardt children.

Earnhardt pictured making a career transition similar to the one Junior Johnson had made decades earlier, giving up his job behind the wheel for the role of NASCAR team owner, fielding racecars for drivers he would handpick. In the meantime, he was getting his racing operation up and running.

The interview continued the next day, when Ron Green Jr. of the *Charlotte Observer* and I met Earnhardt for lunch at the Speedway Club overlooking the frontstretch of Charlotte Motor Speedway. Despite the on-track slump that had the garage buzzing, he was in a good mood and joked about hoping that McReynolds, his crew chief, would cut practice short later that day after only a few laps. He never looked at his watch, never seemed impatient, was courteous to the waitress, and broke his train of thought only once when he saw a track worker watering the frontstretch grass.

"He shouldn't be doing that *now!*" Earnhardt snapped. "Somebody could slip and get hurt. *Me,* for instance."

Then it was back to the conversation, which unspooled easily with two of us doing the prodding. The banter had no meaningful chronology but skipped from topic to topic: his memory of the day his daddy surprised his momma with a brand-new car, a laid-back, beige, 1972 Plymouth Fury III; the joy he got from sleeping with the windows open at night so he could listen to the geese down at his lake; and the wrenching emotion of having to get out of his racecar at Indianapolis the previous year, when he nursed the broken bones.

"I just didn't want to give up," he said. "I think the giving-up part—the feeling like I was letting the team down part—that was the biggest thing. Then that probably contributed to me staying in the car at Watkins Glen, where I *should* have got out of the car. Go out there and beat yourself up more than you did . . ."

He would reminisce, crack a joke, and then suddenly say something serious.

"I'd give up everything I got to have my dad back," he said with a wistful flatness. "People make statements like that, but I *would*. He was a neat person. I knew him, but I didn't realize what you had when you had it. When he said something, you didn't listen. You listened, but you didn't listen. I wish I could have learnt a lot more than I have learnt."

Asked what lesson stayed with him the most, he said, "Stay in school," with a self-deprecating laugh. "Oh, a lot of things. But in general, about being a man and being responsible. The responsibility thing was a big thing with my dad."

The question of retirement had clearly been on Earnhardt's mind. And when it came up, he talked about his mixed feelings and recalled a conversation he'd had a few years earlier with best friend Neil Bonnett, who had been killed in a crash at Daytona in 1994 while trying to make a comeback after suffering a serious head injury.

"I think I could enjoy it," Earnhardt said of retirement, with more than a trace of reservation in his voice. "But I also worry because I remember when Neil Bonnett was hurt in 1990, and he went through some trying times recovering. We were sitting, talking at his trailer where we deer hunt, I can remember him telling me, 'I used to think, man, I wish I had more time to go hunting or go fishing, but I had to go to the racetrack to test or something. Man, I'd give anything just to go test. Just to get in a racecar.'

"I worry that when I do say, 'Hey, I'm gonna retire, the year 2005 or whatever it is, whether I really can retire? Can you comfortably retire and walk away from it? Maybe the race team ownership type thing and being involved that way . . . *This* is what I'm thinking: Dale Jr.'s coming along, and say, five or six years down the road, Dale Jr. is starting to make it. And if I'm involved with him, or if he's involved with our program, then it may be easier to retire.

"I surely don't want to race too long. I think A. J. Foyt raced too long. And I think Richard Petty would really have liked to have retired a little earlier. But I bet Richard has the fire inside of him that he would *still* enjoy the driving part of it. So I mean, I don't know. That's the part I worry about. When I *do* think it's time—or when *time* says it's time—if, inside, I can accept it? And I can retire? . . .

"I mean, everybody has their time. And I'm still having mine. And I'm enjoying it. Maybe I'm not right at the peak of it as much as I was. But I'm still there. And I'm still a factor and a contender and by no means ready to throw in the towel and give up and hand over the flag. Son-of-a-bitch is gonna have to take it from me."

Chapter 5

THE WONDER BOY
AND INDY

Jeff Gordon tried his best to convey adulthood when he arrived on the NASCAR scene at age nineteen. But until he strapped in a racecar, he was hard for fans to take seriously—scarcely bigger than a jockey (five-foot-six, 145 pounds), sporting a pencil-thin mustache that was more fuzz than facial hair, and carrying a briefcase whose contents consisted of a Game Boy and a handful of stock-car racing magazines.

While Earnhardt conjured up the image of a big-game hunter, Gordon conjured up Milton Bradley's 1960s-era board game Mystery Date, in which little girls took turns opening a door to reveal one of four images: three dream dates, each dressed in a different outfit for a fabulous outing (a tuxedo to take you to the prom, pressed khakis to go bowling, swim trunks for a beach picnic), and one dud. Until 1992, most NASCAR drivers looked like the dud dressed in grimy dungarees, as if their idea of a date was taking you to a dirt-track race and making you pay. Jeff Gordon was the first NASCAR driver to look like a dream date.

It was no accident that Gordon showed up in NASCAR well-groomed and well-spoken—not only ready to meet your parents but also ready to make a sales pitch to a corporate CEO. The California native had been coached for this moment from age five, when his stepfather, John Bickford, first put him in a tiny, quarter-midget racecar. Over the next fourteen years, Gordon progressed up the ranks of open-wheel racing under Bickford's watchful eye, from quarter midgets to go-karts to the lightning-fast sprint cars, following the same path that had led generations before him to a ride in the Indianapolis 500. Just as assiduously Bickford coached the painfully shy child in making a strong first impression, fully able, from age thirteen, to make eye contact with adults, extend a firm handshake, and field reporters' questions with engaging sound bites.

The result was a sponsor's dream and a hellacious talent behind the wheel, with nearly as many years' experience in racing as Earnhardt, who was twenty years his senior. Indeed Gordon was the total package by the time he abandoned his dream of racing in the Indianapolis 500 for a future in southern stock cars. He had phenomenal racing skills, good looks, polish, and, in short order, a ride with a front-running NASCAR team and a beauty-queen bride.

All of that was reason enough for longtime NASCAR fans to cast a wary eye. In their view, the California phenom hadn't paid his dues the same way Dale Jarrett or Dale Earnhardt had, forced to prove themselves in mediocre racecars before getting a chance with a championship-caliber team. After the twenty-four-year-old Gordon bumped Earnhardt from his perch atop stock-car racing in 1995, becoming the youngest to win NASCAR's Winston Cup championship in the modern era, that wariness morphed into overt hatred, fueled by all the resentment scrawny kids feel toward the captain of the football team.

"It's like somebody's writing this script for him, and he has wings," said three-time champion Darrell Waltrip, as Gordon closed in on his second NASCAR title. "He's like an angel. He's too good for his own good."

Gordon's decision to abandon the Indy-car career track for NASCAR had profound implications for American motorsports in the decade that followed. Indy-car racing, which had defined automotive glamour and daring for decades, saw its fan base erode from the mid-nineties on, primarily the result of an ugly power struggle that caused its top drivers and teams to defect and form a rival series. NASCAR, meanwhile, took off—in part because of the sensation caused by Gordon, who would win fifty-five races and three championships before his thirtieth birthday. NASCAR's Wonder Boy raised stock-car racing's profile in the eyes of corporate America and brought legions of new fans to the sport—particularly women, children, and teenagers.

But the telegenic Gordon wasn't the first to shake up stereotypes about NASCAR drivers. Tim Richmond was.

• • •

An Ohio native with a prep-school education, Tim Richmond swaggered into NASCAR in 1981 as the top-finishing rookie (ninth) in the previous year's Indianapolis 500, oozing more raw talent than ever sat in a Winston Cup car. And he crammed more fast laps and wild times than anyone dreamed possible in a brief, often brilliant stock-car racing career. Richmond won thirteen races and nearly $2.3 million in six seasons in NASCAR's top ranks, then left a swirl of controversy in his wake after being run off in 1988 amid allegations of illegal drug use and rumors that he had contracted AIDS.

A sanitized version of his story supplied the plot of *Days of Thunder,* the 1990 star vehicle for Tom Cruise, which sidestepped the private battle Richmond waged against AIDS. The movie was roundly mocked in NASCAR circles for its over-the-top depiction of stock-car races as demolition derbies. But its principal characters, while mythologized and caricatured, were drawn from Richmond and his circle of friends and rivals, with Cruise portraying the hotshot racer Cole Trickle (based on Richmond), Robert Duvall as the wily crew chief Harry Hogge (based on Richmond's veteran crew chief Harry Hyde), Randy Quaid as NASCAR team owner Tim Daland (a thinly veiled Rick Hendrick), and Michael Rooker as Trickle's legendary on-track foil Rowdy Burns (inspired by Dale Earnhardt).

"All the big Hollywood people that came in here to do this movie, they sat right there where you're sitting," Harry Hyde said one afternoon in 1994 as I sat in his mobile home on a hillside next to Hendrick Motorsports, interviewing him for a story to mark the fifth anniversary of Richmond's death. "They had three tape recorders running, and they had twenty-five rolls of tape in a two-day session. I don't know why they didn't tell the story like I told it to 'em. They had to go put all that Hollywood stuff in it, and they just about covered Tim up. As far as I'm concerned, they jimmied up the movie real good."

Earnhardt represented NASCAR's bedrock culture in his too-tough Wrangler jeans, denim shirt, and cowboy hat in the early 1980s. Richmond represented a culture clash—the first stock-car racer to sport Armani suits, silk shirts, and a Rolex watch. But pitted against each other on the racetrack, Earnhardt and Richmond were electric, staging some of the most thrilling battles NASCAR fans had ever seen, diving into the corners nose-to-tail and barreling down the straightaways on the brink of losing control.

Richmond's driving was worth paying to see, especially in qualifying runs or on road courses, where he'd sling the car so hard into the corners it would exit sideways with all four tires off the ground. And no one brought out his best quite like Earnhardt. As far as Richmond was concerned, Earnhardt was the only other driver in the race. "He'd rather race Earnhardt than eat," said Hyde.

Richmond didn't waste his time doing anything he *didn't* enjoy, in fact. Having fun was his credo. Every day was Christmas on Tim Richmond's calendar, and every night was Saturday night.

Richmond never won a Winston Cup championship, but he had a tuxedo custom-made for the occasion, with a silk shirt patterned after a checkered flag. He envisioned his race team riding up the East Coast from Florida on a high-speed cigarette boat to collect the trophy. He even charted the course they'd take to a dock on Long Island, where they would hop in to a limousine for the ride to NASCAR's season-ending banquet at New York's Waldorf-Astoria.

"He was going to start at the top and go from there," Hyde said.

Richmond's first NASCAR team had trouble building cars and engines to withstand his go-for-broke driving style. But if the engine could keep from blowing up, Richmond could make a decent car look good. And he could make a good car win.

"Tim had very little knowledge of the car, but he had a sixth sense about him," recalled Buddy Barnes, a member of that Blue Max team. "He had the absolute no-fear driving style. He was so confident in that racecar, he'd say, 'Just get it close! Just get it close!' We wrecked a lot of cars because Tim would just drive so hard trying to make up the deficits."

But the guys on his crew loved him for it. Richmond wrung everything possible out of his racecar and staged a hell of a show in the process. Plus, his wild driving style meant job security for them. There was never an idle moment as long as Richmond was wheeling the car. There was always something to fix.

"To finish second . . . he'd just as soon finish last or wreck," Barnes said. "He loved putting on a show for the media and the fans. He wanted everyone to have fun because he was having fun. He just had this aura about him. When Tim Richmond was around, something was going to happen. Fireworks were going to go off."

Richmond reveled in doing things other NASCAR drivers didn't. Driving around Tampa once he told a buddy he had to stop for coffee and took him to a topless coffee shop. On the way to the track in Dover, Delaware, one fall he made his team stop at a haunted house. He showed up at Atlanta's superspeedway once with three NFL Falcons cheerleaders in tow and gave each some fast laps around the track, saving his fastest, wall-scraping lap for the most prissy one, who

ran shrieking and cussing from the car. He had a flair for grand en-
trances, whether by limousine, Harley-Davidson, screeching Corvette, or lavish motor home with all the frills. And more often than
not, he was dangling a stunning woman on his arm when he exited—
if not one on *each* arm.

NASCAR officials weren't quite as enthralled with Richmond's
antics. And they were particularly irked by his vocal criticism of the
circuit's trackside medical services, which were a far cry from the
standards Richmond had witnessed in Indy-car racing. Of the handful of NASCAR drivers who had the nerve to question the way Bill
France Jr. ran NASCAR, none did so publicly. Richmond didn't give
a rip for politics-as-usual and harped on the need for more safety
workers at the races, for water-barrel barriers on road-course turns,
for skilled medical personnel at each track, and helicopters to ferry injured drivers to hospitals.

"If something was wrong, Tim didn't care if it had been Jesus
Christ himself—he would have got up in his face," Hyde said.
"NASCAR was not big to him."

"It was ironic," recalled Harold Elliott, his former engine-builder.
"Tim always thought about safety . . . except when he got in a racecar and tried to put a six-foot racecar in a one-foot hole."

Richard Petty suspected Richmond's on-track daring was partly
fueled by drugs. Others in NASCAR were suspicious of his Hollywood friends. Richmond flaunted the fact that he didn't fit stock-car
racing's mold. He ran in wildly different circles that rarely intersected:
bikers, actors, rock stars, truck drivers, and a millionaire businessman
named Bob Tezak, who bankrolled his Indy 500 ride and later served
time in federal prison for two counts of arson. Richmond had a personality for every pair of sunglasses, every hat, every leather jacket, and
every pair of Italian loafers and snakeskin boots he owned.

Said third-generation NASCAR racer Kyle Petty, who counted
himself a friend: "A lot was made about the way he dressed, but I don't
think he dressed that different from anybody else in the world. He just

came into a sport that had not realized the significance of natural fiber yet. If it didn't have a racing logo on it, or it was wasn't Sansabelt slacks, it was different."

Despite Richmond's flamboyance, he was the only choice of NASCAR team owner Rick Hendrick when Procter & Gamble offered its Folgers coffee brand to sponsor a new race team in 1986. For a company as straitlaced as P&G, Richmond was a hard sell. As one of his buddies cracked years later, "Tim was the driver most likely to be found sitting on a pile of pot buck-naked with a sixteen-year-old girl." But Hendrick was adamant, telling P&G executives that he wanted Richmond to drive the No. 25 Folgers Chevrolet or no one.

Then, after selling the sponsor on Richmond's potential, Hendrick paired his hotshot driver with a crew chief who was thirty years his senior and a world apart in every regard. Not surprisingly, Richmond and Hyde got off to a rocky start. Even basic communication was a challenge, with Richmond incapable of explaining to Hyde how the racecar handled, telling him it was either "looking out" or "looking in" as it rounded the corners. In time, Hyde figured out that Richmond meant that the car's front end was veering toward the wall in the turns when he said it was "looking out," and that its back end wanted to whip around and smack the wall when Richmond said it was "looking in."

Vocabulary was just one aspect of the divide they'd have to brook. Hyde had a hellish time getting Richmond to think about the big picture during races, which often meant paring back his speed to conserve his tires, as smart stock-car veterans learn to do, in order to make a charge at the end. Richmond wanted to run every lap as fast as he could, even if it meant blowing a tire or an engine in the process.

But once they found common ground, they were magic— winning seven races, finishing second four times, and taking eight poles in the second half of 1986.

Said former NASCAR crew chief Robin Pemberton, among the

legions who marveled at Richmond's ability: "Tim was the perfect example of a talent that almost didn't make it until he got with somebody who could put cars underneath him that would stay going. That was Harry Hyde. Until then, he could break an anvil! Harry wasn't the best at some things, but he was great at building cars that didn't fall apart."

Richmond was on top of the world as 1986 drew to a close, and everyone at Hendrick Motorsports fed off his euphoria.

"He just was *wide* open, one hundred percent of the time," recalls former racer Brett Bodine, who built racecar bodies at Hendrick's shop at the time. "He just was all about living life. His abilities as a driver were unbelievable because he didn't know siccum about a racecar. But he knew how to drive. I can remember Rick being mad at him all the time because he never cashed his checks; they'd be sitting on the dash. Tim didn't do it for the money. He did it because he just loved it. He just liked the limelight."

Said Ed Clark, executive vice president of Atlanta Motor Speedway: "The rock 'n' roll crowd loved him. Girls loved him. Cool guys loved him. I don't know if the blue-collar guy who worked at Cannon Mills ever fell in love with him. But that guy's girlfriend did."

At the 1986 season-ending awards banquet, Richmond shared NASCAR's Driver of the Year honors with Earnhardt. But within a week he was hiding behind the name "Lee Warner," Case No. 1-861-775-7, at Ohio's Cleveland Clinic, where, on December 10, he was diagnosed with acquired immune deficiency syndrome.

Hendrick had never heard of AIDS until Evelyn Richmond, Tim's mother, telephoned to explain the diagnosis. "I didn't know what she was telling me," Hendrick recalled. "I was confused. I didn't know what it actually meant, what the prognosis was. The more you found out, the more you just . . . It hurt, and it killed you."

Richmond and Hendrick kept the condition a secret. But the rumors started flying after Richmond missed the 1987 Daytona 500 with what reportedly was double pneumonia. Some said he was in rehab for a cocaine addiction. Others whispered he had AIDS. Kyle Petty didn't believe either story, fearing his friend had cancer. Hyde wasn't sure what was wrong and didn't want to know.

"Tim Richmond had pride that was beyond anybody's imagination," Hyde said years later. "He was never going to tell nobody. The more I looked at him, and the more I saw, the more I realized. . . . But didn't anybody know a lot about AIDS then."

Richmond was too weak to run a full-length race until June, when he showed up for the Miller 500 at Pocono Raceway in Pennsylvania, where he had swept both NASCAR races in 1986. Most drivers steered clear of him in the garage.

"He never was accepted when he came back," Richard Petty said. "Everybody knew he had trouble."

Meaning AIDS?

"Yep," said NASCAR's King. "Whether it was true or not, everybody said that's it. And so everybody kept their distance."

But just before the start of the Pocono race, Richmond's old buddy Dale Earnhardt walked up and slapped him on the back. "You ready to get it on?" Earnhardt asked, grinning.

"Yeah," Richmond said. And he climbed in his Folgers Chevy, roared onto the giant racetrack, and led eighty-two of the two hundred laps. And won.

Richmond cried so hard on the final lap that he couldn't see the checkered flag. And he wept all the more when Earnhardt, Bill Elliott, and Kyle Petty, who were battling for the season's championship, drove alongside to congratulate him. Richmond circled the track one extra time, despite the objection of NASCAR officials, so he could compose himself before pulling into Victory Lane. It didn't do any good. He was too choked up to speak when he climbed out of the car. So was the sobbing Miss Winston, the sport's beauty queen, who had to excuse herself from the festivities because she wasn't allowed to show any emotion but happiness after a race. As flashbulbs popped,

Richmond hugged his mother, whipped a towel in the air, and poured beer on everyone in sight.

Richmond won the next race, too, on the snaking road course at Riverside, California. Barry Dodson, his former crew chief with the Blue Max team, had watched his own car fall out of the race earlier that day. So he hopped in his rental car and drove to a hillside over-looking the track to watch Richmond tear through the course's famed turns. Dodson had a feeling it might be his last chance to see Richmond's magic at work.

"He wouldn't just run through them like an old lady," Dodson said. "He'd sashay through there, slinging the car into the corners, passing on the inside in Turn 8."

It was Richmond's last NASCAR victory.

In the months that followed, Richmond couldn't hide the fact that his health was deteriorating. And his fellow drivers, convinced his problem was either AIDS or a drug addiction, started pressuring NASCAR to keep him off the track. Richmond had checked back into the Cleveland Clinic about the time Hendrick got a call from NASCAR's competition director, Les Richter, who said, "Your driver doesn't look in any shape to drive." That September, Richmond re-signed from Hendrick Motorsports.

Five months later, he was battling NASCAR again—this time for the right to run one more race, the 1988 Busch Clash, the invitation-only event that preceded the season-opening Daytona 500.

NASCAR had developed its first drug-testing policy in the months leading up to the 1988 season. Richmond suspected it was created expressly for him. As a precaution he stopped taking his AIDS medication, AZT, six weeks before so it wouldn't be detected. Nonetheless, NASCAR announced Richmond had tested positive for a banned substance and suspended him indefinitely.

Richmond demanded a second test. He passed. Within days NASCAR amended its initial report, acknowledging that the first test had detected only large doses of over-the-counter cold medicine.

The second test was clean. NASCAR lifted Richmond's suspension but announced he couldn't compete unless he turned over his medical records from the Cleveland Clinic. Richmond refused.

Richmond filed suit against NASCAR in April 1988, seeking $15 million in actual damages and $5 million in punitive damages for defaming him through the drug test. NASCAR countered by demanding eight years of his tax returns; the results of every test of his urine, blood, and bodily fluids; and his medical records from the Cleveland Clinic and from his personal doctor in Florida.

After a judge ordered him to turn over the records, Richmond dropped the suit. He died in a West Palm Beach hospital on August 13, 1989, at age thirty-four, shut out by nearly everyone in racing.

According to Hendrick, Richmond considered making his AIDS diagnosis public shortly before he died. "The country really wasn't ready for it," Hendrick said. "We all prayed there would be a cure. We chased everything we could find."

Charlotte Motor Speedway held a memorial service the following week. About two hundred people attended. One of Richmond's helmets was displayed, but racing's biggest names were absent.

"It's something a lot of people in racing would like to forget happened—that there even was a Tim Richmond, that Tim Richmond died the way he died," said speedway president H. A. "Humpy" Wheeler. "But he proved that you could come down in a southern culture and go completely against the grain and be accepted. Though maybe not by everybody."

At the request of Richmond's parents, Dr. David Dodson announced AIDS as the cause of death days later, adding that he was convinced Richmond contracted the disease through heterosexual sex.

Years later a former model named LaGena Lookabill Greene came forward and accused Richmond of knowingly infecting her with the virus. Greene said their relationship was consummated only after he proposed marriage in September 1986. Richmond's family said he was diagnosed with the virus that December. A 1986 story in the *Miami Herald* suggested that Richmond may have spread the disease unchecked for as long as eight years.

It was hard to find evidence of Tim Richmond around NASCAR's tracks after his death. There were no grandstands named in his honor, no statues erected in his memory.

But Harry Hyde devoted an entire room in his mobile home to mementos: boxes of videotapes of Richmond's races, cases of Folgers coffee, and stacks of Victory Lane photographs. Racing together those eighteen months, Hyde said, had been the best time of his life.

"He wasn't going to be like you wanted," Hyde said. "He wasn't going to be like his mama wanted. He wasn't going to be like Harry Hyde wanted. Or Folgers. Or Rick Hendrick. Now, if you can blame a guy for that . . ."

Said Hendrick: "Tim was good for the sport. In my opinion he helped change the sport for the better—for the flamboyance, the excitement, and just the fact that you don't have to be from the South to come in and drive. You don't have to be a good ol' boy. You can be a young, good-looking, fun-loving Hollywood kind of guy and do well."

• • •

In many respects Jeff Gordon picked up where Tim Richmond left off, minus the controversy. Gordon could handle an out-of-control racecar with the same authority as Richmond. When a victory was on the line, Gordon raced with the same breathtaking abandon. And when it came to luring a broader audience, Gordon fulfilled Richmond's promise tenfold. Best of all, Gordon arrived in NASCAR at precisely the moment stock-car racing was looking for a new driver with broad appeal.

It wasn't that the garage lacked personality after Richard Petty retired. In many ways the sport's popularity was at an all-time high. The success of Petty's Fan Appreciation Tour in 1992 had revealed that the public's appetite for NASCAR outstripped the supply. Everywhere Petty raced that season, track owners sold tickets as quickly as they could print them. Souvenirs flew off the shelves. And corporations that had never marketed their products through stock-car racing suddenly ponied up hundreds of thousands of dollars just to be linked with Petty's all-American image.

So when Petty tipped his cowboy hat good-bye in November 1992, NASCAR was eager to exploit the momentum. What stock-car racing needed was a driver who could leverage the mania over the next five or ten years. It needed a guy who could win races *and* sell tickets, move merchandise, and hook corporate America. And it needed a "white hat" to play off Earnhardt's black-hat persona.

There were a few obvious candidates. One was Georgia's Bill Elliott, NASCAR's 1988 champion, who perennially led the voting for the sport's most popular driver, although insiders suspected his vigorous public-relations machine had a hand in swaying the outcome. But Elliott was a pure racer, with scant interest in courting corporate sponsors or pitching their wares. He seemed to resent any obligation that took him away from his racecar. Plus, Elliott's thick southern accent made him a poor candidate for being anointed NASCAR's new national face.

There was Alan Kulwicki, the only college-educated NASCAR driver at the time, who had scored a victory for brainy underdogs everywhere by winning the 1992 championship in a Ford Thunderbird that he owned himself. But Kulwicki was a Wisconsin version of Elliott—happier burying his head in a racecar's engine than fraternizing with the public.

Three-time NASCAR champion Darrell Waltrip was as glib as Elliott was aloof, taking to the spotlight like a flea on a sweaty dog. But Waltrip's front-running days were winding down in the 1990s, so he wasn't the driver to propel NASCAR into the twenty-first century. Rusty Wallace was just as eager an interview as Waltrip and a hellacious racing talent, but he spewed a profanity (albeit good-natured ones) roughly once every fifteen seconds. Davey Allison and Kyle Petty were also in the mix, with their famous names and innate warmth.

But if Bill France Jr. wanted stock-car racing to transcend its regional stereotypes, he needed a new ambassador. What he needed was a driver capable of putting the "national" in his National Association for Stock Car Auto Racing. He needed a Bill Elliott without the accent and a Tim Richmond without the baggage.

Jeff Gordon was it. He had grown up understanding that auto racing was a business as well as a sport—a big business that involved not only selling his skill behind the wheel, but also selling his image, his sponsors' products, and the excitement of whatever racing series he represented. On all those fronts, Gordon was as determined to do his job the right way as Richmond had been determined to do things *his* way. The result was a different sort of stock-car racer, and legions of hopeful parents and ambitious NASCAR owners would soon clamor for a prodigy just like the one John Bickford had reared.

Gordon's parents had divorced when Jeff was one, and his mother married Bickford, a Californian with a love of racecars, an inventive mind, and more initiative than capital. Jeff was an energetic boy but extremely small for his age. So Bickford custom-built his stepson a BMX bicycle to keep him busy, cutting down the standard parts to suit his tiny frame. Then, on the eve of Jeff's fifth birthday, his stepdad brought home a quarter-midget racecar with its pedals and steering wheel sized precisely for a thirty-pound boy who stood just thirty-eight inches tall.

Bickford had wanted to work on racecars as a teenager, but his parents didn't approve of racing or the crowd it attracted. So his deferred passion became Jeff's first love. It was an activity father and son could do together. Bickford finally got to build racecars, serve as a chief mechanic, and, through Jeff, get the thrill of competition.

"Jeff was actually living my childhood for me," Bickford said.

From the start Bickford treated Jeff's racing as a structured, serious pursuit. He built Jeff the fastest cars he knew how. Jeff was expected to get them to the front—and to do it in a respectful way, without bumping the other kids or wrecking. And even though he was in elementary school, Jeff was also expected to conduct himself like a professional out of the racecar. His uniform was always clean— never cluttered with patches. And he wasn't allowed to go to the track until he could prepare himself to race without his parents' help. So he practiced the ritual at home and repeated it like clockwork when he got to the track: putting on his jacket, getting in the car, buckling the seat belt, laying his gloves on the steering wheel, putting his helmet on, rocking it on his head to straighten it out, putting on his right glove and then his left.

At age seven he taped his first TV segment: a day-at-the-track feature on the local racing prodigy. The only problem was Jeff didn't utter a word as the reporter and cameraman followed him around. He was so shy that some suspected he had a speech impediment because he wouldn't talk. So Bickford went to work on that, mindful that if his son was going to make it in racing, he'd have to learn to cultivate corporate support. They started with the basics: don't stare at your shoelaces; look people in the eye; shake their hand; think before you speak.

As Jeff got better at interacting with adults, Bickford suggested they study how professional athletes handled themselves on TV. They'd sit and watch postrace interviews, then talk about who was boring, who was interesting, and what made the difference. With help from a local TV reporter, Bickford learned more about what TV producers wanted from athletes, and he explained that to Jeff, stressing the constraints of a thirty-second segment, the importance of being enthusiastic, and the value of providing specific insights and inside information in a few, quick sentences. In time, Jeff knew exactly what to do when a TV reporter asked "How's the track?" Jeff pounced on the question as if it were a racetrack to be conquered.

"It's gonna be *great* for the fans!" he'd say. "You drive down into

Turn One, and there are two holes, so I gotta be really careful to watch out for the holes! But it's really slick in Turn Three, so I have to get out of the gas early. But the place to watch? That's Turn Four! Lots of bite! *Everybody* is going to be coming off of Turn Four hard, so tell the fans to watch Turn Four!"

Meanwhile, Jeff's on-track skills progressed at an even faster pace. With Bickford preparing his racecars, Jeff had the fastest car most everywhere they went. He was remarkably comfortable at high speed and showed an uncommon knack for getting his car to the front cleanly. So Bickford accelerated Jeff's learning curve by putting him in sprint cars at thirteen—an age most car owners and promoters considered foolhardy (and the state of California deemed illegal) to race such fast, dangerous machines.

One indication of the difficulty of controlling a particular racecar is its speed-to-weight ratio. On that count sprint cars, with their 850-horsepower engines and 1,400-pound bodies (roughly equal the horsepower but less than half the weight of NASCAR's stock cars), are among the more daunting contraptions on wheels. Topped by a wing to keep them from flipping, sprint cars are still apt to somersault as they slide sideways around slippery dirt-track corners, often running three and four abreast. Jeff showed so much promise in the wicked fast cars that the Bickfords uprooted the family and moved from California to Indiana, where the age restrictions weren't as stringent.

After he had proved himself in sprint cars, the next logical step was Indy cars. But the doors were closed. Jeff needed more than talent to get a quality ride in the Indianapolis 500. He needed a multimillion-dollar sponsor or a wealthy benefactor. He had neither.

Stock-car racing was the next best alternative—a form of motorsports in which ability still counted for more than deep pockets. So Bickford contacted NASCAR racer Ken Schrader, who had come up through the open-wheel ranks, and asked how his son could get a foothold in the sport. Schrader steered the family to Buck Baker's three-day racing school at the North Carolina Motor Speedway. Bickford had to barter for the $3,000 tuition, arranging for an ESPN crew to film a sequence on Jeff's lessons if Baker would waive the fee.

The next time Bickford heard from Jeff he was shrieking over the telephone from North Carolina. "Sell everything!" he screamed. "We're going stock-car racing! This is what I want to do the rest of my life!"

. . .

Unlike Tim Richmond, who roared into NASCAR with the show-manship of P. T. Barnum, the nineteen-year-old Gordon wanted to blend in without fanfare. He knew he needed time to adjust to the heavier stock cars, and he threw himself into his apprenticeship on NASCAR's Grand National circuit, racing the Baby Ruth–sponsored Ford for car owner Bill Davis, who paired his prospect with an inventive mechanic and former modified racer from New Jersey named Ray Evernham.

Gordon still looked like a kid. And he acted like one, too, away from the track. He played video games and loved to break-dance. He goofed around with basketball and sported a mullet haircut with skinny mustache. "I think some of that was eyebrow pencil," Evernham later joked. But Gordon was all business in the racecar.

He won three races in just his second Grand National season—at Atlanta's 1.5-mile superspeedway and at Charlotte, where he swept the spring and fall 300-mile races. He turned the fastest qualifying lap to claim eleven poles that year, too—a testament to his nerve and Evernham's skill.

It was during practice for the Atlanta race that Gordon caught the eye of Rick Hendrick, who had yet to find a driver to equal the talent he had lost in Richmond. Suddenly here was this kid zooming around one of NASCAR's more treacherous tracks on the brink of crashing, and Hendrick stopped to watch the wreck that was about to unfold. But Gordon never lost control. Hendrick couldn't believe it. And when he found out Gordon wasn't under contract for the 1993 season, he signed him to a contract at once, touching off a firestorm of criticism from Ford officials who felt they had nurtured the young-ster's progression.

With Evernham joining him in the move to Hendrick Motor-sports, Gordon made his Winston Cup debut in the 1992 season finale at Atlanta. His unremarkable performance in a Hendrick Chevrolet was overshadowed by the day's major story: the retirement of Richard Petty. But Gordon was on top of the world.

"Right now, the way things are going for me, I wouldn't want to change anything in the world," Gordon told *Stock Car Racing* maga-zine on the eve of NASCAR's 1993 season. "I want to make a name for myself. I want to win races, to be in Winston Cup for a long, long time."

. . .

There are a handful of venues in sports where great achievements live on long after the trophies are carted home. And the moment you walk through their gates, you feel history come alive; it's embedded in the playing field, lingers in the air, and echoes amid silence.

Wimbledon is like that. It's impossible to look down on its man-icured Centre Court, threadbare after each fortnight's pounding, and not see Bjorn Borg crumpling to his knees in triumph.

Churchill Downs is like that, too. They say you can walk through the stalls and feel the presence of the great horses. And when you gaze on the famed track, you still see the mighty chestnut colt, Secretariat, ears pinned back, steam billowing from his nostrils, running each quarter-mile faster than the one before in his charge from dead-last to first in the fastest Kentucky Derby on record.

In the sport of auto racing, that place is Indianapolis Motor Speedway.

So when word leaked out in 1992 that NASCAR was preparing

to stage the first stock-car race on the world-famous oval, which historically hosted only one event each year—the Indianapolis 500—it conferred immediate legitimacy. It was as if NASCAR, derided for so long as the homely stepchild of motorsports, had suddenly married into royalty.

It had taken decades of wooing on the part of NASCAR's founding France family, whose overtures to bring their show to Indy had been repeatedly spurned by speedway officials. Allowing NASCAR to race on the sacred oval was unthinkable to Indy car purists, who feared the 3,500-pound taxicabs would diminish the mystique of the Indianapolis 500.

But in the early 1990s the speedway's young CEO, Tony George, had a change of heart. With the famed facility aging and an ugly battle brewing over control of open-wheel racing, George saw the wisdom of adding a new revenue stream. But before making the pact official, George and France agreed to hold a "feasibility test" to make sure NASCAR's hulking stock cars could produce an entertaining show on the flat, 2.5-mile behemoth. They had a second agenda in mind, as well: gauging the sentiment of midwestern Indy-car fans. No one was sure whether they would greet the arrival of stock cars at Indianapolis with picket lines or with open arms and wallets.

NASCAR tapped nine of its biggest stars to take part in the June 1992 test: Davey Allison, Dale Earnhardt, Bill Elliott, Ernie Irvan, Mark Martin, Kyle Petty, Ricky Rudd, Rusty Wallace, and Darrell Waltrip. To a man, they were awestruck over the prospect of racing on the same track where champions like Graham Hill, Mario Andretti, Al Unser Sr., and Rick Mears had triumphed. They were just as awed by the turnout, considering absolutely nothing was at stake.

A NASCAR test with nine drivers is no more meaningful than a blocking drill during spring football practice. The premium is on repetition, not competition. Still, thirty thousand fans showed up for the NASCAR test—more than attend the NBA All-Star Game—clamoring for a glimpse of a Petty or an Allison or the Man in Black.

Petty carried a video camera everywhere he went to chronicle the historic day. Wallace begged to be the first driver on the track. To avert a squabble, NASCAR decided the only fair thing to do was send the cars on track according to their number. Wallace was thrilled. He drove the No. 2, and there was no car No. 1. Not only would he be the first NASCAR driver out, but Earnhardt, in his black No. 3, would be staring at his bumper the whole time!

Wallace's heart was racing. He had never felt so proud.

Indianapolis Motor Speedway was hardly a stranger to the roar of racecar engines. But the deep-throated rumble of just nine NASCAR engines was a jarring, shocking assault. Indy car engines emitted a high-pitched squeal that sounded like a swarm of wasps. The thunder of NASCAR's engines sounded as alien at the famed oval as an Aerosmith concert at La Scala Opera House.

Wallace led the parade into the first and second turns, disappeared behind the tree line and roared onto the backstretch. He was approaching 170 miles an hour, but the 559-acre complex was so vast it felt as if he were motoring down a country road, with blue skies above and trees on either side. Wallace had goose bumps as he rounded Turn 3. The grandstands came into view, and he glanced in his rearview mirror. There, hurtling toward him like a maniac, was the black No. 3 Chevy.

Earnhardt!

"That son of a bitch!" Wallace thought. "He's trying to beat me to the line to lead the first lap!" And Earnhardt did.

Wallace laughs about it today. "I never even *thought* about gassing it and running it real hard," Wallace says. "All that was on *his* mind, by God, was, 'I'm gonna lead the first lap!'"

In August 1993, NASCAR staged a two-day tire test at Indianapolis and invited its top thirty-five drivers. While ostensibly for the benefit of Goodyear engineers, the test was largely designed to drum up excitement for the inaugural race, scheduled for August 6, 1994.

Many feared NASCAR's ballyhooed Indy debut would be a flop. Indy cars whipped around the speedway at more than 230 miles per hour. Stock cars were nearly 70 mph off that pace, so there was reason to worry they'd look like tortoises by comparison. Once again it was up to NASCAR's drivers to win the crowd over. Richard Petty had established the protocol decades earlier: treat fans as equals and thank them for their support with an autograph, a wave, or a friendly word.

As an insurance policy, NASCAR's competition director, Les Richter, called drivers to a meeting on the eve of the test to stress the importance of making a good first impression. Racing at Indianapolis was a privilege, Richter reminded them, sounding like a school-teacher preparing third-graders for a field trip to the state capitol. Drivers needed to be on their best behavior. He told them not to bitch at the security guards in the yellow shirts. He reminded them to accommodate the media and be friendly to fans. Above all, he begged, make it look "racy." Run the cars in thick packs; don't let them get strung out over the giant oval.

"There was a lot of squeamishness over the Brickyard deal," recalls Wheeler, the Charlotte promoter who had worked for Firestone at the Indianapolis 500 in the late 1960s. "If NASCAR was going to Indy, then it needed to look better than the Indy cars. The race needs to be better; the crowd needs to be bigger. Well, how many people are going to come—100,000, 200,000? Nobody knew. To a certain extent, it was a gamble."

The speedway charged fans five dollars to attend the test. This time, fifty thousand came. Many had driven two hundred and three hundred miles just to see the NASCAR stars and their American-made racecars up close. In a front-page story in the *Indianapolis Star,* Charles Powers, who had traveled from Burlington, Iowa, explained why. "I like it because you can relate to it," Powers said. "These cars are basically what you can see at your dealer's. It just seems closer to home."

Earnhardt and Gordon had already set up their souvenir rigs outside the speedway even though the inaugural Brickyard 400 wouldn't be run for another year. Business was brisk. Inside the track, midwestern fans packed the grandstands that lined the front straightaway and dangled autograph pens and caps on ropes so the NASCAR drivers below could sign them as they walked to the track.

Drivers were just as giddy. Before they pulled onto the track for the first time, the three Bodine brothers arranged for a photographer to take their picture as their racecars roared down the front straightaway nose-to-tail. "It was *that* special to us," said Todd Bodine, the youngest. "We wanted that picture. It was hallowed ground, and everybody felt the same way."

Every chance drivers got, they paid homage.

"This place is awesome, incredible, like I knew it would be," said Gordon, after his first few laps. "I'd been around in my pickup truck and the tour bus, but it was a whole different perspective today."

Even Earnhardt was humbled: "I'm still awed because I never thought I'd be here, much less NASCAR. I don't want to spoil any of the tradition of the Indy 500 or the month of May, but hopefully we can create some of our own excitement for the month of August."

NASCAR had yet to run a competitive lap at Indianapolis, but already it had tapped into a new fan base at the geographical center of the country. Expanding the sport's footprint was critical. At the time, fifteen of NASCAR's thirty-one races were run in essentially the same market: the Carolinas, Georgia, and Virginia.

"To a large population in this country, us racing at Indy legitimized the sport of stock-car racing," Kyle Petty later said. "Until then, you'd go somewhere and people would say, 'You drive a racecar? When do y'all run Indy?' "

"We don't run Indy," Kyle would explain. Their faces would invariably fall.

"We don't run Indy." He had said it so many times over the years. Now, he'd never have to say it again.

. . .

Gordon had already scored one huge victory in his second season on the Winston Cup circuit—winning the sport's longest race, the Coca-Cola 600, in May 1994 thanks to a gamble by crew chief Ray Evernham to change only two tires rather than four on the final pit stop. But for the most part, Gordon and Evernham were finding it was tough being competitive as a second-year team when they raced on tracks that had been part of NASCAR's circuit for decades. Veteran teams had thick notebooks filled with data on each track's characteristics and nuances; Evernham and Gordon were starting from scratch, working from a notebook filled with nothing but clean sheets of paper.

Finally, heading to Indianapolis for NASCAR's inaugural Brickyard 400, they were on equal footing. No NASCAR team had experience at Indy. And Evernham was determined to outwork them all in an effort to build a car that could get his little buddy to Victory Lane in what promised to be the sport's biggest race since the inaugural Daytona 500.

Even though Indianapolis Motor Speedway is the same size as Daytona, its configuration is altogether different. It's more narrow and almost flat, banked just 9 degrees in the corners compared with Daytona's 31. Its turns are closer to right angles than sweeping curves. If you could slice into its thirteen-inch depth, you could date the track like a live oak. At its base is masonry sand and the remnants of 3.2 million paving bricks laid down in 1909. Atop that is layer after layer of tar, asphalt, and bituminous binder.

Evernham researched the track as if he were writing a master's thesis, grilling Indy car veterans for their insights. He phoned Pancho Carter, who competed in seventeen Indianapolis 500s, and he spent time with four-time Indy 500 champion A. J. Foyt. He asked every question he could think of. How smooth was the surface? How did the track respond to changes in temperature? In humidity? Then he designed a special car with trick features to exploit what he had learned.

The key to going fast at Indy, he found, was "light, low, and left." In other words, you wanted a racecar that was as light as possible, had as low a center of gravity as possible, and had the balance of its weight on the left side.

Evernham learned that Indy's surface was far smoother than the rutted, bumpy tracks on NASCAR's circuit, so he added pans underneath Gordon's car to increase its downforce in the front. He installed a sway bar in the rear so the car's weight wouldn't shift as it rounded the turns. He built special brake ducts that gave the car an aerodynamic edge. And he tweaked its front-end suspension to help it negotiate the corners more easily.

The car proved so fast in the first practice of race week that Evernham skipped the final practice, fearing he might screw things up if he kept tinkering. The entire garage took note, with opinion split over whether Evernham was an arrogant idiot or a genius hiding a rocket.

It wasn't until race morning, when teams pushed their racecars onto the starting grid, that Evernham fully grasped the magnitude of the moment. There he was, a former Modified racer who had given up his dream of racing cars after confronting the fact that he had likely peaked in winning the track championship at Wall, New Jersey. And now, he was rolling a racecar he had designed and built and nurtured like a baby onto the track at Indianapolis Motor Speedway.

"I walked up and down and saw all those people and the scoreboard and realized that we were at Indy, it really hit me," Evernham said. "It choked me up because I thought to myself, 'Oh my *God,* we are at Indianapolis! We're on hallowed ground. And we've got a shot of winning this thing.' You almost feel like, 'I don't deserve to *be* here.' "

But he did. Lap after lap Gordon's Chevy got faster, just as Evernham had designed it to. And Gordon's young voice got more manic over the radio as the race hurtled toward its conclusion. He was out front, leading the Brickyard 400, until Ernie Irvan passed him with twenty-one laps to go.

"Just pace yourself," Evernham said over the radio. "You'll be all right."

Gordon screeched back, "I'm going to get his tires hot!" He nosed his Chevy under Irvan's bumper and retook the lead with sixteen to go.

"Okay, I got him passed!" Gordon said.

A few laps later he was screeching again. "He's doing the same thing to me! He's getting my tires hot! I'm gonna lose it! I'm gonna lose it! I can't keep him on the outside!"

Gordon let Irvan pass and settled in to regain his composure and rethink his strategy. Evernham started counting down the laps remaining, trying to keep his driver's confidence up and his anxiety down.

"Eleven to go. You're the man!" Evernham said.

"Ten. You're the man!"

"Nine. Watch your corners."

"Eight. Hit your marks."

"Seven. You're the man!"

Gordon ducked to Irvan's inside exiting Turn 2 with six laps to go, and their cars touched lightly. Moments later Gordon shrieked again, "He's got a flat! He's got a flat!"

Irvan's right front tire shredded, and Gordon roared past to reclaim the lead with five to go. He was still screaming, with Evernham screaming right back, when he took the checkered flag more than a half-second ahead of Brett Bodine.

NASCAR's gamble had paid off.

Before a crowd estimated at 300,000 and a national TV audience tuned to ABC, the inaugural Brickyard 400 came to a storybook end—won by the youngest driver in the field, who had attended his first Indianapolis 500 at eleven and had clung to a fence that day to get Rick Mears's autograph. It was won by a transplanted Californian who spent his teenage years in the shadow of the great track and cut high school to sneak into Carburetion Day the week of the Indy 500. It was won by the open-wheel racing phenom who had been spurned by Indy cars because he couldn't bankroll a ride. Two days after turning twenty-three, Gordon found himself in Indianapolis Motor Speedway's Victory Lane with tears in his eyes as he accepted a trophy that outweighed him by twenty pounds.

No one was happier that day than Jeff Gordon.

But NASCAR president Bill France Jr. might have been more proud. "You've got to remember one thing," said France, whose father had worked on the winning car of the 1938 Indy 500. "Every driver that was driving in America, by and large, always wanted to drive at Indianapolis. I can remember my father saying that back when he was driving years ago. The only way you could race here would be driving an Indianapolis-type, open-wheel car. If a driver had picked a stock-car career, he didn't have an opportunity to race here. Now, there's another route for someone to race at Indianapolis. That's through NASCAR."

Chapter 6

THE CHAMP AND
THE CHALLENGER

With his storybook victory at Indianapolis Motor Speedway in 1994, Jeff Gordon won the trophy that every stock-car racer coveted. But Dale Earnhardt won the second running of NASCAR's Brickyard 400 the next year. Then he went on *Late Night with David Letterman* and bragged that he was the first *man* to win a stock-car race at Indy, landing another well-placed jab at the youngster he loved to needle as "Wonder Boy."

The forty-four-year-old Earnhardt had a son older than Gordon, who was then twenty-four. Earnhardt was also a grandfather, though "Grandpa" wasn't a nickname anyone in the garage dared call him. The Intimidator didn't particularly like answering to "Senior," either, for that matter, after his second son, Dale Jr., joined him in NASCAR's top ranks a few years later.

Despite their generational divide, Earnhardt and Gordon gave NASCAR a delicious pair of protagonists once again—a contemporary Petty versus Allison—with starkly contrasting personalities and widely divergent appeal.

Earnhardt, just over six feet, loomed larger when riled. The 145-

pound Gordon simply refused to grow. And when he got excited in a racecar, his chirpy voice seemed to jump an octave.

Outside of racing, Earnhardt loved nothing better than hunting and fishing. Gordon favored scuba diving and playing video games.

Earnhardt looked like a modern-day Samson in his open-faced helmet—his bushy mustache obscuring everything from his nose down to his chin strap. Gordon's baby face totally disappeared behind his brightly painted, closed-faced helmet, which, when paired with his bright red-and-blue racing suit, made him look like a Ninja Turtle.

Even their racecars evoked opposites. Earnhardt's No. 3 Chevy was coal black: a force of evil on wheels. Members of his pit crew rode their Harleys to the races if the track was within a few hundred miles. They also posed for a promotional photo sitting atop an automotive scrap heap, proclaiming themselves "the Junkyard Dogs." Gordon's rainbow-schemed No. 24 Chevy seemed to spread optimism and good cheer with every lap. It was serviced by color-coordinated crew members known as "the Rainbow Warriors," who had their own personal trainer.

But there wasn't the vast difference in the routes the two drivers took to NASCAR's top ranks that fans wanted to believe there was. Earnhardt had come up through a hard-knocks school, no question. And he was deservedly proud of the calluses that proved it. But Gordon's path hadn't been paved with gold, as so many suspected. He had clawed his way into stock-car racing, too, with his parents staking their livelihood on his ability to make it.

Gordon's stepfather, John Bickford, was earning $7.50 an hour in the mid-1970s designing vehicles for people with physical handicaps. His wife, Carol, earned $4.90 an hour working for the federal government. They had a young son and daughter to support, and Bickford put everyone at risk when he quit his job in August 1976 to start his own manufacturing company with $30,000 from an investor.

Bickford worked from 7:30 in the morning to 11:00 at night to get the business going. His wife took a second job. They slashed expenses every way possible. Still, there was little left to bankroll Jeff's budding racing career. That's where Bickford's ingenuity and the family's determination took over. Bickford traded parts he manufactured to buy Jeff a used sprint-car chassis. He bought used motors, but for safety's sake he paid the going rate for new tires. He sold the sedans he and his wife drove to work so he could buy a pickup truck to tow Jeff's racecar around the country. They limited their hotel stays on the road, bunking with friends along the way or, if need be, sleeping in the truck.

"That's how we lived for the summer," Bickford recalled. "It was kind of like camping."

By the time Gordon made it to NASCAR, he had raced nearly as many years as Earnhardt had. The Man in Black started in his midtwenties; Wonder Boy, shortly after turning five.

Time spent behind the wheel of a racecar goes a long way toward seasoning drivers. It's called "seat time," and there's no substitute. It's how drivers pick up wisdom that isn't taught in racing school, and it has nothing to do with nerve or bravery.

It's being able to react to trouble on the track without panicking.

It's knowing how close you can run to another racecar without wrecking—*and* knowing that the answer differs on a straightaway as opposed to a corner, on a short track as opposed to a superspeedway, while racing side by side as opposed to three or four abreast.

It's recognizing that a lug nut is loose by sensing a subtle vibration in a wheel.

It's realizing that a tire is rubbing against a fender and liable to go flat by the smell of tire smoke.

It's anticipating how a gust of wind will affect the car's handling by noticing the way a hot-dog wrapper skitters across the racetrack a few hundred yards ahead.

While Gordon boasted plenty of seat time when he arrived in NASCAR, Earnhardt had a huge head start when it came to handling the heavy, often balky, stock cars. Gordon was acutely aware of his deficit and unashamed about throwing himself into remedial work. Who better to learn from, he thought, than the master?

Each time Gordon pulled his No. 24 Chevy onto the track, whether during practice or a race, he sought out the No. 3 and fell in behind. And nowhere did he work harder at mimicking Earnhardt's moves than on the sport's two largest speedways, Daytona and Talladega, where NASCAR had mandated the use of carburetor restrictor plates to reduce horsepower and keep speeds under 200 miles per hour. With all the cars running at essentially the same top speed, the key to passing was exploiting the powerful aerodynamics at play. And no one did that better than the Intimidator. Air was invisible to most drivers. Earnhardt, they said, could see it. And Gordon felt sure he'd learn to see it, too, if he could just hang on to that black Chevy's bumper.

Earnhardt seemed flattered that Gordon was trying to download his brain with every lap. And as Gordon improved, Earnhardt reveled in having another foil join the ranks of his most worthy rivals—Rusty Wallace, Mark Martin, and Dale Jarrett, chief among them. Racing wasn't half as much fun, after all, if you couldn't beat the best. Just as in hunting, the bigger the kill, the better the marksman.

But Gordon's learning curve accelerated faster than most anyone thought possible. No driver won more NASCAR races than Gordon in 1995. He visited Victory Lane seven times and proved a quick study in racing with restrictor plates, winning the 400-mile race at Daytona in July. And though Gordon would squander most of a 205-point lead down the stretch, he became, at twenty-four, the youngest driver in the modern era to win a Winston Cup championship. Gordon edged Earnhardt for the title by 34 points. In doing so, he denied Earnhardt the eighth championship that would have broken his tie with Richard Petty and established him, without dispute, as history's greatest stock-car racer.

Gordon was sensitive to the awkwardness of the occasion as

NASCAR's top drivers, accompanied by their bejeweled wives, donned tuxedos to fete him at the season-ending awards banquet in New York that December. So from the stage of the Waldorf-Astoria's ballroom, the young champion proposed a toast to Earnhardt, who looked on from his table, dressed to the nines. On cue, a waiter carrying a silver tray strode on stage and presented Gordon with a crystal flute filled with milk. Gordon turned to Earnhardt and raised his glass, conceding he probably was too young for champagne, anyway.

Earnhardt roared.

And the seven-time NASCAR champion raised a glass of champagne in reply, saluting the driver who was, undeniably, stock-car racing's future.

. . .

NASCAR starts each season with its biggest event, the Daytona 500. The winner collects the same number of points toward the annual championship as the victor of every other NASCAR race. But the Daytona 500 payday is far more lucrative. And all the money in the world can't buy the prestige. Drivers spend lifetimes dreaming of the Daytona 500 trophy. Engine builders indulge in the same fantasy, as do NASCAR mechanics, who live for a chance to have a hand in assembling the winning car.

But if thirty-eight runnings of the Daytona 500 had proved anything, it was that the trophy didn't necessarily go to the most courageous driver or the fastest car or the hardest-working crew. Winning the Daytona 500 was as vexing a challenge as there was in stock-car racing. Few knew this better than Earnhardt, who had won everything else on Daytona's high banks—125-mile qualifying races, 300-mile Grand National races, 400-mile Winston Cup races—but never the 500.

Just to be in contention for the victory, a driver had to have a loaded hand. For starters: a powerful engine, despite NASCAR's horsepower-choking restrictor plates; an aerodynamically sleek car that could slice through the air with the ideal balance of downforce and drag; presence of mind (keen awareness of the caliber of cars and drivers around him); drafting help from another driver to pull off the critical passes; plenty of patience; and a little luck.

Mused NASCAR team owner Robert Yates, who built multiple Daytona 500–winning engines: "The Daytona 500 usually comes down to the guy that's the smoothest, coolest, and shows the most patience—not usually the guy that storms off with it."

Earnhardt had fallen short eighteen times, and his record of futility included some memorable gaffes and misadventures. He ran out of gas with three laps to go while leading the race in 1986. He led on the final lap in 1990 only to cut a tire and limp home fifth. In 1991 he plowed into a seagull on the back straightaway, damaging his car's snout and doing far worse to the bird. He led on the final lap again in 1993 but was passed by Jarrett, who had studied the champion's drafting technique over the years as closely as Gordon would later.

In 1997, Earnhardt found himself again in a position to win. Two-time Daytona 500 winner Bill Elliott led the race with eleven laps to go. On his bumper were five cars running nose to tail at more than 190 miles per hour. Earnhardt was second, followed by Gordon, Jarrett, Irvan, and Terry Labonte, each separated by less than a car length.

That's when Gordon made his move, pulling up on the inside of Earnhardt. "Ooh, this is gonna be close," Gordon thought as he squeezed past. Earnhardt's car skimmed the outside wall, bounced back, and brushed the No. 24, then got rear-ended by Jarrett. The contact turned Earnhardt's Chevy sideways, and it flipped end over end down the backstretch before finally coming to rest, a smoking wad of sheet metal.

The caution flag flew. Amid the hush that followed, Earnhardt crawled from the wreckage, waved to the screaming fans, and headed toward the waiting ambulance. He took one last look at his car and stopped. All four wheels were on and reasonably aligned. He walked over and asked a track worker to try firing the ignition. The motor roared to life.

"Give me my car back!" Earnhardt snapped. And he climbed in the window, steered back onto the track, and fell in line under the caution, determined to complete all two hundred laps and earn whatever points were still in play for his run at the season's title.

Meanwhile, up at the front of the field, Elliott had no teammates to help fend off the Hendrick onslaught. It was one car against three, and Elliott knew it was hopeless.

With six laps to go, Labonte and Ricky Craven fanned out to the high side. Gordon dove low, and Elliott didn't know which line to block. He tried nudging Gordon low, nearly pushing him onto the racetrack's apron—the flat shoulder of a track that's not meant for racing. It didn't work. Gordon sped by, pulling Labonte and Craven with him for a 1-2-3 Hendrick sweep.

But in the eyes of many, Earnhardt stole the show, refusing to quit in his mangled No. 3.

"That's the toughest man alive right there," Earnhardt's car owner, Richard Childress, told Jeff Owens of *Winston Cup Scene* afterward. "He deserves to win this race more than anybody ever has."

• • •

For Gordon fans, his 1997 Daytona 500 victory was only the beginning of a glorious year. The twenty-five-year-old had set yet another NASCAR record, becoming the youngest driver to win the Daytona 500. He would go on to win nearly a third of the season's races, pulling his No. 24 Chevy into Victory Lane ten times in thirty-two starts.

Three-time champion Darrell Waltrip said that Gordon's dominance had NASCAR officials scared. "Why?" Waltrip said. "Because they can't make enough rules to keep him from winning all the races!"

Others groused that NASCAR was tilting the playing field in Wonder Boy's favor. Whether true or not, it was undeniable that Gordon and his Rainbow Warriors were improving at a scary pace.

Gordon worked hard at getting better behind the wheel. He focused on his physical conditioning so he wouldn't tire as easily on those sweltering days when four hundred laps in the racecar felt like roasting in a Crock-Pot for four hours, leaving him mentally and physically fried. He forced himself to balance his aggression with patience so he could be around at the finish of more races. He experimented with different lines around the racetracks, searching out that elusive sweet spot where the car handled best. He paid particular attention to his entry into the corners, mindful that cornering speed was the key to a fast lap.

Most race fans, and more than a few eager racecar drivers, obsess over speed. They bring stopwatches to the track and cheer whoever runs the fastest qualifying lap. But a fast lap has more to do with how well a car corners than how fast it runs down the long straightaways. As Bobby Allison liked to say, repeating an adage that had been drilled into him as a young racer: "Every racetrack has two straightaways and four corners. So that means you've got to handle twice as good as you run."

Evernham, Gordon's crew chief, was a tremendous factor in Gordon's success. As a mechanic, he seemed one step ahead of NASCAR's rulebook at every turn, inventing trick features that made the car go faster by exploiting the gray areas of the rules rather than breaking them outright. And as a race-day strategist over the two-way radio, he knew how to coax Gordon's best performance.

"I don't think you could put Jeff with just anybody and have him go out and dominate like he's done," said Jimmy Johnson, general manager of Hendrick Motorsports at the time. "Ray has got a tremendous talent at keeping Jeff calm, cool, and collected. No one else can do that like Ray can."

Evernham deflected all credit to his driver. "He is the Michael Jordan of auto racing," he said. "He's the Tiger Woods of our sport. Every once in a while, someone comes along who has got the gift. He pumps us up. I want to be the best crew chief because I feel he's the best driver."

But the more Gordon won, the more fans hated him. He had a loyal following, to be sure, but it was drowned out by the hecklers during prerace introductions. Gordon-haters booed his car every time it took the lead, and they cheered whenever it wrecked or blew an engine. And when the No. 24 pulled into Victory Lane, they were merciless.

In the eyes of Earnhardt fans, Gordon's crimes were too numerous to count. They resented Gordon for having been handed the sport's savviest crew chief. They resented him for having the best engines. They resented him for having the best-looking wife. Above all, they resented him for standing between Earnhardt and an eighth championship.

Asked why he thought NASCAR fans hated Gordon so much, Jarrett once replied: "He shouldn't be allowed to be that young, that talented, that experienced, and that good-looking."

Gordon tried looking on the bright side. He remembered riding around a racetrack in the back of a convertible with Earnhardt in the moments following driver introductions at a race in 1993. And he was shocked by how much the Intimidator was booed and heckled as he circled the track, waving to the fans who paid his bills. Earnhardt wasn't fazed. "As long as they're making noise . . . " the champ said, grinning.

Still, Gordon couldn't help but be disappointed by his reception.

"Sure if it was my choice, I want everybody to cheer," he said.

"But I also know there are a lot of fans out there for other drivers, and there's no reason there shouldn't be. I've got a lot of fans out there cheering for me. The boos are sometimes louder. . . . They maybe don't want to see us winning every weekend."

Well, too bad.

Gordon kept winning in 1997, showing a special flair for NASCAR's biggest events. In late August he became only the second driver to collect the $1 million bonus staked by series sponsor R.J. Reynolds for winning three of the sport's so-called crown-jewel races. (Bill Elliott had done it in 1985, earning the nickname "Million-Dollar Bill.") Gordon clinched the bonus by winning the Southern 500 at Darlington Raceway, the most challenging track on the circuit.

Jarrett and Martin battled him for the series title down the stretch, but Gordon held them off. In just five seasons, Gordon had amassed twenty-nine victories, two Winston Cup titles, and more than $16 million in winnings. NASCAR's Wonder Boy was everywhere, it seemed. And corporate America was scrambling to latch on to his rainbow-colored cape.

•   •   •

For NASCAR, it was a moment of sheer serendipity. Poised to pop the cork on its fiftieth anniversary, the sport had found its driver of the future.

What set Gordon apart from previous NASCAR champions was a fan base whose demographics debunked nearly every stereotype about stock-car racing. Market research conducted for JG Motorsports, the company that Gordon had recently formed, indicated that 50 percent of his fans were female. They tended to be technologically savvy. And they listed golf as their favorite pastime. Gordon was smart enough to play to his audience, becoming the first NASCAR driver to have his website address embroidered on the back of his racing suit.

What all this suggested was that Gordon was the man to deliver the broader audience that stock-car racing coveted. He and his team of advisers were eager to get started.

"Our goal," said Bob Brannan, Gordon's personal business manager and vice president of JG Motorsports, "is to hook Jeff up with the right companies to help him transcend our sport. And in doing so, bring the sport to a new audience that might not currently follow our sport."

A former executive at Wachovia Bank, Brannan had replaced Gordon's stepfather in managing the driver's business opportunities. And he went to work extending Gordon's personal "brand" in the marketplace.

At the time, Earnhardt was still NASCAR's highest-paid stock-car racer, appearing eighth on *Forbes* magazine's 1997 ranking of the world's forty highest-paid athletes. Of his $19.1 million earnings, $15.1 million came from endorsements: sales of T-shirts and souvenirs; deals with Anheuser Busch, Coca-Cola, Burger King, and Wrangler Jeans. Gordon was the only other NASCAR racer to make the cut, making his first appearance on the list at number thirty-two, credited with $10.3 million in earnings, of which $6.5 million had come from endorsements—among them Pepsi, Ray-Ban sunglasses, and Edy's Ice Cream.

But after Gordon won his second Winston Cup championship, the price of doing business with him escalated overnight. Depending on the specifics of the contract—the number of personal appearances it guaranteed, the use of Gordon's image in his NASCAR uniform, the use of images of him with his No. 24 racecar—signing Gordon to pitch a product had become a seven-figure proposition by 1998.

"Considerably more," Brannan added with a smile, "depending on what rights go with the deal."

Gordon loved the marketing aspects of the sport. He was positively starstruck over the experience of filming his first national TV commercial for Pepsi, which had signed him in 1997 as one of its "GeneratioNext" sports celebrities, along with Shaquille O'Neal,

Derek Jeter, Deion Sanders, soccer's Mia Hamm, tennis champion Andre Agassi, and Olympic skier Picabo Street. The filming took place at Universal Studios in Los Angeles, and Gordon arrived to find he had been assigned his own trailer, with his name on the side!

"Then John Travolta goes walking by, like it's no big deal," Gordon said during a telephone interview from the set. "That was sort of a highlight right there!"

Everyone wanted a piece of NASCAR's prodigy, including the world's largest talent agency, William Morris, which signed him to a roster of clients that included Clint Eastwood, Cindy Crawford, Bill Cosby, and former president Gerald Ford. The agency's goal was to place Gordon in all areas of entertainment—TV sitcoms, feature-length movies, publishing, everything. To that end, he was assigned a team of agents to expand his "image-based marketing."

It was alien terrain for a NASCAR racer. But Raul Mateu, Gordon's lead agent at William Morris, said the relationship made perfect sense. "Every day the worlds of sport and entertainment are becoming closer," Mateu said. "They're becoming one. In the end, somebody's paying for a ticket to go see this guy race, which is no different than somebody paying to see a movie."

But first, Gordon had to undergo surgery to remove ten polyps from his vocal cords. He had granted so many TV and radio interviews after winning his second championship that he'd lost his voice. The procedure was scheduled three weeks before the awards banquet so Gordon would have time to recover before arriving in New York for the celebration.

Speaking barely above a whisper, Gordon joked the day before his surgery that he had asked the doctors if they could deepen his voice in the process. The doctors just laughed.

• • •

Meanwhile, Earnhardt's 1997 campaign ended as miserably as it began. For the first time since 1981, he failed to win a race all season—hardly what was expected from his highly touted pairing with crew chief Larry McReynolds. Moreover, on the day Gordon was collecting his million-dollar bonus at Darlington, Earnhardt was rushed to a Florence, South Carolina, hospital for a battery of tests on his brain and heart after he blacked out on the first lap of the Southern 500.

It wasn't uncommon for the seven-time champion to take a cat-nap in his black No. 3 before the start of a race or during a red-flag delay. And that's what he did before the start at Darlington. He kissed his wife, Teresa, and said "Catch you later," as he climbed into his racecar. Then he strapped in and dozed off.

But his business manager, Don Hawk, thought it was odd that Earnhardt was still sleeping when the time came for drivers to start their engines. Hawk had to rouse him. The driver seemed groggy; his voice was slurred. Earnhardt fired up the car and joined the parade for the three pace laps that preceded the start. He spoke only once over the radio, which was also odd. And Childress could tell that his voice wasn't right. From his perch atop the pit box, Childress tried getting Hawk's attention to tell him to ask NASCAR to add a few more pace laps so he could bring his driver in and check on him. But there wasn't time.

The flagman signaled green. The crowd sent up a hellacious roar. And forty-two racecars took off at full throttle—all but the No. 3, which lagged off the pace and veered toward the wall in Turn 2. It smacked the concrete once, continued on and hit again, with Earnhardt saying nothing over the radio.

"Park the car!" Childress screamed into his microphone. "Dale! Park the car now! Stop the car!"

"I'm sorry," Earnhardt finally mumbled. "I saw two racetracks."

He steered onto pit road the next time by. The crew helped him from the car, and Hawk grabbed his wrist to take his pulse. Earnhardt's was notoriously low, measured at 55 beats per minute—half that of most racers. His pulse was normal by his standards, but his body was

The precursor to Daytona International Speedway was an oval that had one straightaway on the beach and the other on a portion of state highway A1A. Here, Buck Baker (301) and Fonty Flock (500-B) battle in a NASCAR race, February 1956. DOZIER MOBLEY

Richard Petty (left) joined his father, three-time champion Lee Petty, on NASCAR's circuit in 1958. Here, they stand beside Lee's racecar at Darlington, South Carolina, in 1960.
RACING ONE/
GETTY IMAGES

The author interviews Richard Petty, stock-car racing's king, at Charlotte Motor Speedway in 1991. MARK SLUDER

Richard Petty signs a young fan's shirt during a July 1992 open house at Petty Enterprises' Level Cross, North Carolina, compound during his final season as a NASCAR driver. MARK SLUDER

Bobby Allison receives congratulatory kisses from Unocal's Race Stoppers, the beauty queens hired to promote the sport's official fuel, after winning the World 600 at Charlotte Motor Speedway in May 1984.
MARK SLUDER

Bobby Allison celebrates his victory in the 1988 Daytona 500 with his elder son, Davey, who finished second. Four months later, Bobby would lose all memory of the achievement after suffering career-ending injuries in a crash at Pocono Raceway.
RACING ONE/
GETTY IMAGES

A fan mourns Davey Allison outside his funeral service in Bessemer, Alabama, on July 15, 1993. The license plate, which Allison had autographed after his victory in the 1992 Daytona 500, was placed on his casket and buried. MARK SLUDER

Wrangler Jeans, Dale Earnhardt's first major sponsor, branded him "One Tough Customer." And he surely was, pictured here at Charlotte Motor Speedway in 1981 at age 30, still struggling for job security.
MARK SLUDER

Earnhardt made millions from his Intimidator persona but was a prankster outside of his racecar. Here, he tells the author how to do her job at Charlotte Motor Speedway in the early 1990s.   MARK SLUDER

The sight of Earnhardt crouched low behind the wheel of his black No. 3 Chevy was something no NASCAR driver was thrilled to see in his rearview mirror.   MARK SLUDER

Earnhardt hugs the Winston Cup trophy—the fourth of seven that he would eventually win—after edging Mark Martin for the championship at Atlanta Motor Speedway in November 1990.
MARK SLUDER

Tim Richmond, the 1980 Indianapolis 500 Rookie of the Year, shook up NASCAR in the mid-1980s with his raw racing talent and love of the spotlight. He poses on one of his boats at a marina in Daytona Beach, Florida, in February 1986. MARK SLUDER

Jeff Gordon, 23, had it all in 1994: a storybook victory in NASCAR's inaugural Brickyard 400 at Indianapolis Motor Speedway, a trophy that weighed more than he did, and former Miss Winston Brooke Sealy (left), his fiancée. GETTY IMAGES

Gordon's fast rise in NASCAR owed a sizable debt to crew chief Ray Evernham (right), who led him to three championships in four years. Here they discuss his car's handling at North Wilkesboro Speedway in 1995.
MARK SLUDER

Earnhardt's No. 3 Chevrolet leads Gordon's No. 24 around the track during a 1995 race at Martinsville, Virginia. It was a familiar sight as Gordon was honing his stock car racing skills.
MARK SLUDER

The on-track rivalry between Earnhardt (left) and Gordon thrilled fans, but they got along well off the track, photographed here in the North Wilkesboro Speedway garage in 1995.
MARK SLUDER

Three decades after retiring as a driver, NASCAR's original hard-charger, Junior Johnson, strolls around his home track, North Wilkesboro Speedway, which was shuttered in 1996 following its sale.

MARK SLUDER

Three generations of Pettys celebrate in Charlotte Motor Speedway's Victory Lane following Adam Petty's first victory in an ARCA series race, September 1998. From left: Grandfather Richard; Adam, 18; and Kyle, the proud father.   MARK SLUDER

Dale Earnhardt (left) congratulates his son Dale Jr. on his winning his first NASCAR Winston Cup race at Texas Motor Speedway, on April 2, 2000. Dale Jr. drove the No. 8 Chevrolet owned by his father.
COURTESY OF TEXAS MOTOR SPEEDWAY
PHOTO ARCHIVE

Within hours of the death of seven-time NASCAR champion Dale Earnhardt on February 18, 2001, grief-stricken fans had created a shrine of flowers, caps, cards, and candles in front of his race shop in Mooresville, North Carolina.   MARK SLUDER

Stock car racing's iconic beauty queen, Linda Vaughn, circles Daytona International Speedway atop a float as Miss Hurst Golden Shifter, one of her many honorary titles, in the early 1960s. DOZIER MOBLEY

R. J. Reynolds created spokesmodel Miss Winston to promote its brand after the tobacco maker signed on to sponsor NASCAR's top division in 1971. From left, Juliet Ashborn, Jenny Lynn Andrews, Marilyn Chilton, Angelia Gale, and Noneen Hulbert. DOZIER MOBLEY

R. J. Reynolds sports-marketing executive T. Wayne Robertson pilots a Winston-branded modified show car with Miss Winstons Sonja Matthews and Noneen Hulbert aboard in the early 1970s. Their outfits are adorned with the phrase "How Good It Is!" DOZIER MOBLEY

NASCAR raised its national profile by moving its annual awards banquet to New York's Waldorf-Astoria in 1981. Here, Terry Labonte and Miss Winston Renee Perks high-five his 1996 title in front of the Park Avenue landmark.

DOZIER MOBLEY

Wendell Scott competed in NASCAR's top ranks without help from Detroit automakers or a major sponsor. Pictured here at 50 before the 1972 World 600, Scott remains the only African American to win a major NASCAR race.
MARK SLUDER

Janet Guthrie became the first woman to compete in the Daytona 500 in 1977 and battled for the season's rookie-of-the-year honors. Like Wendell Scott, she campaigned despite lean financial support and often icy attitudes.
GETTY IMAGES

Colombia's Juan Pablo Montoya (left) made headlines worldwide by jumping from Formula 1 to NASCAR in 2007. Here, he talks with former open-wheel racer Adrian Fernandez of Mexico before that year's Busch Series race in Mexico City. MARK SLUDER

Brian Z. France, grandson of NASCAR founder "Big Bill" France, became the sport's third-generation CEO in 2003 and ramped up efforts to diversify stock car racing's fan base and extend its global footprint. MARK SLUDER

Open-wheel prodigy Kasey Kahne followed Jeff Gordon and Tony Stewart into NASCAR and won rookie-of-the-year honors in 2004. Boyish good looks and clever marketing earned him a fervent female following.
GETTY IMAGES FOR NASCAR

Kahne, shown here in the infield of Las Vegas Motor Speedway in March 2007, upholds Richard Petty's credo of being good to NASCAR fans and generous with autographs.   MARK SLUDER

With sponsorship for a front-running NASCAR team costing $20 million a year, drivers are expected to market their benefactors' products as well as drive. Two-time champion Tony Stewart is a master at product placement.   GEORGE TIEDEMANN

NASCAR opened an office in Los Angeles to cultivate ties to Hollywood. One result: celebrities Ben Affleck and Whoopi Goldberg serve as the grand marshal and honorary starter, respectively, for the 2004 Daytona 500.
GETTY IMAGES

Teresa Earnhardt embraces her stepson Dale Earnhardt Jr. after his victory in the Busch Series race at Daytona in February 2002. Strained relations between them would lead him to leave the team founded by his late father.
GEORGE TIEDEMANN

A fan of both Earnhardts displays the extent of his allegiance as he monitors activity in the NASCAR garage before the August 2007 race at Watkins Glen, New York.
MARK SLUDER

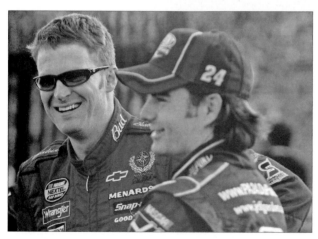

Dale Earnhardt Jr. (left) and Jeff Gordon joke around at Lowe's Motor Speedway in May 2007. Two weeks later Dale Jr. would announce he had signed a five-year deal to join Gordon at Hendrick Motorsports starting in 2008.   MARK SLUDER

limp. Hawk set him down behind the pit wall. Someone hooked him up to an oxygen tank.

Earnhardt was forty-six—one year older than his father had been when he died of a heart attack. That was Childress's first concern. Others wondered if his violent crash the previous year at Talladega had damaged his brain.

A brain-wave test at the Florence hospital showed nothing amiss. Neurosurgeon R. Joseph Healy suspected that Earnhardt's unusually low heart rate, which slowed under stress rather than sped up, was a factor. If it was vasodepressor syndrome, beta blockers or a pacemaker might be required.

Earnhardt was held overnight and instructed to bring Dr. Healy's notes when he went to see another specialist at the Bowman Gray Medical Center in Winston-Salem, North Carolina, later that week. Healy had treated racecar drivers before, including Earnhardt's best friend, Neil Bonnett, after the 1990 Darlington crash that left Bonnett with temporary amnesia, and he knew their tendency to feel invincible. So he sat Earnhardt down before releasing him the next morning and told him, bluntly: "My track record in this area is not good."

Healy went on to explain that Bonnett had signed himself out of that same Florence hospital against medical advice after regaining his faculties. He had promised to follow up with his own doctor in Alabama, but Healy wasn't sure he ever did. Three years later Bonnett got a doctor who agreed to clear him to race again. In less than six months, he was dead after hitting the wall on the high banks of Daytona.

"Obviously something greater than myself or something greater than yourself stopped you from doing your job," Healy told Earnhardt. "You need to stop and think about that."

But the tests that followed over the next three days found nothing wrong with Earnhardt's heart or brain. He returned to racing that Saturday night at Richmond.

Six weeks later at Talladega, Earnhardt spoke about the mysterious sequence of events. He confessed that he had been afraid of undergoing the MRI, unsure what doctors might find. And he got irritated when doctors made him swallow "this damn camera" that looked in the back of his heart.

"Too much technology there," he snorted.

Maybe aliens had taken possession of his body at Darlington, he kidded. Either way, he was in good health and good humor now, despite his winless streak. The doctors had checked everything there was to check, he said, except to see whether he was pregnant.

"Teresa is wanting me to eat healthy, and they tell me I *am* healthy," Earnhardt said. "So I went and had me a steak and a Coca-Cola. Not a diet one, neither! I had me a Classic!"

• • •

Earnhardt was keenly aware that his racing career was heading in the opposite direction from Gordon's. He knew that Gordon had only begun to tap his potential. There would be more championships to come. And he was sensitive about it. The surest way for reporters to piss him off was by asking what made Gordon so good.

Gordon's golden halo also annoyed Rusty Wallace to no end. But unlike Wallace, Earnhardt decided it was smarter to embrace the fact that Gordon was the sport's future—and use it to his advantage—than to fight it. In a sense, he borrowed a page from *The Godfather.* As Don Corleone counseled, "Keep your friends close and your enemies closer."

Fans wanted to believe that Earnhardt hated Gordon to his very marrow. Certainly Earnhardt wanted to beat Gordon on the track every Sunday. But as a businessman, he saw no reason why they shouldn't join forces. He viewed Gordon as an ethical, admirable young man—the kind of guy he could trust. So where was the shame in doing business with him, Earnhardt thought, if it made them both some money?

The stock-car racing souvenir business was an ad hoc affair as late as the 1980s, with each driver running his version of a sidewalk lemonade stand on the grounds of every NASCAR track. Drivers would get somebody to whip up a few T-shirts and hire family and friends to hawk them from souvenir trailers that traveled the NASCAR circuit.

Earnhardt was a step ahead. He had recognized the value of his name, nickname, image, and likeness early in his career, and he was the first NASCAR driver to trademark them. That gave him a legal club to combat the makers of bootleg Intimidator T-shirts and caps, which weren't earning him a dime.

By the mid-1990s, the sport's more prominent drivers had followed suit and signed over their rights to one of two major companies, Sports Image (which controlled Earnhardt's trademarks) and Motorsports Traditions (partly owned by Rick Hendrick, which controlled Gordon's trademarks, as well as those of a few other drivers and the Winston Cup series itself). The two companies focused their sales efforts at the racetracks, where 70 to 80 percent of their merchandise was sold.

Eager to exert more control over the fast-growing enterprise, Earnhardt bought Sports Image outright in December 1994. That way he could steer the industry's growth while hauling in a larger percentage of the proceeds. He and his wife, Teresa, tapped a business-man with an accounting degree, Joe Mattes, to manage the company.

Even though the sport was booming in the mid-1990s, and Earnhardt fans in particular were gobbling up everything with the No. 3 on it, NASCAR memorabilia lagged behind that of other professional sports in terms of quality, distribution, and sales. Mattes was quick to recognize that for the company's growth to continue, it had to reach fans who didn't go to the races. Earnhardt needed a foothold in retail outlets.

Ken Barbee, a partner in Motorsports Traditions, saw the wisdom. He and Mattes had become friends over the years. And they realized that even though their companies represented on-track rivals, they weren't competing for the same business. No Gordon fan was going to buy an Earnhardt hat, just as no Earnhardt fan would be caught dead wearing a Gordon T-shirt. Their real competition, they concluded, came from the NFL, Major League Baseball, and every other sports league that sold its gear in the nation's major retail stores, like JCPenney and Sears. That's where the real money was.

So Barbee and Mattes arranged a meeting with a Dallas-based buyer for JCPenney and brought samples of various drivers' T-shirts to make their sales pitch. It bombed.

"Look at this hodgepodge of shit!" the buyer told them, sifting through the shirts—some cotton, some not; some made by Hanes, others by Fruit of the Loom. "That's just not something I can really market effectively. Go get me a brand and come back and see me."

A single brand for drivers who bent each others' fenders for a living?

They saw the potential upside, but selling Earnhardt and Gordon took some work.

The rivals had already pooled their marketing clout for a series of commemorative trading cards after Gordon's victory in the inaugural Brickyard 400. The idea came from series sponsor R.J. Reynolds, and it had been a success, with fans gobbling up the forty-two-card set that was packaged in a fancy gold box and billed as "The Champ and the Challenger: Honoring Dale Earnhardt and Jeff Gordon."

Launching their own brand was a larger proposition. Mattes and Barbee devised a concept for a company called Chase Authentics, which would manufacture NASCAR's first quality line of apparel, and they made their presentation in a meeting with Dale and Teresa Earnhardt; Jeff and Brooke Gordon; and the drivers' respective business managers, Don Hawk and Bob Brannan. As founding owners, Earnhardt and Gordon would be principals in the company. But to broaden the brand's credibility and appeal, Mattes and Barbee told them they needed to include other drivers in the Chase brand.

Earnhardt resisted, arguing that he and Gordon had enough clout to make it successful by themselves. Mattes told the Intimidator he was wrong. Earnhardt relented. And he and Gordon handpicked the rest of the Chase family, agreeing to invite Rusty Wallace, Dale Jarrett, and brothers Terry and Bobby Labonte into the venture and offer each an ownership stake.

None was initially keen about going into business with Earnhardt and Gordon. But all did and were rewarded handsomely. After eighteen months, Chase Authentics was bought by Action Performance, the major player in NASCAR's memorabilia market. The sale returned fifty times the initial investment, according to Barbee. For every $10,000 each of Earnhardt's buddies had invested, he made roughly $500,000.

From there, Earnhardt and Gordon went into real estate. The opportunity arose after Action Performance bought Earnhardt's Sports Image and the Gordon-dominated Motorsports Traditions. Gordon's stepfather, John Bickford, was put in charge of finding a suitable piece of land for an expanded office. After hearing about a 106-acre parcel abutting Charlotte Motor Speedway that was ripe for development, Bickford contacted Barbee, who contacted Earnhardt, the moneybags of the bunch.

Earnhardt was on board at once. He knew the land, and he loved dirt as much as Scarlett O'Hara. He could have afforded it outright, but he refused to invest unless they split it three ways, with Barbee and Gordon owning equal shares. Gordon hesitated; Earnhardt insisted. It ended up another shrewd investment.

"Dale always looked at the sport as a business," Barbee said. "He loved to compete. But it was a business."

Meanwhile, Earnhardt was building another empire closer to home: Dale Earnhardt Inc., the race team he had started years earlier as a hobby in a small, brick building on his property. By 1997 it had mushroomed into a multimillion-dollar enterprise, housed in a 104,000-square-foot race shop and museum, that fielded a NASCAR truck team, a Busch Grand National team, and, starting in 1998, a Winston Cup team for driver Steve Park.

DEI, as the company was known, was intended to keep Earnhardt occupied, and his family provided for, long after his driving days were over. And increasingly, it was becoming a proving ground for another Earnhardt—Dale Jr., who had come up through the late-model ranks, an entry-level form of racing in which the cars were lighter and less powerful, and was preparing to succeed Park in the Grand National car. That series was akin to Triple A baseball, just one rung below the elite Winston Cup.

About sixty miles up the interstate, the Pettys were grooming their own legacy in Level Cross. Richard's grandson and Kyle's eldest son, Adam Petty, was learning the family trade as well, competing mainly on midwestern short tracks in the ARCA series. He and Dale Jr. were quickly finding out that racing with a famous name was basically like painting a bull's-eye on your bumper. There simply was no greater thrill for racers eager to make a name for themselves, it turned out, than to spin out a Petty or wreck an Earnhardt.

But Dale Earnhardt Sr. wasn't ready to ease into retirement just yet. There was an eighth championship to win.

And that damn Daytona 500.

•　•　•

For months, NASCAR's best marketing minds had been planning the yearlong celebration to mark the sport's fiftieth anniversary. The party got started, naturally, with the 1998 Daytona 500.

In the weeks leading up to the race, people kept telling Earnhardt that it was his year. And despite nineteen years of disappointment, he was starting to believe it. He had won another 125-mile qualifying race at Daytona—the ninth of his career—and won it in spectacular fashion, leading every lap from start to finish. He was fast in every practice session, although "fast" was discernible only to those with stopwatches, because the lap times of the fastest forty cars were separated by just two-tenths of a second.

But something didn't feel right about the motor during Saturday's final practice. The team took a close look and found a problem with one of the pushrods. They had no choice but to switch engines, with no chance to test the new motor before the race. It was late afternoon, and the garage was almost empty. All the fans had gone home. Most of the drivers had left. Reporters were writing their stories for the next day's papers. All that remained were a few dozen mechanics making last-minute adjustments to their cars.

Earnhardt's fame had gotten so unwieldy that he could barely step outside the No. 3 transporter truck without getting mobbed by TV cameras, tape recorders, and autograph-seekers. But with the garage almost deserted, he wandered out in his street clothes to check on his car, which had its hood up and half a dozen crew members buried underneath it. He talked to McReynolds a bit. Then he talked to Childress, cutting his eyes at the racecar every few seconds. Then he turned, gave the car a good-night pat on its spoiler, and walked off.

The next day, a roar went up from the grandstands when the green flag signaled the start of the fortieth Daytona 500. It erupted again on Lap 17, when Earnhardt took the lead. All afternoon the No. 3 Chevy was the best car on the track, running near the front, never falling from contention. Its edgy driver set the pace for more than half the two-hundred-lap distance, but he spent as much time eyeing the challengers in his rearview mirror as he did looking out the windshield.

Bobby Labonte's Pontiac, which had won the pole with the fastest qualifying lap, was strong. So was Gordon's Chevy and Wallace's Ford. But Earnhardt's No. 3 was better, and it was in the lead again with sixty laps to go. Gordon's day soon ended with a broken engine valve. But Labonte and Wallace stayed in the hunt.

Earnhardt still held the lead on Lap 199—just one lap to go—when John Andretti and Lake Speed spun on the backstretch, bringing out the final caution. All Earnhardt had to do was fend off the furious charge from Labonte as they raced toward the flag stand, and the Daytona 500 would finally be his.

Earnhardt did it. And tears started welling in his eyes as he drove that final lap. It was a lap that seemed to take forever. It was a lap that had taken twenty years.

"My eyes watered up in the racecar," Earnhardt later confessed. "I don't think I really cried. My eyes just watered up on that lap to take the checkered."

The fans cheered like mad as he rounded the track and steered onto pit road, where dozens of mechanics from every team and several fellow racers had swarmed to slap his hand, extend a thumbs-up, or simply touch his black car as it inched toward Victory Lane. Earnhardt stuck his left arm out the window and got a lifetime's worth of high-fives.

Then he veered onto the infield grass and spun the car in celebratory circles, cutting deep ruts in the turf. Once he drove off toward Victory Lane, his masterpiece was unveiled: Stock-car racing's master had carved the number "3" in the grass with his tires.

"The Daytona 500 is ours!" Earnhardt shouted. "We've won it! We've won it! We've won it!"

And for the only time in his twenty-seven years as NASCAR's president, Bill France Jr. joined the celebration in Victory Lane.

After the champagne and fireworks and photographs, Earnhardt swaggered into the press box atop the front grandstand, grinning like some deranged animal, with a pooch in his midsection. He hopped up on a swivel chair facing reporters, his back to the huge picture window overlooking the frontstretch.

"It sure feels good to get that monkey off my back!" he said. And at that moment, he pulled a stuffed, toy monkey from his racing suit and flung it across the room.

Earnhardt thanked the Lord and every living person who had helped him chase his dream of racing stock cars. He thanked every past winner of the Daytona 500 because, he said, they taught him how to race the track. And he thanked the loved ones he had lost: his father; his hunting buddy Neil Bonnett; and his mentor, T. Wayne Robertson, the force behind R.J. Reynolds' NASCAR sponsorship. They had been watching from heaven, Earnhardt felt, keeping him safe on every lap.

"I thank everybody that touched my life in racing and helped me get where I am," he said. And he asked reporters to put it in their stories just like that.

Someone pointed out that a crowd of fans had wandered onto the frontstretch grass below and were digging up clumps of dirt and grass that his racecar had kicked up in its celebratory spins. Earnhardt spun around and looked. He would earn no income from *these* unlicensed souvenirs, but it didn't bother him a bit.

"Now *those* are some good race fans!" he said, waving at the adoring throng below.

And though the champion must have been impossibly small to their eyes, peering down from a press box that was twelve stories high, the fans knew it was him and frantically waved back. Then, like a high school marching band, they formed themselves in the shape of a giant "3." Earnhardt laughed. Then they scrambled around and re-formed in the shape of an "8," for the eighth championship he wanted so badly. Then they dropped to their knees, flung their arms above their heads, and bowed.

Earnhardt smiled so broadly that his mustache stretched across his grizzled mug.

"It's just unbelievable that you could win another race and feel more excited than you feel about the last one," he said. "But the Daytona 500 tops them *all,* buddy. It tops them all."

• • •

A few months later I got a call at the *Washington Post* from Earnhardt's public-relations man, J. R. Rhodes. Dale was coming to Washington to speak at the National Press Club, an honor normally reserved for heads of state, national political figures, and titans of industry.

Could I come? Could I come early? There was a reception beforehand, and Earnhardt wouldn't know anyone.

I found him that day standing in the middle of the reception, dressed in a suit and tie, his hair neatly combed. I had never seen him so nervous—his posture rigid, his eyes uncertain. The room was packed. But the guests seemed frozen in the Intimidator's presence, marveling at him as if he were a shark in a glass tank. They were awed, yet afraid to go near.

Just stand with him, I was told. Just stay with him.

He cracked a faint smile when I said hello.

"I wish you'd written my speech," he muttered under his breath.

Oh, no! I said. It's going to be great.

"Could you ask me the first question?" he mumbled. "I don't think people are going to ask me any questions."

Sure they will, I told him. But I'd have one ready, just in case.

I felt like one of those stable ponies they put next to a thoroughbred racehorse to calm him down. Only Earnhardt's nerves were making *me* nervous. I started wondering if it was going to be a disaster.

The reception mercifully ended, and he was whisked away to the thirteenth-floor ballroom and seated on the stage along with NASCAR president Bill France Jr. and a host of Press Club dignitaries. Earnhardt was the first stock-car racer to address the august body, and his speech was being broadcast on C-SPAN.

I took a seat in the back of the room.

"It's intimidating to stand up here and talk," Earnhardt began, his voice slightly quivering. "When they first asked me, I asked them, 'Are you sure you want me up there?' I don't get really excited about too much off the racetrack. But really, I had trouble sleeping last night. I kept waking up and thinking about it and wondering, 'What am I going to talk to those people about?' I've only got an eighth-grade education, and to be speaking to the National Press Club. . . . Well, I knew I couldn't talk politics. But I can talk racing—where we come from and where we're going."

The more he talked, the more comfortable he became. His voice returned to its normal register. And every time he made a joke, the audience of 150 or so responded with gales of laughter. The Intimidator was finally strapped in and up to speed.

He talked about how proud he was to have won seven NASCAR championships. He spoke about his son Dale Jr., who was then twenty-three and off to a promising start as a rookie in the Grand National ranks. He talked a little about Jeff Gordon, whom he referred to as "that kid," drawing even more laughter. And when it was time for questions, he was bombarded from every direction.

What did he think about restrictor plates?

What really went on between him and Rusty Wallace in the tussle during practice at Michigan the previous weekend?

What did he think of Ford's new Taurus?

What advice would he give for dealing with road rage on Washington's notoriously congested Beltway?

"You've got to give a little," Earnhardt said, borrowing a line from the prerace drivers meeting he had to sit through every Sunday. "Just be nice and hope the other guy is, too."

Earnhardt charmed them all and was rewarded with two standing ovations—a first, as far as anyone could recall, for a National Press Club speaker.

First, Jeff Gordon had charmed Madison Avenue. Now, Dale Earnhardt was commanding standing ovations from official Washington. NASCAR was changing, all right. But in the years that followed, not everyone, nor every place, would be able to keep up with its frenzied pace.

As I headed toward the exit I took one last look over my shoulder. NASCAR's seven-time champion was basking in a sea of adoration, signing autographs, and posing for pictures with TV cameras all around him.

Earnhardt had conquered a new realm. And it seemed as if he'd go on forever.

Chapter 7

BRIGHT LIGHTS, BIG CITIES

N o sport grew faster in the 1990s than NASCAR. Race-day attendance nearly doubled during the decade as fans swarmed
to the tracks to bellow and bray at the latest installment of the
Champ-versus-Challenger morality play. And for the zealots who regarded *every* Chevrolet driver as the enemy, NASCAR races offered
the chance to cuss Earnhardt and Gordon alike while cheering on the
Ford brigade led by Rusty Wallace and Mark Martin.

Meanwhile, other American sports were tending to their own
self-inflicted wounds. Major League Baseball fell silent for 232 days in
1994 as a players' strike cost team owners $1 billion in revenue,
cost players $400 million in salaries, and achieved what neither World
War I nor World War II managed: it canceled the World Series.
Alienated fans responded by shunning the sport when the millionaire
athletes returned to work the next season. Game-day attendance
dropped 20 percent, plunging from an average of 31,256 in 1994 to
25,022 in 1995.

Baseball fans weren't easy to win back, either. Attendance in
1996 inched up only 2 percent, to 25,509. By contrast, Charlotte

Motor Speedway was drawing bigger crowds for a Thursday-night NASCAR qualifying session, mind-numbing in its monotony, in which one racecar circled the track by itself, and nothing was at stake but the starting order for Sunday's race.

At the same time, open-wheel racing in the United States was driving itself into a ditch as a power struggle between its top race teams and the only track that mattered, Indianapolis Motor Speedway, cleaved the sport in two. The most famous drivers and best teams went one way, forming their own racing circuit, Championship Auto Racing Teams. And the heir to Indianapolis Motor Speedway, Tony George, went another, forming the rival Indy Racing League, based on technological specifications that effectively barred the fastest cars from his Indianapolis 500.

The sad, sorry result was obvious to everyone except the power-brokers in the boardroom: despite their famous last names, the Unsers and Andrettis had no meaningful stage without the world-famous Indianapolis 500; and the Indy 500, by extension, was reduced to a bland parade without its high-wattage stars.

"When they split, it completely killed everything," said Rusty Wallace, whose NASCAR team owner, Roger Penske, also owned the most decorated team in open-wheel racing, with ten Indianapolis 500 victories to his credit at the time of the split. "I would have loved to have been in that room with all those directors making that decision and said, 'You guys are about ready to run off the track!' "

Baseball's troubles and the open-wheel morass may not have spawned outright converts to NASCAR. But in the mad scramble for sports fans' attention, their woes certainly opened a generous passing lane for stock-car racing. And NASCAR took swift advantage, becoming the country's preeminent form of auto racing. Among American sports leagues, only the NFL attracted more regular-season TV viewers.

From a management perspective, NASCAR's popularity surge in

the 1990s also represented an endorsement of the France family's business model: a closely held, vertically integrated company in which immediate family owned the core product, controlled its distribution, and owned many of its major venues. Once again the lesson seemed to be that in an arena as dynamic and aggressive as auto racing, nothing good could come from power-sharing in any form, whether with a players' union, a board of directors, or any group with bargaining rights. The iron fist worked best.

• • •

NASCAR's bright future, however, didn't bode well for everyone in the sport. If you took a map of the United States in 1996 and stuck a pushpin where each NASCAR race was held, you'd come up with a dense cluster of pins jammed into a single region defined by a three-hundred-mile radius. Of the thirty-one races on the schedule that year, fourteen were in Virginia, Tennessee, or the Carolinas. If stockcar racing was supposed to be a national sport, why was it selling itself over and over in the same market? It made no sense to anyone but the sport's historians.

The challenge was that NASCAR's schedule was so long, spanning mid-February to early November, that the sport couldn't add any more races. If it wanted to expand to new markets, it would almost certainly have to leave an existing market behind. And if culling had to be done, it was easy to spot the weak sister: North Wilkesboro Speedway, the sport's oldest track, perched by the side of U.S. Highway 421, the famed moonshine-running route through western North Carolina.

Enoch Staley had carved his oval out of the Wilkes County soil in 1947, with none other than Big Bill France supervising the work. In the decades that followed, local hero Junior Johnson thrilled the fans by barreling down the frontstretch and up the back, slinging his monstrous Ford around its turns and busting through the retaining walls on occasion. Fireball Roberts raced there. So did Bobby Isaac, the Flock boys from Georgia, three generations of Pettys, and two generations each of Allisons and Jarretts.

Apart from touting itself as "the moonshine capital of the world," the town of North Wilkesboro staked its identity on its two annual NASCAR races. Every stock-car racing fan knew about its role in giving birth to the sport. Even the New York literati knew about it, thanks to a magazine reporter who showed up in 1964 looking for Junior Johnson.

Junior, whose fame as a hard charger was unrivaled in the era, was reared to be polite to strangers—at least until they proved they didn't deserve the courtesy. But he couldn't help but laugh to himself when this particular fellow turned up in the dead of summer wearing a brownish-green wool suit when everybody else, Junior included, was wearing a T-shirt. From the way the reporter dressed and talked, Junior suspected he was from England. He wanted to know about stock-car racing, and Junior was happy to tell him a few things. But when he took out his notepad and started asking more personal questions, Junior shook his massive head.

"You're gonna hafta go out and get the information you're looking for from the people of this county," Junior said. "Now, what *I'll* tell you will probably be favoritism to me and not be the real, true story. If you get the story from the people, you'll have the right story."

So off the reporter went. For several days he went around the county, introducing himself to the local folk. And stories of the encounters eventually trickled back to Junior.

"Forgive me," the reporter would politely begin, "but would you tell me a little bit about, say, Junior Johnson?"

"What kind of person is he?"

"What does he stand for?"

That fall the reporter came back to North Wilkesboro's track to watch the Wilkes 400 stock-car race.

Recalls Johnson, in his singular vernacular: "He weren't a pushy person. He was very well dressed, and he stayed that way. That day and every day I seen him thereafter he had on that sorta brown, green suit. All he'd do is keep wiping the sweat off him."

In March 1965, *Esquire* magazine published "The Last American Hero Is Junior Johnson. Yes!" As it turned out, the author hadn't come from England, after all. Tom Wolfe was born in Richmond, Virginia, just a few hours up the road. And he was born the same year as Junior, in 1931.

"Ten o'clock Sunday morning in the hills of North Carolina," Wolfe's essay began. "Cars, miles of cars in every direction, millions of cars, pastel cars, aqua green, aqua blue, aqua beige, aqua buff, aqua dawn, aqua dusk, aqua Malacca, Malacca lacquer, Cloud lavender, Assassin pink, Rake-a-cheek raspberry, Nude Strand coral, Honest Thrill orange, and Baby Fawn Lust cream-colored cars are all going to the stock-car races, and that old mothering North Carolina sun keeps exploding off the windshields.

"Seventeen thousand people, me included, all of us driving out Route 421, out to the stock-car races at North Wilkesboro Speedway. . . ."

And no finer story has been written about the sport than the one that followed.

• • •

Every NASCAR track has a personality—not just a personality based on the sort of food it sells at the concession stand, but a personality that has a direct bearing on the competition. It's no different from baseball parks or golf courses. Fenway Park, with its short left field, favors right-handed hitters. Yankee Stadium, with its short porch in right field, favors left-handed hitters. Augusta National smiles on golfers who can crush the ball 330 yards, preferably from right to left.

Racetracks differ in obvious respects, including length, layout, and banking. At one extreme is Martinsville Speedway, just over one-half mile around, shaped like a paper clip and nearly flat (banked 12 degrees in the corners). Pocono Raceway is about five times bigger, 2.5 miles around, and shaped like a lopsided triangle, with three turns of different angles and pitch. South Carolina's Darlington Raceway is in between, 1.366 miles around, but more egg-shaped than oval, with no two corners the same. It also has a mean streak that no engineer can explain: a tendency to reach out and grab a car and slap it into the concrete wall.

Within those variations, the same track can differ from one race to the next, one day to the next, and one hour to the next. Racetracks aren't just slabs of asphalt or concrete. They're living, organic beings whose characteristics change as they age and whose traits vary according to the amount of sun or cloud cover, humidity or wind.

Typically, the older the racetrack, the more pronounced its quirks, especially in the South, where short tracks would often spring up at local fairgrounds or be carved in barren fields by a guy on a tractor who had no use for a blueprint. The terrain dictated the shape.

North Wilkesboro Speedway fell into that category. It started out as a dirt track and was transformed to an asphalt oval in 1957. For racecar mechanics, it was a puzzle to be solved. Building a car that would be fast at North Wilkesboro was a bit like girding for a fight with a stubborn spouse. Outright victory was too much to expect; the best you could hope for was a compromise you could live with.

The trick was getting the car to stick. Speeds on the Wilkes County oval never topped 120 miles per hour, so that meant the cars had more power than the drivers could use. Getting traction was the challenge; the wheels would spin so easily that some drivers said racing at Wilkesboro was like driving on a thin sheet of ice. By the mid-1990s the track's asphalt surface was so worn that the cars slipped more than ever. Getting a car to stay planted as it whipped around the corners boiled down to sacrificing speed for stability.

. . .

But to look at North Wilkesboro, you might think anyone could strap in a car and race a few hot laps. Even yourself. How hard could it be? I remember thinking that I might have excelled at this common-man's sport, too, if I had only started early enough. Then, one day in 1997, I got to ride in a real stock car at close to top speed with one of NASCAR's best drivers, Mark Martin. And I never indulged the notion again.

The setting was the Road Atlanta race course, a winding circuit that wasn't part of NASCAR's schedule but was used for sports-car races, driving schools, and testing. As an auto-racing writer for *USA Today,* I was invited to join guests of Roush Racing for a few laps "at speed" in a racecar that had a passenger seat bolted next to the driver's. It was serious business, and everyone taking part had to suit up in full fireproof racing gear and helmet and get strapped in with the elaborate five-point harness that drivers wear.

The team had prepared several cars for the day, each piloted by a different driver in Roush's multicar stable. Several guests were clearly nervous while strapping in the cars; several more climbed out ashen from the experience. But I had no qualms, knowing I was riding with Martin, one of the sport's more skilled road racers. Still, I had *no* idea how wild the ride would be—how frenzied Martin's job really was— as he slung the car around the tight corners. And I had no appreciation for how violent the sensation of the gravitational forces could be.

From the moment we pulled out, Martin's feet and legs were in constant motion—clutch, brake, clutch, brake—manipulating the pedals faster than an Irish step dancer. But his upper body was totally relaxed. In my mind (as well as in the movies), drivers raced with their shoulders up by their ears, fists clenched on the wheel, veins bulging from their necks. Yet while Martin's feet were a frenetic blur, working the throttle and clutch and brakes, his left elbow was propped on the window ledge as if he were out for a Sunday drive. His right hand guided the steering wheel and manipulated the gear shift—also at a frenzied tempo. But not for one second did he act tense or stressed in the slightest. He even peered over every few seconds to see if I was panicking. I wasn't; I was just in awe.

In driver's education I had been taught to put one car length between my bumper and the car ahead for every 10 miles per hour I was traveling. This ratio flashed in my mind at that moment, and I almost burst out laughing as Martin flung the racecar around hairpin turns with total commitment. He couldn't see what was around the bend, yet he threw the car forward with no thought that a hazard might lie ahead—a puddle of motor oil, a stalled car, a deer or a raccoon. It was as total a leap of faith as I could imagine. More than marriage. More than a religious conversion. It was a faith, I felt sure, that I could never have. We made several laps—each faster than the one before. And I climbed out utterly humbled. I wrote about this sport for a living, yet I understood so little about what it actually required.

•　•　•

What North Wilkesboro required of NASCAR drivers, above all, was patience and restraint. Success on this ribbon of weary apshalt wasn't as simple as mashing the pedal to the floor and running flat-out. It called for some creativity behind the wheel. The track's corners were wide enough to accommodate multiple angles of attack, so the smart drivers experimented with their entry to each turn. High, low, middle—any one of several approaches might be fastest through a given corner at a particular point in the race.

"You really had to drive that track," recalls Brett Bodine, who won three North Wilkesboro poles, as well as its spring race in 1990. "You could just spin the tires any time you wanted to. It was *so* hard to get around because it would be so slippery, and the tires would just wear out. It was old school. O-o-ld school!"

Other drivers like to describe the challenge of various NASCAR tracks in terms of percentages, distinguishing between how much the driver had to do with running well as opposed to the car. Some tracks might be 20 percent driver and 80 percent car, they'd say. Other tracks might be 50 percent driver and 50 percent car. But North Wilkesboro was 80 percent driver and 20 percent car. As a result, drivers who won there came away with a well-earned sense of pride.

Yet, increasingly, drivers came away with little else.

North Wilkesboro was packing 50,000 race fans in its grandstands in the mid-1990s—enough people to nearly double the population of Wilkes County. Still, that was the smallest race-day crowd on the NASCAR circuit, eclipsed slightly by North Carolina Motor Speedway and Martinsville Speedway in southwest Virginia. And it was paltry compared to the crowds of 150,000 that were flocking to the superspeedways in Charlotte, Atlanta, and Daytona.

Its payday was meager, too. NASCAR dictated the size of the purse for each of its races, telling track owners how much prize money they had to pay competitors. At the time, that amount was based on a hodgepodge of factors. Among them: the number of seats in the grandstands, the number of suites, the perceived prestige of the event, the fee that the racetrack owner got for selling its broadcast rights, and anything else Bill France Jr. deemed relevant. On all those measures, North Wilkesboro ranked near the bottom. As the cost of fielding a front-running team escalated, the track's purse couldn't keep up. The posted award for winning North Wilkesboro's spring race in 1996, for example, was $57,325. But the weekend's expenses for a NASCAR team often ran significantly higher than that. The winner of that year's Daytona 500, by contrast, earned $360,775.

North Wilkesboro didn't measure up in the eyes of the corporate sponsors who were footing the race teams' bills, either. It didn't have plush luxury suites for entertaining clients. Instead, it offered dignitaries a spot in an air-conditioned, cinderblock booth atop the frontstretch. And there wasn't a fancy chain hotel or an elegant steakhouse within fifty miles.

But North Wilkesboro did offer simpler charms. The track was close to home for nearly all of NASCAR's drivers, mechanics, and much of the press corps. They had been coming there for so many autumns and springs that it had the familiarity of home.

You could almost feel the pages of the calendar flip backward as you made the drive up the Brushy Mountains on race weekends. Time seemed to regress by the decade the closer you got—from the 1990s, to the '80s, '70s, '60s until it stopped in an era that could have passed for the '50s. Still, North Wilkesboro didn't necessarily feel bound by time. It was set in what's called a "hollow" and moved at its own pace, just as it produced its own corn liquor, made its own strain of bluegrass music, and answered to its own mores.

The locals still revered their legendary bandits, including Tom Dula (immortalized by the Kingston Trio as "Tom Dooley") and a car-thieving ladies' man named Otto Wood, who was killed in a gun battle with police in 1923 after busting out of jail for about the tenth time in his thirty-six years. Wood's crime had been killing a Greensboro pawnbroker after he went back to the shop to reclaim a pocket watch he'd hocked. The pawnbroker had sold it, not realizing it contained a picture of Wood's mother.

Seventy years later, a virtual convoy of NASCAR mechanics would hop on their Harley-Davidsons at 5:30 a.m. in Charlotte and roar up to North Wilkesboro every spring and fall, freezing in the early-morning chill. And they'd ride their motorcycles home along the back roads that night. In between they'd work like dogs under the hoods of racecars. But in the getting-there and getting-back, they were Peter Fonda in *Easy Rider.* And as workday commutes go, it was as big a rush as any wage earner could hope for.

Most of the reporters spent race weekends at local motels—the fifty-dollar-a-night sort where you could pull your car right up to the front door. You'd go to dinner at Harold's Restaurant and fall asleep listening to the visiting scribes sitting outside, telling racing stories and drinking warm beer.

Enoch Staley had subscribed to a fundamental creed since building North Wilkesboro Speedway: good racing at a fair price. Fans parked free on the grassy hillsides of his track. A bag of potato chips cost fifty cents; pork rinds, a dollar. The bleachers sat so close to the asphalt surface that fans could see the drivers' faces through the windshields. And after the fans got home that night, those who had watched from the front rows picked shreds of tire rubber out of their hair—a badge of honor or an annoyance, depending how deeply their love of racing ran.

But Staley's death in May 1995 set off a troubling chain of events. Charlie Combs, Staley's founding partner in the track, sold his 50 percent stake to Bruton Smith. A Charlotte auto magnate, Smith was a racetrack impresario who was in an aggressive expansion mode after taking his track-owning company, Speedway Motorsports Inc., public earlier that year. Smith floated multiple offers to buy the remaining half, which was controlled by Enoch's only son. But Mike Staley chose instead to sell to New England businessman Bob Bahre, who owned New Hampshire International Raceway just north of Boston.

The rush to buy North Wilkesboro had nothing to do with its facilities or real estate. Its chief asset was the two NASCAR Winston Cup races it hosted each year. Smith could build all the new racetracks he wanted, but if he didn't host Winston Cup races to draw the fans, his Speedway Motorsports stock wasn't going anywhere. He needed a show.

With NASCAR president Bill France Jr. controlling the schedule, Smith reasoned that the surest way to get a Winston Cup date for the new speedway he planned to build in Texas was to buy a track that already had a race and move it to his bigger venue. The switch required France's blessing, of course. But how could France refuse a businessman who was offering to foot the bill for taking NASCAR where France wanted it to go anyway? In this case, to a major metropolitan area west of the Mississippi.

Bahre had a similar agenda in mind when he bought the remaining half of North Wilkesboro. His New Hampshire track, which had opened in 1993, hosted only one NASCAR Winston Cup race. A second annual race would vastly improve its bottom line.

The sale of North Wilkesboro was like putting a roast turkey on the dinner table between two starving men and handing each a carving knife.

Neither Bahre nor Smith attended NASCAR's last race at North Wilkesboro, the Tyson Holly Farms 400, in September 1996. They weren't speaking to each other, and they certainly weren't speaking to local officials or to reporters about what the future held for the track. But it was clear that its two Winston Cup races were going away. Smith was taking the spring race for the 160,000-seat superspeedway he was building in Texas; Bahre was moving the fall race to his track in New Hampshire.

So for the ninety-third and final time, race day dawned at North Wilkesboro Speedway with the same rituals as always.

Enoch's widow, seventy-nine-year-old Mary Staley, rose at four-thirty to start frying bushels of chicken in the trackside kitchen for the reporters' lunches. By six a.m. Shorty Folds had taken his post by the back gate to let the racers in, just as he had done for the last forty years, since he was sixteen. And the Wilkes County Sheriff's Department, backed by fifty-five North Carolina state troopers, braced for the arrival of fifty-thousand fans.

It was a sad day for the locals who had grown up alongside stock-car racing. But there was little remorse among the NASCAR drivers.

"It might be that we're getting away from our roots," conceded Richard Petty, who had won more races at North Wilkesboro (fifteen) than any driver. "But you got to figure that they don't play with leather football helmets anymore, either."

Rusty Wallace, who swept the 1993 races on the devilish short track, was equally pragmatic.

"Staying in North Wilkesboro is only sentimental," Wallace said.

"This is really an expensive sport, and you can't fault anybody for wanting to leave a track that pays the least and seats the least people for something that's going to be super big and super nice."

It was fitting that the final race was won by Jeff Gordon, a driver with old-school driving smarts and new-era appeal. Gordon led 207 of the 400 laps to beat Dale Earnhardt by 1.73 seconds.

"It's ironic, really," said Gordon, twenty-five, after picking up his tenth victory of the season. "You look at this racetrack and see where we've been. And the fact that we're not coming back anymore is another sign of how far we've come."

. . .

To Bruton Smith, chairman of Speedway Motorsports Inc., stock-car racing was no different from any other business. To thrive, it had to be in the right markets—not hostage to the past, but responsive to the present.

"Let's look at facilities other than racetracks. Let's look at McDonald's," Smith once explained. "Wherever they built one, maybe it was good for twenty-five or thirty years. But then you have to raze it and go build one somewhere else."

An auto dealer and stock-car racing promoter, Smith had gotten in the racetrack-owning business in 1959, helping finance construction of a 1.5-mile superspeedway just north of Charlotte that gained instant notoriety as host of NASCAR's longest race—the World 600. Determined to make his racetrack profitable, Smith took a look at his race-day crowds in the years that followed and didn't like what he saw. Only about 10 percent of the audience was female: a missed opportunity, he decided. So he set about sprucing up his track to attract women. He planted 250 trees around the grounds. He hired a horticulturist who added hundreds of shrubs, flowers, and grass. And he built ladies' restrooms. Lots of them.

In 1990, Smith bought the 1.5-mile superspeedway in Atlanta

and gave it a makeover, too. If his tracks were going to pay dividends, they had to attract a better clientele. Then, with NASCAR's popularity taking off, Smith decided in 1994 that he wanted to build a new superspeedway west of the Mississippi. He planned to take his company public on the New York Stock Exchange, and a major building project would make the bold corporate statement he wanted.

He considered three markets: St. Louis, Las Vegas, and Dallas–Fort Worth, studying each for its suitability to host a major NASCAR race. Were highways in place to move seventy thousand or more cars in and out of the track on race day? Was there a major airport nearby? Did historic weather patterns indicate the likelihood of a dry race weekend or a rainout? Was the population dense, affluent, and unserved by a major NASCAR track for a few hundred miles around?

Dallas–Fort Worth had it all. Plus, Smith liked the fact that so many great racers had come from Texas—A. J. Foyt, Johnny Rutherford, and the Labonte brothers among them. He also had a well-placed friend in the region, Ross Perot Jr., who was eager to help him find the ideal parcel of land.

That April, Perot invited Smith and Eddie Gossage, who would be charged with getting the superspeedway built, aboard his helicopter and flew them over a 1,450-acre tract north of Fort Worth. It was perfect.

In November, Smith announced he would build his superspeedway in the Dallas–Fort Worth market but stopped short of committing to a site. Both cities jockeyed for the project. Finally, in February 1995, Smith announced he had chosen Fort Worth, where city officials pledged $11 million toward the project to extend road, water, and sewer systems. The same month, Speedway Motorsports Inc. went public—a move that ramped up Smith's expansion agenda and touched off a building boom that would see new racetracks sprout up in southern California, Las Vegas, Chicago, and Kansas City over the next six years.

For Smith's Speedway Motorsports, the next acquisition was the half-mile track in Bristol, Tennessee, that seated 71,000. After buying the venue in 1996, Smith refused to let its cramped quarters make it obsolete, as had happened in North Wilkesboro. Instead, he built grandstands to the heavens, turning Bristol Motor Speedway into a 158,000-seat Roman Colosseum in the Tennessee hills, topped by nearly 200 luxury suites. The company also bought Sears Point Raceway in Sonoma, California, later that year, which extended its portfolio coast to coast.

It was as if Smith were playing Monopoly, buying properties, building houses, and upgrading to hotels as quickly as his cash flow permitted. Given NASCAR's rate of growth, it was a smart play.

"You simply have a company and an individual who want to grow a business and realize that they're holding on to the fins of a rocket that's moving very fast," said Tom Thomson, a motorsports industry analyst for Wheat First Butcher Singer at the time. "That rocket isn't Bruton Smith, but the industry itself. You have a limited number of Winston Cup dates, and you probably have a limited amount of time before all the tracks in the country that can run these dates are gobbled up."

NASCAR races had made Smith a multimillionaire. Still, he was on the outside of NASCAR's power structure. He wasn't a NASCAR shareholder, of course, because he wasn't a member of the founding France family. But he wielded considerable clout as head of the company that now owned more racetracks than the France-controlled International Speedway Corporation.

It was a symbiotic, yet strained, alliance.

To a large extent, Smith's profit margin—and that of every other racetrack owner on the circuit—was dictated by NASCAR president Bill France Jr., who succeeded his father as the sport's CEO in January 1972. France decided how many Winston Cup races each track hosted. He set the annual sanctioning fee that track owners had to pay

NASCAR to host one of its races. He determined the date of each race, which alone could dictate whether an event was successful or not. And he assigned races on an annual basis rather than for multiple years, which gave him enormous leverage over track owners as he could threaten to take a race away from a track. He could also exert his power more subtly, informing a track owner, for example, that NASCAR couldn't return for the next season unless certain conditions were met. The track needed to sweeten the purse, for example. The track needed better guardrails, or a new racing surface, or a bigger press room, or better facilities for the broadcast media. Each "deficiency" that had to be addressed affected the track's bottom line.

Still, Smith was hardly deferential. He pushed France every way he could to negotiate favorable business terms for his company. And when he found opportunities to make money despite NASCAR's far-reaching power, he jumped on them, whether it was charging into the Dallas–Fort Worth market or outbidding the France-controlled International Speedway Corp. to buy Las Vegas Motor Speedway in 1998.

Smith's initial vision for his Texas property was to build a $75 million superspeedway that seated 75,000. By the time it was completed, in April 1997, the track had more than doubled in size and tripled in cost.

As in Charlotte and Atlanta, Texas Motor Speedway was more D-shaped than oval, with most of the seats overlooking the frontstretch, which bowed out as if it had a front porch. That way it accommodated more seats with a view of the frenzied action in the pits and at the start–finish line. And frontstretch seats sold for more than backstretch seats.

Borrowing a page from the NFL's playbook, Smith created a two-tiered experience for spectators. Of the roughly 113,000 seats along the frontstretch, nearly one-third (36,000) were sold to season-ticket holders who paid a premium for lifetime rights to the seats, which were equipped with arm rests and conferred access to club-level amenities, for every race on the speedway's annual calendar.

The frontstretch also boasted 50 "Victory Lane" club suites and 114 luxury suites for another 13,000 who were willing to pay top dollar to be insulated from the rabble. And, as at his speedways in Charlotte and Atlanta, Smith built trackside condominiums for well-heeled Texans who loved racing so much that they wanted to stake a property claim at the venue. Finally, Smith built restrooms, more than 2,000 of them—twice as many for women as for men.

• • •

A few months after the opening of Texas Motor Speedway—a forgettable race and a lamentable debut that was marred by days of rain, horrible traffic snarls, and a fourteen-car pileup on the first turn of the first lap—another new NASCAR track opened. This one was in southern California and was built by industrialist and former racer Roger Penske, a third player in the racetrack-ownership arms race.

NASCAR had raced in the region years before. But both of the venues, Ontario Motor Speedway and the Riverside road course, had gone out of business, crippled by a heavy debt load and waning interest.

Penske felt the timing was right to try the market again. He constructed the 2-mile California Speedway about 50 miles east of Los Angeles, on the site of an abandoned steel mill. It was a D-shaped oval, similar in layout to Michigan International Speedway, which Penske also owned. Its racing groove was sufficient to accommodate three-wide racing. And its seating capacity was roughly half that of Smith's Texas track. As racetrack operators, they stood in sharp contrast. Smith followed his gut and was given to bold visions; Penske was obsessed with detail and favored conservative business plans. He was also compulsive about neatness and customer service.

Ticket holders at California Speedway were referred to as

"guests" rather than "fans." Weeks before the inaugural NASCAR race, each guest was mailed a thirty-two-page guide with directions to the track. Even-numbered ticket holders were routed one way for a smooth traffic flow; odd-numbered ticket holders were routed another.

Once at the track, guests were greeted by vest-wearing customer-service ambassadors who steered them to shuttle buses, first-aid stations, ATMs, or nooks to diaper the baby. Drunkenness, profanity, and offensive signs were banned in the infield. Greg Penske, the track's president, had "benchmarked" standards for cleanliness by studying Disneyland and borrowing the idea of putting three hundred Boy and Girl Scouts on a tidiness patrol. Every child twelve or younger was issued a plastic wristband with his name, address, section, and seat location. Kids also got a commemorative speedway coloring book and colored pencils. NASCAR drivers had access to a private infield health club. Pizza- and newspaper-delivery services were available to infield motor homes. Employees disguised as ticket holders roamed the grounds to ferret out unfriendly coworkers; rudeness was cause for dismissal.

"There's a lot of competition for that entertainment dollar," said the younger Penske, noting the proximity of Disneyland, Dodger Stadium, and southern California's beautiful beaches. "You have to treat every guest like guests in your own home."

•　•　•

While Penske and Smith were wooing NASCAR guests trackside, the fans who watched from home were having a terrible time simply finding the races on TV each Sunday afternoon.

With each speedway negotiating its own broadcast deal, NASCAR races were scattered among several different networks—most of them cable outlets. Assuming fans could find the race, the broadcasts had a disjointed feel, with little continuity from one event to the next. And the rights fees didn't make much sense, with the value of each deal skewed by the negotiating skill of the track operators.

Sports properties were hot commodities in the 1990s, triggering fierce bidding wars among traditional networks and cable upstarts. And Bill France Jr. couldn't help but take note of the escalating rights fees that other professional sports leagues were getting each time they put their broadcast contracts up for bid. In the case of the NFL, networks were willing to pay far more for broadcast rights than they could recoup through advertising sales. But TV executives considered the transaction worth it just to have the identity of being an NFL partner. Plus, broadcasting NFL games, even at a loss, paid dividends if it enabled a network to promote its other programming on the back of professional football.

There were many aspects of the NFL that Bill France Jr. did *not* admire. Its players' union, for one. Its collective-bargaining agreement. And the bad publicity that came with the off-the-field shenanigans of so many high-profile players. But France coveted the prestige and the lucrative payout that the NFL enjoyed through its national TV deal.

Even though France had no role in brokering the various speedways' TV deals at the time, NASCAR collected 10 percent of every contract's value from the track owners. The rest was split between the track (65 percent) and the drivers (25 percent, which went into the race purse).

Given stock-car racing's explosive growth, France decided that it was time to change the way stock-car racing's broadcasts were sold, bundling the entire season into a single package that could be put out for bid. NASCAR couldn't claim to be a major-league sport as long as it had a minor-league TV contract. With a national TV deal, NASCAR could maximize profits, reach a broader audience, and make it easier for fans to find the races on TV.

The first step was persuading track owners to turn over their negotiating rights to NASCAR. For the most part, the men who owned a single track on the circuit—such as Joseph Mattioli (Pocono Race-way), Clay Earles (Martinsville Speedway), and Bob Bahre (New Hampshire International Speedway)—saw the wisdom at once.

Smith, whose Speedway Motorsports Inc. now owned six NASCAR tracks, was an early advocate of consolidated TV rights. But it took a full year of negotiating to convince Smith to go along with NASCAR's proposal for structuring the deal. He finally relented, and the result, unveiled in November 1999, was a six-year contract worth more than $2.4 billion, in which Fox Sports and NBC would become stock-car racing's new home.

It represented a fourfold increase in revenue—up from $100 million a year to more than $400 million. Only the National Football League and National Basketball Association had negotiated higher rights fees. And everyone would benefit—NASCAR, track owners, and drivers.

That's not to say Smith didn't object to aspects of the deal. Each race on the schedule was classified as either an A, B, or C event, with the classification dictating its share of the TV revenue. Only one race—the Daytona 500—was classified as an A race. Its share was nearly triple that of races in the next category, which irritated Smith then as it still does today.

"Too much money goes to Daytona," Smith said years later. "It's not criminal, but it's damn near close to it. NASCAR is cutting up the pie, but they also hold the knife. I want to get my hands on the knife and be fair about it."

Regardless, Smith's chief lieutenant, H. A. "Humpy" Wheeler, says the national TV deal was one of the three most significant developments in NASCAR history—if not *the* most significant.

It signaled NASCAR's acceptance on a major-league level. It moved more races off cable channels and onto major networks. It gave NASCAR two committed TV partners, whose return on their investment depended on their success in promoting the sport. And, not least of all, it made everyone involved in this once poor-man's sport rich, which had a way of muting any lingering discontent.

With roughly fourteen months' lead time, Fox Sports started preparing for its first NASCAR broadcast, the 2001 Daytona 500—a race that would change the sport forever.

Chapter 8

"WE'VE LOST DALE EARNHARDT"

It was a day for celebrating the promise of NASCAR's future. It was April 2, 2000—a day that 150,000 race fans at Texas Motor Speedway witnessed a gleaming superspeedway in a vibrant, major market mint the next generation's heroes.

For two months, twenty-five-year-old rookie Dale Earnhardt Jr. had been causing a sensation just by showing up at NASCAR's race-tracks with his famous last name and bright red No. 8 Chevrolet. Dale Earnhardt's second son had won back-to-back championships in stock-car racing's Grand National series, one rung down. But he wasn't yet confident that he had the mettle to compete with the sport's greatest drivers, including his intimidating father, in NASCAR's Winston Cup circuit. And he felt sure that he hadn't earned the hearty cheers he was getting from fans during the prerace driver introductions.

But that afternoon, when he roared across the start–finish line in Texas after out-dueling his legendary father and forty-one other drivers to win his first Winston Cup race, it was all the validation he needed. And a thousand pounds of emotion flew out of his chest, as he'd later describe it.

Earnhardt Jr. destroyed his racecar's clutch doing the biggest celebratory burnout of his young life, so his crew members, as delirious as their driver, pushed the No. 8 Chevy to Victory Lane, where Earnhardt Sr. was waiting, having hopped out of his own car and run to meet his son. Still dripping with sweat in his racing uniform, Earnhardt poked his head in the driver's-side window and told Dale Jr. how proud he was and how much he loved him. Savor the moment, he told him. And then he scooted away, ceding the stage to his boy, who climbed out to deafening cheers that he finally felt he deserved.

Also competing that day was nineteen-year-old Adam Petty, who was making his first start in the Winston Cup series. In doing so, he became NASCAR's first fourth-generation driver. Adam didn't finish the race. His engine gave out shortly after the halfway point. But it was an encouraging start for NASCAR's first family, which looked to Adam to carry the Petty legacy forward once he moved up to the Winston Cup ranks full-time in 2001.

Adam was just seven months old when he took his first spin in NASCAR's Victory Lane, perched atop his grandfather's shoulders after Richard won his seventh Daytona 500 in 1981. The littlest Petty had an air of destiny about him that day, people said. But he came to his stock-car calling by choice, deciding as a teenager that he wanted to be just like his father, his grandfather, and his great-grandfather Lee, who had won NASCAR's inaugural Daytona 500.

Like Dale Jr., Adam hadn't yet reached his potential as a racer. But it stood to reason that with the right preparation he would grow into his racing ability just as he would grow into his lanky frame. There certainly was no mistaking he was a Petty, with that affable manner and huge smile. If genes and desire were part of the equation, he couldn't miss.

Six weeks later, on May 12, Adam Petty was killed in a crash at

New Hampshire International Speedway. He'd been preparing to qualify for the weekend's Grand National race and was hurtling down the backstretch, the fastest point on the track, when his racecar failed to negotiate the third turn and slammed headfirst into the concrete wall. The Winston Cup circuit had the weekend off, and Kyle had taken Adam's younger sister, Montgomery Lee, on a trip to London. Within hours he got a call from Mike Helton, then NASCAR's chief operating officer.

NASCAR fans nationwide grieved for the sport's first family. And fifteen hundred of the Pettys' closest friends and relatives filled High Point University's convocation center the following week to celebrate his life. They were joined by NASCAR president Bill France Jr. and dozens of team owners, racetrack operators, and drivers, including Bobby Allison and his former wife, Judy, who had set aside their differences to attend the service together. Montgomery Lee delivered the eulogy, vowing that her first child's name would "definitely" include her brother's name. Adam's body was cremated; his racecar was buried on the grounds of the Petty family's Level Cross compound.

It had been six years since a Winston Cup driver was killed on the track, and Adam's death jolted the sense of well-being that had crept over the sport in the interim. New Hampshire wasn't a track where you'd expect a fatality. It was hardly bigger than a mile and gently banked, with top speeds about 135 miles per hour. To those at the track that day, it looked as if the racecar's throttle had stuck. If so, it would have been all but impossible to control.

Then, eight weeks later, NASCAR's 1998 Winston Cup Rookie of the Year, Kenny Irwin, was killed at the same track, in the same turn, in near identical circumstances. NASCAR officials impounded Irwin's racecar for further study, as they routinely did after on-track fatalities. But unease spread among the drivers. Had a stuck throttle been to blame? Should the track's turns be reconfigured? Was it time for NASCAR to start experimenting with the new "soft-wall" technology that supposedly cushioned the blows of particularly violent crashes?

Three months later, a third NASCAR driver died from injuries suffered in a crash—this one during a truck race at Texas Motor Speedway. Contact with another racer sent Tony Roper's truck nose-first into the wall, and the vehicle burst into flames. The next morning, Dean Roper, a former dirt-track champion, became the latest to join the fraternity of racing fathers who had lost sons to the sport. Roper's death, NASCAR's third in six months, intensified the questions about the sport's safety.

Again, NASCAR officials impounded the vehicle but said little after investigating. They found no hazards that needed to be addressed at the track. And they apparently saw no need for drivers to take extra precautions, such as wearing the so-called HANS device (which stood for "head and neck support") that biomechanical engineers said could limit the potentially fatal whiplash motion of the head during the most jarring collisions.

NASCAR officials mandated a "kill switch" on the cars' steering columns, similar to those used in other forms of racing, that drivers could flip to cut off an engine in an emergency. But neither NASCAR nor the circuit's track owners were ready to endorse the use of energy-absorbing barriers on stock-car racing's oval tracks.

"If you say it's a coincidence, it sounds flippant," Texas Motor Speedway president Eddie Gossage said of Roper's death in an interview with the *Dallas Morning News*. "But I think this is a coincidence. This was totally unlike the other accidents. . . . I've never seen a car or truck turn and take a bite and go head-on into the wall like that. Usually it glances off the wall."

Nonetheless, a few NASCAR drivers, such as Brett Bodine, had already started wearing HANS devices. Others, like Dale Earnhardt, stuck with what had served them well in the past. In Earnhardt's case, that was an open-faced helmet and a basic metal seat, with the seat belt brackets mounted to his liking. That's the way old-school drivers had done it. But by 2000, most drivers were wearing full-faced helmets and installing more substantial seats in their racecars—seats that encased the torso and thighs almost in a cocoon.

Earnhardt wasn't flouting more contemporary safety measures for the sake of his "tough guy" image. He simply put his faith in the equipment he knew best. His life depended on his peripheral vision, and he felt that his helmet and seat gave him the latitude to use his vision to its full extent. That was part of what he believed had kept him safe in the racecar for more than twenty years.

•   •   •

Earnhardt was forty-nine when NASCAR's 2001 season dawned. He hadn't won a Winston Cup championship in seven years but had come close in 2000, finishing second to Bobby Labonte. No driver older than forty-five had ever won a championship in stock-car racing's top division. But in Earnhardt's mind, the eighth title that would distinguish him from Richard Petty was still within reach. Few of his peers doubted it.

Earnhardt had signed one last contract extension to drive the No. 3 Chevy for Richard Childress through 2003. Without fanfare they had hired Chuck Spicer, Richard Petty's former PR representative, to start planning the merchandising campaign that would be built around Earnhardt's final season as a NASCAR driver.

Meanwhile, Earnhardt had expanded the team he planned to oversee during his retirement years, Dale Earnhardt Inc., adding a third car for Michael Waltrip, who held the dubious record of the longest winless streak—462 races—in NASCAR.

Earnhardt arrived in Daytona for the hoopla that preceded the Daytona 500 claiming to feel better than he had in years. He had undergone neck surgery prior to the 2000 season to fix an injured disk, likely suffered during his 1996 Talladega wreck or the following year's crash at Daytona. His focus was locked on winning an eighth title.

The week before the season opener, the *Orlando Sentinel* published a series of stories about NASCAR's shortcomings regarding drivers' safety. Reported by Ed Hinton, the series identified basal skull fractures as the principal cause of NASCAR's on-track fatalities during the preceding decade. And it explained that two innovations—the HANS device and soft-wall technology—would likely have prevented the deaths of Adam Petty, Kenny Irwin, and five of the six other NASCAR drivers who had been killed since 1991.

The series characterized NASCAR as the most secretive and least proactive of all major racing series regarding issues of driver safety. And it raised questions about NASCAR's spending priorities, and those of the stock-car racing industry as a whole, in investing so much in the sport's growth yet so little in developing technology to keep drivers safe.

The Indy Racing League had taken the lead in developing energy-absorbing walls, with its high-speed Indianapolis Motor Speedway in mind. Championship Auto Racing Teams had made the HANS device mandatory equipment for its drivers beginning that year.

NASCAR drivers were divided on the merits of the head-restraint system. Some said it felt too confining and feared it would interfere with their ability to get out of the racecar during a fire. But several Ford drivers reconsidered that position after attending a safety seminar in January 2001 in which engineers told them the HANS device might have prevented seven of the sport's last eight deaths.

NASCAR officials remained skeptical of the so-called soft-wall technology, citing concerns that the barriers could have unintended consequences. They might heighten the severity of a crash rather than blunt it, for example, if they grabbed hold of a racecar that otherwise might skid along the wall and shed its energy over an extended period of time. The longer it took for a crash to unfold, oddly, the safer it was for the driver. It was the sudden, abrupt crash that was more likely to prove fatal. "Soft walls" might also prove a nuisance, others pointed out, by breaking into millions of little bits and pieces that required a lengthy cleanup each time they were hit during a race.

Earnhardt's response to such arguments, as quoted by the *Sentinel:* "I'd rather they spent 20 minutes cleaning up that mess than cleaning me off the wall."

· · ·

The 2000 Daytona 500 had been a resounding bore, with only nine lead changes—the fewest in thirty-five years. TV ratings slumped to their lowest level in five years. And Earnhardt grabbed headlines afterward by grousing that the race was so tedious that NASCAR founder Bill France was probably rolling over in his grave.

NASCAR officials fixed that, modifying the rules that affected how the cars handled at its two biggest speedways, starting with the fall 2000 race at Talladega Superspeedway. The change produced a staggering forty-nine lead changes. And Earnhardt won it in larger-than-life fashion, whipping past other cars as if they'd run out of gas to storm from eighteenth to first over the final five laps. His late-race assault reconfirmed his mastery of turbulent air and debunked any notion that he had lost his edge.

Everyone acknowledged that Earnhardt was the best at restrictor-plate racing. So it was natural that on the morning of the 2001 Daytona 500, rookie Kurt Busch was instructed by his spotter to pull in line behind Earnhardt once the race got going and follow him no matter where he went. "Even if he stops to get a hot dog," Busch's spotter added.

With the new aerodynamic rules in effect, the 2001 Daytona 500 had the makings of a great show for fans. None other than Earnhardt guaranteed it. But not all drivers were as enthused as the season-opening spectacle neared. They viewed the new rules as ratcheting up the risk for the sake of staging a more crowd-pleasing show. "It *is* more scary when there are forty-five lead changes—trust me," Bobby

Labonte said the day before the 2001 Daytona 500. "Whether you like it or not, you're here. You've got to do it."

NASCAR was unique among professional sports in rewriting its rulebook to recalibrate the playing field and jazz up the entertainment value on impulse. It also was unique in starting each season with its biggest event. There was a certain brilliance to the idea. On one hand, the stock-car racing season had morphed into a ten-month ordeal that never seemed to end. But after the engines fell silent each November, nothing sounded so powerful or felt so electric as the roar of forty-three racecars on the high banks of Daytona International Speedway the following February. By then, everyone was hungry for an adrenaline rush. And Daytona felt like the epicenter of excitement.

The 500 was preceded by ten days of preliminary events, including the Bud Shootout, pole qualifying, the 125-mile qualifying races, the International Race of Champions event, and the 300-mile Grand National race. Each was a show in its own right yet also served as a preview of the 500. The buildup was orchestrated like a Broadway overture that had fans cheering before the curtain ever rose. And in 2001, with dozens of racecars swapping positions on every wild lap of the 500's companion events, it seemed certain that a show-stopper was in store on Sunday.

Fox broadcast executives were as giddy as the NASCAR bosses. It would be the first Daytona 500 for the network under NASCAR's national TV deal, and three-time Winston Cup champion Darrell Waltrip would be the lead announcer in the booth.

The race was as wild as predicted, with cars whipping around each other all afternoon. And with 30 laps to go, every driver was racing like mad—even the cautious ones who had lurked near the back for the first 150 laps to avoid the wreck everyone dreaded. It came with 26 laps to go, when Robby Gordon tangled with Ward Burton on the crowded backstretch. The contact turned Burton's car into Tony Stewart's, which was punted in the air and flipped several times.

In the 190-mile-per-hour mayhem most drivers could only see dirt, smoke, and dust. Their only sense of direction came from a spotter hollering in their ears, "Go low! Go low!"

Bobby Labonte tried ducking low, but he got rammed, turned sideways, and jolted even harder when Stewart's airborne car landed on his windshield. By the time the crashing ended, nineteen cars had been collected—nearly half the field. Labonte was among five drivers taken to the infield care center, where the injured are quickly evaluated and released if their conditions aren't serious. Stewart, suffering a concussion and severe shoulder pain, was transported by ambulance to Halifax Medical Center less than a mile away. Labonte, his teammate at Joe Gibbs Racing, rode with him and was encouraged when Stewart was able to tell him who the president was.

Earnhardt had been running just ahead of the pack when the melee erupted. His black No. 3 was unscathed. But the backstretch was littered with so much debris that the race was halted sixteen minutes so track workers could clean the mess. Meanwhile, drivers whose cars had been totaled in the pileup were barely able to hide their anger.

"I'm sorry, but that's not racing," said Dale Jarrett, a three-time Daytona 500 winner. "It may be a great show out there, but from a driver's perspective, that's not it. That's no fun to me at all."

Mark Martin couldn't believe a massive wreck hadn't happened sooner, given the crazy way the cars were running. "I really hope everybody is satisfied with that race," Martin said after he climbed out of his crumpled car. "I feel like we have to entertain them, and I hope that was enough entertainment to that point."

As the drivers who were still in contention waited out the delay, strapped in the racecars they'd parked on the track's high banks, Earnhardt's spotter came over the radio. "You're doing a good job, Champ," Danny Culler said.

As Earnhardt's spotter, Culler had one of the most thankless jobs in the sport: clearing the ornery racer through traffic in the hairiest moments. It required a thick skin. Earnhardt raised hell and cussed over the radio if Culler messed up, and he never said a kind word when Culler did his job well.

But on this day, as he waited for the final charge to Daytona's checkered flag, Earnhardt keyed his microphone to reply. "You're doing a good job, too, Danny," he said.

It was shaping up to be a memorable day for the Earnhardts. Dale Jr. was leading, with his father right behind, when the race was restarted with twenty-one laps to go. The No. 8 and No. 3 Chevys hugged the low groove, nose to tail, as they flew around the speedway. Two laps later Sterling Marlin snatched the lead, then Earnhardt snatched it back. Michael Waltrip, driving the Earnhardt-owned No. 15 Chevy, then passed his boss for the lead. And when the white flag flew, signaling one lap to go, Waltrip, Dale Jr., and Earnhardt were running 1-2-3.

"Come on, buddy!" Darrell Waltrip shouted from the Fox broadcast booth, frantically urging his younger brother on, just as Ned Jarrett had done for his son Dale in the 1993 Daytona 500. "One to go, buddy! Keep it low! Don't let 'em run up on you."

Marlin and Ken Schrader closed on the front-runners coming down the backstretch. Marlin ducked low, thinking Schrader would follow him. But Schrader went high, which left Earnhardt in the middle of a three-wide pack rounding the third turn. Once their cars were three abreast, they lost their aerodynamic advantage. Waltrip and Dale Jr. extended their lead up ahead, while another pack of cars led by Rusty Wallace closed from behind.

Earnhardt started blocking as hard as he could. He was a master at this, too—skilled in the thuggish art of winning races despite not having the fastest car. It meant looking out his rearview mirror nearly as much as he looked out his windshield and *deliberately* not getting so far ahead of his pursuers that they would be able to pull off a pass.

Blocking faster cars was Earnhardt's trademark. In racers' terms, he knew precisely how to make his racecar's rear end wider than everyone else's.

Meanwhile, nearly all eyes were focused a few hundred yards ahead, where Waltrip was barreling toward the finish line with Dale Jr. in tow. And as Michael's Chevrolet took the checkered flag, Darrell shrieked: "You *got* it! You *got* it! You got it! *Mike-eeey!*"

Larry McReynolds, who had been Earnhardt's crew chief for his 1998 Daytona 500 victory, was first to tell TV viewers that the black No. 3 had crashed on the final turn. "How about Dale?" McReynolds said. "Is he okay?"

The camera angle shifted to Earnhardt's wrecked car, which had slid down the 31-degree banking in Turn 4 and come to rest on the frontstretch grass. Waltrip's tone turned anxious. "I just hope Dale's okay," he said, a tremble in his voice. "I *guess* he's all right, isn't he?"

The car's window net hadn't been lowered, which is how a driver signals rescue workers that he's not seriously injured. "Dale, are you okay?" Richard Childress said to his driver over the radio. "Talk to us. Talk to us."

Schrader, whose car had plowed into the right side of the black No. 3 and come to a halt, climbed out and ran to check on Earnhardt. It took a moment for what he saw to sink in. Schrader motioned for rescue workers and got out of the way.

When Childress couldn't get an answer from Earnhardt over the radio, he sent teammate Mike Skinner to check.

Reporters swarmed around the other drivers as they climbed from their cars. Most were still disgusted with the nineteen-car pileup earlier in the race and were only vaguely aware that Earnhardt and Schrader had crashed just a few hundred yards before reaching the finish line.

"It's inevitable," said Jeff Burton, surrounded by TV cameras and microphones. "You can't put that many people in one pack and expect that something is not gonna happen. I know it's exciting to watch. And I understand that last year's races weren't as exciting as they needed to be. But Earnhardt's hurt. They're down there cutting the roof off his car. Stewart's in the hospital. And if we keep doing this, it won't be the last one."

Said Rusty Wallace: "We tore the hell out of just about every car out here with these new rules. I don't like them at all. But *hey,* a couple fans like them. . . . I hope Dale's okay. I heard he had to get cut out of the car. He's a pretty tough guy. It's pretty hard to hurt him, so I hope he's gonna be okay."

The sequence of events still wasn't clear to the TV audience until Fox returned from a commercial break and showed a replay of the last-lap crash. Jammed in between Schrader and Marlin, Earnhardt's car wobbled, then darted low, hit Marlin's, and shot back up across the track. In a flash, the No. 3 was hit by Schrader's car, which turned it nearly headfirst into the concrete. It was traveling at about 160 miles per hour when it crashed.

In the manic aftermath, a TV reporter and cameraman grabbed Schrader just as he turned away from Earnhardt's car window. Schrader's face was ashen. His voice quivered. "We have to pray," he said.

I'd been watching from the press box twelve stories above the frontstretch. The window net on Earnhardt's car never came down. Ambulances raced toward the car. Dale Jr., who finished second to Waltrip, had joined his teammate for the celebration in Victory Lane. He asked a TV reporter what he knew about his father. When he didn't get an answer, he abruptly turned and headed toward his wrecked car. I kept looking for signs that it would be okay— alternately scanning the track below and watching the broadcast. The moment Schrader spoke on TV, I knew.

Dale Earnhardt was dead.

Two paramedics and a trauma surgeon climbed inside Earnhardt's car. One stabilized his neck. One gave him oxygen; and one, CPR. Firefighters cut off the car's roof so he could be extricated more easily. An ambulance took him to Halifax Medical Center. His wife, Teresa, and Dale Jr. went, too.

Childress couldn't find anyone who knew about his driver's condition, so he went looking for Schrader, the last to have seen him before he was pulled from the car. He found him in the infield care center. Childress yanked back the curtain in the treatment room where Schrader was being examined. "How bad is it?" he asked.

Schrader paused, groping for words. "It ain't good," he said.

"Is he gonna be out awhile?" Childress asked.

Schrader didn't know how to answer. "*Richard!* I'm not a doctor," Schrader finally said. "But it ain't good."

As was custom after serious wrecks, NASCAR officials provided precious little information to reporters. It was nearly five p.m., and most journalists in the press box had started writing their stories.

I called my office at the *Washington Post* and asked for the sports editor in charge. It was a slow Sunday, and Courtney Crowley, twenty-two, was running the sports section for the first time that night. I told her that Dale Earnhardt had been hurt and that I thought it was serious. I explained that NASCAR wasn't giving any information. After most fatal wrecks at racetracks, it was common for the Associated Press to report that a driver had been killed before NASCAR officials confirmed the death. I assumed it would happen that way again. Then I started saying words I couldn't believe.

"If he's dead, you have to tell the news side; it's an A-one story," I said over the phone. "And if he's dead, you'll find out before I will. So call me on the cell phone as soon as you hear something."

I hung up. I felt numb—not believing what my eyes and brain and instincts were saying.

My deadline was about two hours away. I felt that if I wrote Earnhardt had died, it would make it so. So I told myself he had been injured. Probably seriously. The details would come later.

And I started typing. It was something basic, like, "Michael

Waltrip held off a furious last-lap charge to win the Daytona 500 Sunday . . ."

No other reporters in the press box seemed panicked, so I kept writing.

". . . but the victory was overshadowed by a serious injury suffered by seven-time champion Dale Earnhardt. . . ."

Then I typed "xxxxxxxxxx" where I planned to add details of the injury and the outlook for his recovery.

Part of me knew Earnhardt had been killed, part of me wouldn't accept it.

I took a breath and tried to exhale all emotion. I thought of the story as a stack of building blocks composed of paragraphs. And I started writing.

An hour passed, and there was still no word from NASCAR.

I kept stacking paragraphs.

Another thirty minutes passed. The story was almost done. Earnhardt would probably be okay in time, I decided. All I needed was NASCAR's injury report. If it wasn't as bad as I feared, I could move the second paragraph about his wreck farther down in the story.

The cell phone rang.

"I'm sorry . . ." is all I remember Courtney saying.

And I cried.

The newspaper wanted two stories, she explained. One about the fatal wreck; the other, an appreciation of Earnhardt's life. They had to be written quickly.

After a few minutes, NASCAR president Mike Helton walked into the press box and picked up a microphone.

"This is undoubtedly one of the toughest announcements that I've ever personally had to make," Helton said. "But after the accident in Turn 4 at the end of the Daytona 500, we've lost Dale Earnhardt."

• • •

Dr. Steve Bohannon, the track's director of emergency medical services, provided details. He had been on one of the ambulances that had rushed to Earnhardt's wrecked car. From there he accompanied the driver's body to the hospital. My fingers typed as quickly as they could, but I could only make out partial phrases.

". . . a very bad situation—a load-and-go situation . . ."

"A full trauma team there to meet him . . ."

"We all did everything we could. . . ."

"He never showed any signs of life. . . . Pronounced dead by all the physicians in attendance at 17:16."

"Head injuries, particularly at the base of the skull . . . ended his life."

After leaving the track that night, I went to a bar with an old friend and former coworker, Tom Sorensen of the *Charlotte Observer,* who had been in the press box, too. We would just sit awhile, we said. There wasn't any need to talk. And everyone in the bar seemed to feel the same. It was filled with numb, dazed people—big, burly men in studded leather vests, their eyes red and swollen; bar maids with no heart for smiles or tips; people too afraid to be alone, too torn up to speak. It was filled with people just like us—sitting quietly, shaking their head.

Earnhardt was the fourth NASCAR driver killed in ten months, yet his death was impossible to accept. The wreck didn't look nearly as bad as countless wrecks that other drivers had walked away from. And Earnhardt was one of the greatest champions the sport had seen, particularly at Daytona, where he had won thirty-four races.

NASCAR racers who had seen everything had trouble believing it, too. They knew death was part of racing. But to a man, they believed there were two people it was never going to get: them, and Dale Earnhardt.

"I thought when he come back around, he'd be out laughing or saying, 'Helluva race!' " Sterling Marlin recalled years later. "But I got back to the motor home, and I heard that he'd been killed. It was just terrible. Everybody was in a state of shock."

Kirk Shelmerdine, Earnhardt's former crew chief, had watched the race on TV with his son in North Carolina. He wondered if Dale was okay; he had seen him crash worse. Then again, Darrell Waltrip seemed awfully concerned. And when Fox aired Schrader's brief comments, Shelmerdine started to worry. He'd never seen Schrader look so scared; nothing scared Ken Schrader. About twenty minutes after the broadcast ended, Shelmerdine's phone rang. It was his friend Will Lind, who had been a crew member on the No. 3 team all those years. Lind was calling from Daytona. "As soon as I recognized the voice," Shelmerdine said, "I knew what he was going to say."

Richard Petty had seen the wreck and didn't think twice about it—other than what a shame it was that Earnhardt had torn up one of Childress's racecars and wrecked two or three others. But that's what Earnhardt got for blocking everybody so bad, he said to himself. Petty headed to the airport after the race ended. That's where someone told him Earnhardt had been killed.

"I said, '*What*? No *way*!'" Petty recalled. "All he done was run into the wall. I mean, I'd hit the wall—and he'd hit the wall—a *lot* harder than that. But there's fate. Circumstances. And you're outta there, man."

Footage of the fatal crash would be replayed for days. And everyone who looked at it, regardless of whether they understood racing or had any insight into Earnhardt, felt sure they knew what his intent had been as he battled so furiously in that last turn to keep the swarm of cars behind him. But there were two radically different interpretations.

To some, including several racers who had dueled against him for years, Earnhardt was just doing what he'd always done when he was about to get passed. He was blocking in the most aggravating way possible, determined to get the best finish he could out of the race.

Every position meant more points toward the championship. And he was hell-bent on getting third.

But in the eyes of others, Earnhardt had abandoned his famous bullying tactics and, for the first time in his racing life, was doing something selfless by blocking so that Waltrip and Dale Jr., who were competing in racecars that he owned, could finish 1-2. Earnhardt, as they viewed it, had sacrificed himself for his son. And in the ultimate irony, he was killed because of it.

Countless stories were written ascribing one or the other intent as a point of fact. But it would never be known. And those who saw it one way would never convince those who saw it another that they were wrong.

Earnhardt's body was taken to the local medical examiner's office for an autopsy that confirmed the cause of death as a severe fracture to the base of the skull. He also suffered eight broken ribs, a broken sternum, and a broken left ankle. His belongings, including his racing suit, gloves, helmet, and shoes, were returned to his wife, who was at his side when he was pronounced dead.

President George W. Bush phoned Teresa Earnhardt that night with condolences and ordered the White House flag lowered to half staff.

NASCAR president Bill France Jr. issued a statement. "NASCAR has lost its greatest driver ever," it read. "And I personally have lost a great friend."

So had veteran promoter Humpy Wheeler back in Charlotte, who had helped Earnhardt during his lean, early years in the sport. "All that stock-car racing was, ran through his veins," Wheeler said. "He was the beginning. The genesis. It was all there. And now it's gone."

. . .

The next morning, stock-car racing awoke without its soul. Yes, the sun rose over Daytona Beach. Waves crashed against the shore, and locals with metal detectors trolled the sand in front of the high-rise hotels, scavenging what race fans had left behind. But fans who loved Dale Earnhardt, and those who had despised him, wept over his death.

They started streaming to Daytona International Speedway before dawn, building a shrine composed of daisies, gladiolas, teddy bears, poems, Earnhardt caps, and Earnhardt photographs near the main entrance. Nearby, giant sheets of poster board were propped up on more than twenty easels. By midafternoon they were covered with hand-lettered messages to the driver whose death moved them so.

"Show me the way, and I will race you to heaven."

"I wasn't your biggest fan, but I respect the man. May God be happy with you."

And in the hand-lettered script of a child: "I am sorry you are gone."

All over the NASCAR circuit—in Atlanta; Bristol, Tennessee; Talladega, Alabama; Las Vegas; and beyond—thousands of fans gathered at racetracks just to stand at a place where Earnhardt had triumphed and to be with others who shared their heartbreak. The mourning wasn't confined to traditional stock-car markets. It was much the same in office buildings, factories, churches, and bars throughout the country. At the Grammy Awards the next weekend, U2's guitarist, the Edge, took the stage wearing a black No. 3 T-shirt.

In Mooresville, North Carolina, the two-lane road that winds from Interstate 77 through the rolling farmland of Iredell County was choked with cars as a somber procession crept past Dale Earnhardt Inc. Several fans reported seeing a cloud shaped like the number "3" appear in the sky. They laid flowers and cards at the black wrought-iron fence in front of the racing compound, congregating in the same way that a generation had flocked to New York's famed Dakota the night John Lennon was shot and mourners had flocked to British embassies worldwide upon learning Princess Diana had died.

"To be honest, it doesn't matter to me now if I never see another race again because my man is gone," said P. J. Craven of Loris, South Carolina "That's the only reason I watched." Added her husband, Ricky: "He represented NASCAR. He represented the American people."

The scene was replayed for days afterward. The cars kept coming—from the Carolinas and from states hundreds of miles away. Members of the North Carolina Highway Patrol and Iredell County Sheriff's Department were posted out front to maintain order, but there was little need. It was a somber, silent crowd.

"I just loved him," said Harold Eudy, sixty-four, as tears welled up in his eyes.

"We came to pay our respects," his wife added. "I loved him because he wasn't a quitter."

For the millions of Americans who had never paid attention to stock-car racing, the magnitude of the shock and anguish triggered by Earnhardt's death was a revelation. It opened a window not only on NASCAR's iconic champion, but on a sport and, ultimately, a whole segment of the population that had been there all along, yet its passions, its longings, and its most fervent beliefs hadn't necessarily been acknowledged.

Earnhardt's death was front-page news in the *New York Times,* the *Washington Post,* the *Los Angeles Times, USA Today,* and nearly every major newspaper. It was the cover story of *Time* magazine. Britain's weekly *Economist* weighed in. And it was the subject of analytical pieces on programs such as *Nightline* and the *MacNeil/Lehrer Report.* Who *was* this racecar driver who had amassed such wealth and commanded such a fervent following? What did he stand for? Why did so many care? And in an era in which the bonds between sports heroes and sports fans were fraying, how did so many come to care so deeply?

• • •

Earnhardt's body was laid to rest at an undisclosed location that Wednesday following a small funeral attended by his immediate family at St. Mark's Lutheran Church in Mooresville.

The next day, Charlotte's Calvary Church hosted a memorial service for three thousand invited guests. There were a dozen busloads of employees from Richard Childress Racing and as many from Dale Earnhardt Inc.; scores of relatives; hundreds of business associates, NASCAR officials, automotive-industry executives, racetrack owners, journalists; as well as his mother, Martha; wife, Teresa; and children, Kerry, thirty-one, Kelley, twenty-eight, Dale Jr., twenty-six, and Taylor Nicole, twelve.

It was the biggest turnout of racers that Junior Johnson had seen in a lifetime of funerals. And it was but one measure of the man. "I've seen Fireball Roberts, Joe Weatherly, and Curtis Turner—all of them guys—pass away," said Johnson, seventy. "But none of them created the multitude of heartbreak as this has. It's been a devastating thing to the sport. It's one of the worst happenings that I've ever seen in auto racing."

Law enforcement officials urged fans to stay away, warning that there was no place to park and nothing to see. A sudden plunge in the temperature, accompanied by a cold, driving rain, helped thin the ranks. Yellow police tape was strung around the perimeter of the church to prevent the curious from peering inside. Police helicopters hovered and TV satellite trucks filled the parking lot.

Inside, the congregation rose as Teresa and Taylor Earnhardt were escorted into the sanctuary by a state highway patrolman. Martha Earnhardt followed, along with the other Earnhardt children, grandchildren, NASCAR's Bill France Jr., car owner Richard Childress, and Earnhardt's extended family.

Floral arrangements filled the massive sanctuary, and local flower shops said they had back orders they couldn't get to for three weeks. There were huge sprays, heart-shaped bouquets, flowers fashioned into "3"s, and simple potted plants sent by the biggest names in racing, as well as fans Earnhardt had never met. The parents of Tony Roper, the NASCAR truck racer who had been killed four months earlier, also sent flowers.

It was a simple service. No program was printed for fear it would become a collectible among fans who were buying and bartering almost anything that bore Earnhardt's name.

The Reverend John Cozart of St. Mark's opened with a reading of scripture and a prayer. He was followed by Dale Beaver, a chaplain with Motor Racing Outreach, NASCAR's traveling ministry. Beaver urged mourners to recall when they first met Earnhardt, share their favorite memory, and laugh, as well as pray, together.

Finally, Teresa Earnhardt was escorted to the stage. She stepped to the microphone, placed her hands over her heart and, in a voice barely louder than a whisper, said, "Thank you."

• • •

The next morning at Rockingham, NASCAR drivers, Dale Jr. included, climbed back into their racecars.

There were numerous unanswered questions about why Earnhardt's wreck had proved fatal. But the next event of the season was scheduled at North Carolina Motor Speedway that Sunday. And after five days of mourning, most drivers wanted nothing more than to seek emotional refuge in their sheet-metal cocoons, flip the ignition, and race.

"We know he's watching us," Dale Jarrett said of Earnhardt. "And we know he's in a better place. . . . I want to be here; I want to race. This is what we do. But I sure want Dale Earnhardt to be here, too."

Said Dale Jr., "I miss my father, and I've cried for him. But my own selfish pity is the reason for those emotions. I just try to maintain a good focus for the future and just remember that he's in a better place—a place we'll all want to be."

Attendance was heavy at the prerace chapel service in the garage, where Dale Jr., Jarrett, Schrader, John Andretti, Jeff Gordon, Michael Waltrip, Jeff Burton, Bill Elliott, Jimmy Spencer, Ricky Craven, Matt Kenseth, Johnny Benson, and dozens of wives, children, and crew chiefs bowed their heads in prayer. Extra chaplains were deployed to help those struggling with the loss.

"We can do everything we want inside the cars to make them safer," Spencer said. "But the bottom line is, I believe in God. I believe I'm going to go to heaven. And I believe that every one of us is going to die. And *He*—not you or me—is the only one that knows when that's going to happen."

It was the first NASCAR Winston Cup race without Earnhardt in the starting lineup since 1979. Tributes were everywhere, from the No. 3 caps that drivers wore during prerace introductions to the Earnhardt pennants that fans hoisted in the air at the start of the race.

Under cold, gray skies, the capacity crowd of sixty-thousand came to life only once—when Dale Jr. was introduced before the start. Wearing a red jacket and baggy blue jeans, he waved to the fans, and they greeted him with cheers. Then he embraced Marlin, the driver some irate fans had blamed for causing the fatal wreck, to make clear that there was no bad blood, or blame, between them.

Darrell Waltrip delivered the prerace invocation and asked fans to take the hand of the person beside them and pause to remember the fallen champion.

The race had just gotten under way when a chill went through the grandstands. Dale Jr. hadn't even completed one circuit before his red No. 8 slammed into the concrete wall after being rear-ended by a rookie driver. Rescue workers helped him from his car, and he limped down the track's bank. He was fine, he said. The car was totaled.

Minutes later the skies erupted. Rain halted the race after fifty-two laps. Some saw God's hand in that, as well—evidence that heaven was weeping, too.

"This is a message that Dale is still watching us," said Laura Wyatt, thirty-three, of Charlotte. "I think he always will. He may be gone, but he will be with us forever."

. . .

NASCAR chose the Friday before the race at Rockingham to announce one of the findings of its investigation into the fatal wreck. Earnhardt's seat belt had failed, NASCAR president Mike Helton disclosed during a press conference at the track. The discovery had been made the night of the crash. It was being aired five days later, Helton said, to make other drivers aware before they strapped in their racecars again.

Dr. Steve Bohannon, the emergency medical-services director from Daytona, took part in the press conference, flown in to field questions related to the driver's injuries and medical care. Bohannon stopped short of saying Earnhardt would have survived had his seat belt worked properly. But he said it would have helped. He also said Earnhardt's use of an open-faced helmet, rather than a full-faced helmet, likely exacerbated his injuries.

Almost immediately NASCAR's credibility was suspect. There hadn't been a similar seat-belt failure in the sport's fifty-two-year history. The controversy intensified after one of the rescue workers at the scene told the Orlando newspaper that Earnhardt's seat belt was intact after the crash—a claim that the worker withdrew months later.

Some viewed NASCAR's announcement that the seat belt had failed as a rationalization for yet another driver's death—one that absolved NASCAR of any responsibility. If Earnhardt's death *was* a freakish event, there was no need for NASCAR to make its racecars safer or for track owners to make their venues safer. And there was no need for drivers to question, even after the sport's best had been killed, whether they weren't vulnerable, too.

NASCAR officials said the investigation was continuing. As a result, they said, it was too soon to take any corrective measures. "If we knew that there was something that we could do, we would do it," Helton said. "We don't have a conclusion today that gives us the ability to react to this."

The controversy over the cause of Earnhardt's death raged for months. NASCAR battled in court with Bill Simpson, the seat-belt manufacturer, who argued that his company had been defamed by NASCAR's public statements. According to Simpson, the belt would not have failed had it been installed properly. And the *Orlando Sentinel* battled with Florida officials and Teresa Earnhardt over access to the dead driver's autopsy photos. Earnhardt's widow characterized the newspaper's pursuit as a ghoulish invasion of privacy. The newspaper said that its goal was to investigate what had become a crisis of safety in stock-car racing.

In August 2001, six months after Earnhardt's death, NASCAR issued the findings of its $1 million investigation, which included a detailed analysis of the multiple factors that contributed to the fatal crash. No single factor caused his death, it concluded. Rather, it resulted from a sequence of events, including the angle that Earnhardt's car hit the wall, its velocity on impact, its abrupt stop (which caused the violent whiplash motion of the head and neck), and the "separated" seat belt.

As a result, NASCAR announced it would begin installing so-called black boxes in its racecars to measure the severity of crashes. NASCAR also agreed to hire a full-time medical liaison who would travel the circuit as a drivers' advocate in the event of serious injury. But one more NASCAR driver would die of a basal skull fracture— Blaise Alexander, at Charlotte Motor Speedway in October 2001— before NASCAR required its drivers to use a head-restraint device.

In the months and years that followed, NASCAR's track owners installed energy-absorbing barriers in key sections of their speedways' concrete walls. And in March 2007, NASCAR introduced a radically redesigned racecar, dubbed the Car of Tomorrow, that included several features aimed at keeping drivers safe, including energy-absorbing panels in its side, a relocated seat (closer to the center of the car), a stronger steel floorboard, and steel reinforcements on the driver's side.

The three deaths during NASCAR's 2000 season had prompted NASCAR to take another look at the design of its racecars. But nothing spurred NASCAR to undertake a major redesign until Earnhardt died. Said Robin Pemberton, NASCAR's director of competition: "We were being tapped on the shoulder and failed to acknowledge the fact that we were getting these reminders."

• • •

Many in NASCAR feared that Earnhardt's death would mark the end of the sport's popularity. At Bristol Motor Speedway, where yet another expansion of the grandstands had been planned, track officials discussed abandoning the idea because Earnhardt's following was so strong in the region. Bristol fans were notorious for packing up and leaving in the middle of a race if the No. 3 crashed out. Now, with Earnhardt gone, no one was sure if they'd bother coming at all.

Certainly many of his fans couldn't bear watching the sport anymore. To many, there was only one driver in NASCAR's races: Earnhardt. They had followed his career for two decades, never wavering through his struggles and triumphs. They wore Earnhardt hats and Earnhardt T-shirts. They bought Earnhardt belts and bolted Earnhardt license-plate holders to their cars. They sent their children to school with Earnhardt lunch boxes. And they charted how fair the world was based on how the black No. 3 fared on the racetrack each Sunday.

Others transferred their allegiance to Dale Jr., who assumed a Kennedy-like onus after his father's death, expected to fill the massive void that the seven-time champion had left behind and comfort the grieving while dealing with his own loss, as well. But there were still others who hadn't been able to name a single NASCAR driver before Earnhardt's death, yet they found themselves tuning in—if only to see what the fuss was all about.

Earnhardt's death, it turned out, didn't signal the end of NASCAR any more than Buddy Holly's death signaled the end of rock 'n' roll. "There's no person on earth that's important enough to keep the sun from coming up and keep the sun from going down," Richard Petty said years later. "We get new presidents; we get new popes. If he dies off, we just keep on trucking along. Time takes care of it."

For the rest of the 2001 season, fans paid tribute at the NASCAR speedways by standing during the third lap of every race and raising three fingers toward heaven. Every NASCAR race broadcast fell silent during the third lap. Tracks dedicated grandstands in Earnhardt's name and commissioned sculptures in his image. Tribute pages proliferated on the Internet with such titles as "God Bless the Legend," "Gone but Not Forgotten," and "Heaven's Raceway." And songwriters memorialized him in verse.

Indeed, the sun still rose and set after Dale Earnhardt died. But for many, racing was never the same.

"When we lost him, I just got numb to everybody," recalled Rusty Wallace, his old on-track foe. "Every week there was a race, and there were still all these other drivers. But I used to go to the track thinking, '*That's* the guy I want to beat! *That's* the guy who defines my day, the one I go on my boating trips with, that likes my family. *He's* the guy.'

"When he was gone, nothing tripped my trigger at all. That's bad to say, but nobody ever turned me on. I never got to the track and said, 'I want to beat *that* guy.' There was a huge void in my life with him not being around. When he passed away, it went from everything being a special event for me, to every race just being another race. Show up. Punch your time clock. Drive the car. Go home. Show up. Punch your time clock. Drive the car. Go home."

The sport was changing long before Dale Earnhardt was killed. But when he died, a lot of things died with him. He was stock-car racing's anchor to the past.

Chapter 9

GOOD-BYE, MISS WINSTON

The history of American entrepreneurship is littered with family dynasties that deteriorated after being passed from one generation to the next, whether because of infighting, indifference, or conflicting agendas. That had not been the case with NASCAR and its founding France family. Each generation's vision for stock-car racing was more ambitious than the one that preceded it—mindful of the debt to the past yet determined to build on the legacy.

Big Bill France had taken hold of a wild, regional pastime in the postwar era and turned it into a legitimate sport. Decades later his elder son, Bill France Jr., took that regional sport nationwide. And as the 1990s drew to a close, Brian Z. France, Big Bill's grandson and the only son of Bill Jr., envisioned transforming that nationwide sport into mainstream entertainment.

With no formal business education beyond a few years of college at the University of Central Florida, Brian France learned the family trade by climbing his way up the ranks—first dispatched to run a short track in Tucson, Arizona, and later installed in NASCAR's competition department, where he helped launch its truck-racing series. Later, in charge of marketing, he sized up prospects for the sport's future and concluded that the key to continued success was hooking younger fans. Stock-car racing needed to become cool in the eyes of the next generation. And NASCAR's brand, specifically, had to become part of young Americans' lifestyles at whatever stage they happened to be—toddler, child, preteen, or teen.

Brian France hardly needed a master's degree in business to identify the major roadblock. It was embedded in the sport's very name and exhaled in a single breath: NASCAR Winston Cup racing.

With a cigarette brand as its title sponsor, NASCAR couldn't market its flagship series directly to youngsters. In fact, it was becoming increasingly difficult to market NASCAR at all given the federal government's restrictions on the tobacco industry. At the same time, R.J. Reynolds' Winston brand was losing market share to low-cost, generic brands. And smoking *any* type of cigarette in public was increasingly regarded as socially unacceptable, if not flat-out illegal—particularly in the major markets that NASCAR coveted.

All of those factors undermined precisely what Brian France hoped to accomplish. And it was a slow, painful process before either NASCAR or R.J. Reynolds was ready to concede the obvious: the company that had been stock-car racing's lifeline for so many years was now a liability.

• • •

It began as a marriage of convenience but blossomed into the most fruitful union in sports-marketing history.

NASCAR and R.J. Reynolds joined forces in 1971 when both were in difficult straits. Citing concerns about public health, the federal government banned cigarette commercials from television and radio at the end of that year. NASCAR, at the time, was barely a break-even proposition for most of the participants. Detroit automakers had withdrawn much of their financial backing, which left car owners struggling for parts to keep their teams running. And many racetrack owners teetered on the brink of bankruptcy.

At the time, the tobacco industry was spending $220 million a year on TV commercials—second only to the automotive industry. R.J. Reynolds accounted for more than half of that, according to industry insiders, pouring about $125 million into TV ads that promoted its top brands: Camel, Winston, and Salem.

So when NASCAR team owner Junior Johnson turned up at the company's headquarters in Winston-Salem, North Carolina, looking for a few hundred thousand dollars to sponsor one of his stock cars, the timing couldn't have been better. RJR executives were flush with advertising money but had nowhere to spend it. "When I told 'em what I wanted them to give me," Johnson recalls, "they kind of laughed and said, 'Lord a-mercy! We need something bigger than that, because we've just been taken off from TV!' They were spending more than a hundred million dollars—eye-poppin' to me."

So Johnson put the company in touch with Bill France, and the North Carolina–based tobacco giant signed on to sponsor the whole sport.

RJR executives realized that hitching Winston's red-and-white logo to televised stock cars was one way to outfox the advertising ban. And if the Winston brand could help NASCAR grow, it stood to reason that the sport's loyal fans would show their appreciation by making Winston their brand of choice rather than Marlboro, the flagship brand of Philip Morris, RJR's Richmond, Virginia–based rival.

The result was a five-year deal in which RJR agreed to put up $100,000 a year in prize money to be distributed among drivers based on their finish in a season-long points race. NASCAR, in turn, agreed to rename its top series the Winston Cup and display the Winston logo wherever it might catch the TV camera's eye—on trackside billboards, drivers' uniforms, and racecars themselves.

NASCAR ended up getting far more than cash in the transaction. It got a sorely needed makeover.

Almost overnight, restrooms and concession stands sprouted up at tracks. Treacherous metal guardrails were replaced with cement walls. Dilapidated racetracks got new grandstands, frontstretch suites, fancy scoring stands, and media centers. And every flat surface—whether concrete wall, bleacher seat, or frontstretch roof—got a fresh coat of paint. RJR bought 200,000 to 300,000 gallons of paint, in fact, and turned every NASCAR track red and white—the colors of the Winston brand.

RJR didn't have a monopoly on the insight that sporting events made ideal vehicles for marketing cigarettes in the 1970s. Philip Morris chose Indy-car racing to promote its Marlboro brand. And its Virginia Slims brand underwrote the fledgling women's tennis tour for more than twenty years, using the achievements of the sport's pioneers to remind women that they, indeed, had "come a long way, baby."

But no advertising executives promoted their sporting partner with more zeal than R.J. Reynolds' Ralph Seagraves and T. Wayne Robertson. Seagraves had been RJR's longtime Washington-based lobbyist. He knew every politician who mattered and had enough clout of his own, insiders claimed, to make sure that Air Force One and the Oval Office were always furnished with Reynolds-brand cigarettes. Seagraves also had an innate feel for the common man. If he saw anyone smoking another brand of cigarettes, he'd grab the pack, crumple it up, and give the person *two* packs of Winstons. And he did it in such an affable way that no one minded—except that long-haired fellow who'd been using his empty pack of cigarettes to store his marijuana joints.

Seagraves's first move, after volunteering to run the company's promotional deal with NASCAR, was to persuade Bill France to trim his unwieldy, forty-eight-race schedule nearly in half. Then he used RJR's money to upgrade the thirty or so races that remained. He hired Robertson, an eager, energetic young salesman, for an entry-level sales job towing the Winston show car to racetracks and shopping malls all over the circuit so fans could see firsthand what a NASCAR stock car looked like.

Seagraves's next agenda item was getting more coverage of NASCAR in daily newspapers. And he turned to a time-tested institution for help in ensuring prominent display in the Monday-morning sports pages: the beauty queen.

Every racing promoter worth a ticket stub knew that nothing turned a man's head like a beauty queen—particularly in the South, where they had long held a special status. Every state fair had a beauty queen, as did every azalea parade, every peach blossom parade, and every festival in honor of the peanut and sweet potato. There wasn't a tradition or a tuber that sprang from southern soil that *wasn't* celebrated with a float-riding, tiara-wearing, long-legged beauty. So it was natural that RJR would want its own to preside over the NASCAR Winston Cup Series. Surely, the sports pages would love a picture of a pretty girl planting a kiss on the winner's grimy face in Victory Lane.

It had worked to great effect for Linda Vaughn, a young Georgia blond considered the original queen of auto racing's Victory Lane. A transfixed Tom Wolfe devoted several paragraphs to Ms. Vaughn in his 1965 homage to Junior Johnson, describing her as the "Life Symbol of Stock-car Racing." Vaughn never was a Miss Winston, but she amassed more titles than a romance novelist, including Miss Atlanta International Raceway, Miss Firebird, and, most famously, Miss Hurst Golden Shifter.

In her role as Miss Hurst Golden Shifter, Vaughn was in such demand at racetracks around the country that the gearshift maker hired twelve backups, known as the Hurst-ettes, to fill in when she couldn't appear. As Miss Firebird (Pure Oil's name for its top-flight gasoline in the early 1960s), she whipped crowds into a frenzy as she circled the racetrack wearing only a bathing suit and high heels atop her red custom-built Firebird float, perched between the wings of a giant wooden bird.

"It was quite something to see," recalled veteran motorsports journalist Chris Economaki, whose memory of Miss Firebird remained vivid at age eighty-three. "She would get up on that float and lean against this very phallic thing and heave her bosom, and men would dream about spending private time with her."

But after Ms. Vaughn left Pure Oil, the gas company (later known as Unocal) decided it would be better if its beauty queen weren't quite so famous. So to make sure one girl's fame didn't eclipse that of the product, they hired several beauties on the eve of the 1969 Daytona 500, ushering in the era of the Unocal Race Stoppers—four models in miniskirts and white leather boots.

Explained Unocal's public-relations man Bill Brodrick: "Nobody writes about gasoline or oil unless a car burns up. How do you get some publicity? What better way than put four pretty girls with a race driver?"

Seagraves wanted to achieve the same end on behalf of Winston. But he wanted Miss Winston to be a cut above. As he envisioned her, Miss Winston wasn't simply a beauty. She was a corporate ambassador, subject to strict rules of behavior. She was chaperoned at each of her appearances. She was discouraged from drinking in public. She wasn't required to smoke, but if she did, it had to be Winstons. And she was forbidden from dating drivers (though a few would later marry NASCAR stars, including Pattie Huffman Petty and Brooke Sealy Gordon).

Over the years, Miss Winston's look evolved from hot pants and bouffant updos, to bell-bottoms and floppy hats, to form-fitting jumpsuits and baseball caps. But her assignment never varied. It was to get Winston's name and logo on TV, get stock-car racing in the newspapers, and with every free sample pack of cigarettes, every gesture, smile, and kind word, make NASCAR fans feel good about the Winston brand.

It took a special kind of girl. Miss Winston had to be spunky enough to lug a giant red tote bag that contained cartons of Winstons, free to adults who smoked, around the garage. She also had to be sufficiently poised to dress up in a red evening gown and represent Winston at the season-ending awards banquet. But her chief duty came in Victory Lane, where she needed to maneuver herself next to the winner and make sure her smile and her Winston uniform were captured in the photographs and on the TV broadcast.

While she commanded the cameras' attention, Seagraves and Robertson worked feverishly behind the scenes to build NASCAR in other ways. They coached self-conscious drivers in public-speaking skills. They arranged meetings between financially strapped car owners and potential sponsors. And they hired an enthusiastic staff of marketers who shared their commitment to the Winston brand, to NASCAR, and to the future that tobacco and racing could build together.

RJR's marketing staff helped the sportswriters who covered NASCAR—some of them drawing the assignment by choice, others against their will. They compiled NASCAR's annual media guide, supplied reporters with race statistics, suggested topics for feature stories, hosted weekly conference calls with drivers, and arranged one-on-one interviews with the sport's personalities. They also set out an ashtray at each reporter's seat in the press box and stocked the room with cartons of RJR-brand cigarettes.

Just like Robertson, RJR's marketing staff took every slight against stock-car racing and tobacco personally. They wore their employment proudly, adhering to a company policy of sporting Winston-branded uniforms whether at the racetrack or commuting to and from. In the early seventies that meant boarding commercial aircraft wearing loud white slacks adorned with drawings of Winston cigarette packs and the phrase "How Good It Is!"

The goal in all this was to broaden NASCAR's audience by taking stock-car racing out of the garage and into middle America. And before long, the mix of sponsors on the racecars testified that RJR's efforts were succeeding. Richard Petty's famed No. 43 still carried the logo of STP motor oil, of course. But it was now running alongside racecars sponsored by Tide, Maxwell House, Gatorade, and many other products found in suburban grocery stores.

. . .

The corporate headquarters of R.J. Reynolds Tobacco Company dominated the skyline of Winston-Salem, North Carolina, with all the art-deco grandeur of New York's Empire State Building. And its sports-marketing arm, which reached its heyday in the mid-1990s, occupied an entire floor.

Robertson, Ralph Seagraves's protégé, had risen from his job towing the show car to become the division's president. And he had a $100 million annual budget to work with and 110 employees who were paid to travel the world and attend the dizzying range of sporting events that RJR's promotional money made possible—stock-car races, drag races, biker rallies, hydroplane races, bass-fishing tournaments, bowling tournaments, golf tournaments, rodeos, and skiing competitions to name a few.

The Winston Cup sponsorship, Robertson's personal point of pride, eclipsed all investments. NASCAR's annual prize fund, which was bankrolled by RJR, had ballooned from $100,000 in 1971 to $4 million in the mid-1990s. The company poured money into other aspects of the sport, too. It sponsored NASCAR's annual all-star race, The Winston (which was renamed The Winston Select in 1994 to help promote a variation on the brand). It sponsored the annual spring race at Talladega Superspeedway, the Winston 500. It staked the $1 million bonus, known as The Winston Million, for any driver who won three of the sport's four marquee events (at the time, considered the Daytona 500, Coca-Cola 600, Talladega's Winston 500, and Darlington's Southern 500). And, for a time, it sponsored a racecar that only stoked critics' claims that RJR was flouting federal advertising restrictions by using a cartoon character to appeal to children. That car was the No. 23 Smokin' Joe's Ford, which had a purple-and-yellow hood that featured the silhouette of a camel.

The car was promoted with help from a jaunty variation on Old Joe, the cartoon camel that had been lambasted by the U.S. surgeon general for illegally and unethically targeting underage smokers. NASCAR's "Smokin' Joe" was even more eye-catching than Old Joe, sporting black sunglasses, a racing scarf around his neck, and a cigarette dangling from his lips. And he quickly became a lightning rod in the debate over how to curb youth smoking, which had become a priority of the Clinton Administration.

Robertson denied the car was aimed at children. Moreover, he denied that children were an appreciable part of NASCAR's fan base. "Less than 2 percent of the fans that attend NASCAR races are under the age of eighteen," Robertson said in 1994. "So if this is a campaign driven toward kids, we certainly are going in the wrong direction."

RJR eventually removed the camel from the hood of its No.23 car, replacing it with the phrase "Smokin' Joe." But the controversy surrounding NASCAR's young audience only grew more complicated.

Clearly the sport's appeal to youngsters was growing in the mid-1990s. Jeff Gordon's rainbow-colored car was an instant hit with children, who were turning up at racetracks in droves sporting miniature No. 24 T-shirts and caps. Youth-oriented sponsors such as the Cartoon Network, Skittles, Mattel's Hot Wheels, Kellogg's, and the Family Channel charged into the sport at the same time and began plastering racecars with images of Fred Flintstone and Tony the Tiger.

In 1996, the NASCAR Licensing Group, which operated independently of R.J. Reynolds, signed a three-year deal with a company called Toy Biz to produce NASCAR-themed remote-controlled cars, action figures, and educational CD-ROMs. Bill Seaborn, NASCAR's director of licensing, said the deal would give "young fans the opportunity to grow up with toys that represent their favorite NASCAR drivers and teams."

In 1998, NASCAR contracted with Fox Kids network to develop a children's TV series that would showcase NASCAR as a "family-friendly sport that appeals to kids of all ages." At the time, the network was the top-rated content provider of TV programming for children ages two to eleven. Said George Pyne, then NASCAR's vice president of marketing, "Our goal is to build the sport of NASCAR with a younger audience on a worldwide basis."

NASCAR found itself in an awkward, if not untenable, position: aggressively pursuing a youth audience that it felt represented its future, yet pressured to deny, for the sake of its sponsor, that a youth market existed for stock-car racing.

It was hard to get a fix on just how many children followed the sport. The industry's chief lobbyist, the Tobacco Institute, claimed that children accounted for just 3 percent of auto-racing audiences. The Campaign for Tobacco-Free Kids claimed the figures were five times as high.

As criticism of the tobacco industry mounted, NASCAR drivers and track owners rallied to the defense of their sponsor, which was spending roughly $40 million a year to promote NASCAR, characterizing the government's proposed advertising restrictions on the industry as an attack on Americans' free will.

"It's a legal product that the government subsidizes through farm programs in North Carolina, my native Kentucky, Virginia, and every state where tobacco is grown," Darrell Waltrip said. "More and more it seems the government, our government, wants to control the whole world and every aspect of it. I don't smoke, but if I wanted to, I should have that choice. Where does government responsibility begin and personal responsibility end?"

Said Bruton Smith, chairman of Speedway Motorsports Inc.: "They attack red meat, popcorn . . . the latest is they're having congressional hearings about removing Coca-Cola from the schools! I'm a big believer in freedom. Whether I want my popcorn that's maybe been popped in coconut oil, that's my prerogative."

But the campaign to snuff out tobacco's presence in sporting arenas gained momentum. The medical research on the dangers of tobacco was too damning. The political tide was too strong.

The 1998 Master Settlement Agreement between the tobacco industry and the states' attorneys general accelerated the inevitable. It limited cigarette makers to promoting just one sport; RJR naturally chose NASCAR, giving up its support of drag racing, golf, and what other sports properties remained in its budget. The agreement also banned promotional merchandise with cigarette brand names or logos, billboard advertising, and brand-name sponsorship of events primarily attended by youngsters. And it banned all cartoon characters, including Joe Camel, in the advertising, promotion, and marketing of cigarettes.

It was one of two developments that year that signaled the beginning of the end for NASCAR's Winston Cup Series. The other was the death of T. Wayne Robertson, who was killed that January, at age forty-eight, in a boating accident in Louisiana. In an instant, the face of RJR's sports-marketing arm changed. The executives who succeeded Robertson didn't share his commitment to the sponsorship. Nor did they boast his clout with RJR's upper management or NASCAR's France family. To them, supporting Winston Cup racing wasn't a cause. Instead, the $40 million annual expenditure was simply the biggest line-item in the budget.

If you listened closely to the France family's public statements as the 1998 tobacco settlement was being negotiated, NASCAR was sending two different messages. NASCAR president Bill France Jr. adopted a posture of loyalty and tradition in his remarks, hailing R.J. Reynolds as a good sponsor that had every legal right to promote its legitimate product.

Brian France, then NASCAR's vice president of marketing, took a slightly different tack. Brian espoused the optimistic stance of a budding CEO who saw only good things ahead for the sport, regardless of what happened to its major benefactor. He characterized NASCAR as stronger than ever and well positioned to find a replacement for RJR, if need be. It seemed as if Brian was already mulling NASCAR's options in case that day ever came. "We have more momentum than we ever had," he said. "The popularity of our sport pretty much ensures us of being able to pick our new direction, whatever that might be, carefully."

Asked to define NASCAR's target audience heading into the twenty-first century, the younger France replied: "It's a mass audience. A wide spectrum. Obviously, it's middle America. It's the bulk of the population. We think it will remain a heavy focus on the female audience. It will remain a family-oriented approach. So any partner that we choose will have to be able to meet that criteria."

Meanwhile RJR had other troubles. When it teamed up with NASCAR in 1971, it was the country's biggest tobacco company, and its Winston brand had a 15.7 percent share of the domestic cigarette market. By 2002, Philip Morris was the biggest tobacco-producer, and Winston's share of the market had plunged to 4.7 percent.

In February 2003, RJR announced it was willing to step aside as NASCAR's top sponsor if a suitable replacement could be found, citing an uncertain economic climate. Poor sales of its Winston brand no longer justified the lavish marketing expense. Said Ned Leary, president of RJR's Sports Marketing Enterprises: "In those situations, you have to weigh, 'Where am I going to invest my resources?' We simply got to the point that we needed to step back and evaluate everything we were doing. As effective as it was, it still carried a price-tag decision."

At the time, though, RJR had five years remaining on its NASCAR sponsorship. And Shannon Wiseman, a former college cheerleader and member of the Charlotte Hornets NBA Honeybees dance squad, still had a season to fulfill as the sport's last Miss Winston.

Nearly fifty women had worn the title since Seagraves envisioned the ideal Miss Winston in 1971. And for over thirty-three years, Miss Winston remained true to his original vision. She was the southern hostess with good taste and a gift for making everyone feel special. She was the wholesome, energetic girl who was always happy. She was happy that race fans loved the sound of a V-8 engine. Happy that they believed in the supremacy of American-made cars. Happy about the skills and daring of the men who drove them. And happy that NASCAR fans preferred the Winston brand.

Marketing restrictions and shifting social mores refined Miss Winston's job over the years. She didn't hand out free cigarettes as liberally as she once did. She couldn't sign autographs for fans under twenty-one. She no longer kissed the winning driver as he climbed from the car—a few of NASCAR's more influential wives suggested to RJR that the practice wasn't appreciated. She still needed to finagle her way into the Victory Lane photographs, of course, but her role was simply to clap and smile—and not to overshadow the driver's wife.

Wiseman was ideal for the job, with a bubbly personality and a starlet's ambition. Her goodwill seemed boundless, and she sprinkled it freely throughout race weekend, visiting with fans at meet-and-greet sessions, touring the garage to perk up the spirits of the hard-working mechanics, applauding the prospects of each competitor during driver introductions, and, of course, cheering the winner in Victory Lane.

"I just try to be their sunshine," Wiseman explained before the fall race at Richmond International Raceway in 2003.

She had started her day at a trackside autograph session, hopping out of her sporty red Winston jeep wearing black stiletto boots and a tight red racing suit with "Winston" plastered across the bosom. Fans were lined up along the souvenir midway to meet her. Some men were so awed that they couldn't look at Miss Winston directly as she picked up her black Sharpie pen and poured her syrupy southern voice all over them.

"Who to, sweetie?" she'd ask, as they stared at their shoe tops.

A few men were brave, sidling up alongside and blushing when she draped an arm over their shoulder and smiled for the camera. They floated away as if transported on a cloud, clutching an auto-graphed postcard that proved a beautiful woman once stood next to them and called them by name.

Once the race was under way, Miss Winston hopped back into her Winston Jeep for a ride up to RJR's corporate suite overlooking the start–finish line, where she chatted with about sixty regional sales representatives, convenience-store operators, and guests. After a few dozen more photographs and laughs, she made her way back to the infield to touch up her makeup for her appearance in Victory Lane. She put on a red Winston baseball cap, which gave RJR another op-portunity for its logo to be captured on TV, in addition to the "Win-ston" that was splashed across her chest. And she was in place, on time, and all smiles when race winner Ryan Newman wheeled his No. 12 Alltel Dodge onto the stage. She didn't even mind when the spray of champagne matted her ponytail and drenched her red racing suit.

• • •

Brian France took the lead in negotiating the deals that extricated NASCAR from its relationship with tobacco. With five years remain-ing on the contract, there were fine legal points in ensuring R.J. Reynolds a graceful exit, and one that made financial sense to both sides.

"We were trying to be great partners because they had supported us for so long," France explained when the scale weighing the pros and cons of tobacco sponsorship finally tipped, in NASCAR's judgment. "But as we got more aggressive in marketing the sport, those moments where we were bumping into those [advertising] restrictions were just more frequent. Their whole industry took a bunch of legal turns by making the deal with all the states' attorneys general. It made it very difficult. You were hoping it wouldn't get any worse. And then every year, it kind of got worse. . . .

"We probably signaled to them it was getting harder than ever. They knew it. In the end, they came to us and said, 'We know it may be time for us. We're doing more harm than good for the sport.' They were good about that."

The end of tobacco sponsorship made the start of a new era possible. And it enabled Brian France to plunge into the challenge he'd been waiting for: selling the biggest deal in sports.

There was hardly a competitive bidding process—or any bidding at all—when NASCAR first sold the naming rights of its top series in 1971. Stock-car racing and tobacco were two outcasts, in a sense, that desperately needed what the other offered. But by 2003, NASCAR had the sort of momentum that made investors take note. It had a national broadcast deal, a foothold in major media markets, athletes with a squeaky-clean reputation and increasing name recognition, and every indication that TV ratings, race-day audiences, and merchandise sales would continue their robust growth curve.

The trick was establishing the value of naming-rights to its top series. Plenty of major-league sports had sold the name of their ballparks and arenas, like baseball's Coors Field and professional basketball's Staples Center. College football reaped millions for title rights to its major bowl games, including the FedEx Orange Bowl and Nokia Sugar Bowl. But no sport had sold the naming rights to itself.

What was NASCAR's top series worth? Setting a price tag was like selling a home without establishing the value of comparable houses in the same neighborhood.

"No one had sold a $750 million deal before," Brian France said years later. "The amount of rights that were granted, the amount of money we were looking for . . . it hadn't been done. And it hasn't been done since. We had to make a market. Convince people that the opportunity was worthy enough. Find somebody to buy it, but find the right person to buy it. Somebody who would buy it for the right reason, believe in it, and be your partner. It's very tricky to get that right."

What NASCAR needed was a stable American company with a well-known identity, deep pockets, and a product that appealed to all age groups, both genders, and every segment of society. There were obvious candidates, including Coca-Cola, McDonald's, and Visa. But Brian France had an additional quality in mind. He wanted a company with a forward-looking orientation that was primed for dramatic growth in the same markets where NASCAR hoped to make inroads. And if it was an ambitious underdog determined to carve out a future in a competitive marketplace, much like NASCAR itself, so much the better.

NASCAR found its Prince Charming through a "cold call," according to motorsports writer David Poole, who recounted the genesis of the deal in the *Charlotte Observer*. According to Poole, Nextel's CEO, Tim Donahue, had attended NASCAR's Busch series race at Daytona International Speedway as a spectator in February 2003. He was stunned by the crowds, the fanaticism they displayed, and the mania over merchandising. And he returned to Nextel's Reston, Virginia, headquarters convinced that the company needed to find a way to align itself with NASCAR's brand.

NASCAR, meanwhile, had identified Nextel, the nation's fifth-largest wireless communications company, as an appealing prospect for a sales pitch regarding the series sponsorship. That spring executives from both companies met. In June, the respective CEOs took the stage at the NASDAQ headquarters in New York's Times Square to unveil a ten-year deal that renamed stock-car racing's top division: the NASCAR Nextel Cup Series. NASCAR chairman Bill France Jr. hailed it as "a giant step for the future of the sport."

Telecommunications was an industry without the political liability of tobacco or alcohol. Cell phones were a product that everyone could use, from age 2 to 102. And the range of Nextel's wireless products represented the future. "They market to children and families," said NASCAR vice president George Pyne said later. "This is a category for us where the opportunities are endless."

The formal announcement was a polished production in which NASCAR paid tribute to R.J. Reynolds by showing a video montage that highlighted the thirty-three-year association set to Natalie Merchant's song "Kind and Generous," which had "Thank you, thank you" as its refrain. The sport's biggest names, Jeff Gordon and Dale Earnhardt Jr., supplied the star wattage, with Donahue presenting each driver with a prototype of a Nextel cell phone that resembled his racecar.

The Nextel deal was reportedly worth $75 million a year—a $30-million increase over what RJR had been investing each year. Nextel would pay roughly $40 million for sponsorship rights and spend about $35 million to promote the series.

Within months of the announcement, R.J. Reynolds announced it was cutting 40 percent of its workforce, including its entire sports-marketing division. And it pulled the entire advertising budget for its Winston and Doral brands to focus entirely on Camel and Salem.

The moment its break with NASCAR was official, the health-policy advocates who had castigated the sport for years showered praise. "NASCAR has successfully changed auto racing into a family-oriented sport that appeals to a wide range of kids," said William V. Corr, executive director of the Campaign for Tobacco-Free Kids. "The tobacco industry has used that success as a means to glamorize smoking and appeal to kids. The end of tobacco sponsorship is a very positive development."

NASCAR drivers welcomed the new sponsor but were careful not to fawn too publicly out of respect and gratitude for all RJR had done for the sport. Most journalists were wistful—even those who had chronicled the myriad ways in which tobacco had hamstrung NASCAR's efforts to reach a mass audience.

RJR's sports-marketing staff had built tremendous goodwill with the media. Every press conference they staged started on time. Every interview they scheduled was delivered. They knew every reporter by name. More significantly, they had driven home to NASCAR drivers the importance of being accessible and courteous—increasingly rare qualities in millionaire athletes.

I never took advantage of RJR's free cigarettes, but its marketing staff made numerous Valentine's Days easier to bear. There's nothing quite so bleak as being at Daytona International Speedway on Valentine's Day, which invariably falls during the week leading up to the Daytona 500. But the holiday improved immeasurably after RJR started the tradition of inviting all the women who covered NASCAR out for a Valentine's Day dinner at a French restaurant in Ormond Beach—the same restaurant where Jeff Gordon had proposed to Brooke Sealy. We'd file our stories, race back to our hotels, get dressed up, and drive to the restaurant, where a single red rose would be waiting beside our dinner plate. For all I know, the good folks at RJR took the male reporters to strip clubs every other night. But I didn't care.

I was sad to see them go. And I wasn't alone.

Wrote the *Gaston Gazette*'s (North Carolina) Monte Dutton: "Joe Camel never stuck a cigarette in my mouth and offered me a light. I'm not saying there wasn't a dark side. I'm just saying I never saw it."

• • •

In Nextel, NASCAR got a business partner with $8.7 billion in annual revenue, a high-tech image, and coast-to-coast reach. It wasn't the biggest player on the telecommunications landscape, but it had an upstart's plucky attitude.

Meetings soon followed between the two companies' public-relations staffs, with RJR offering to smooth the transition any way it could. Meanwhile the garage buzzed over which aspects of Reynolds's marketing program would be carried on and which would be discontinued.

Would the wildly popular preseason fan fest, named for T. Wayne Robertson, still be held in Winston-Salem each January? Did the annual all-star race, known as The Winston, have a future? Would it remain at Lowe's Motor Speedway (the new corporate name of Charlotte Motor Speedway)? Would Nextel hire RJR's best employees? And what of Miss Winston? Would Nextel continue the beauty queen tradition? If so, reporters loved to crack, would they name her the Nextel Call Girl?

Nextel executives, it turned out, didn't see the merit of a beauty queen. It was the right call in the view of racetrack impresario Humpy Wheeler. "We were always trying to develop a female market, and I just felt like the Miss Whatevers was probably something we didn't need to have," he said. "I think we're past having to put a pretty face in the Winner's Circle."

Miss Winston wasn't the only familiar face to disappear from NASCAR tracks when the 2004 season kicked off. In October 2003, with Bill France Jr. battling an undisclosed form of cancer, Brian France had been named NASCAR's new chairman of the board and CEO.

Unocal, the sport's longtime supplier of racing fuel, was replaced by Sunoco. The fifty-four-year tradition of holding the Southern 500 at Darlington Raceway on Labor Day weekend came to an end. In a dramatic revision of the schedule, NASCAR gave that enviable date to California Speedway, which had been clamoring for a second major race. The Southern 500 was moved to November, a switch that essentially ensured its demise given the unpredictable weather and stiff competition from college football in late fall. And indeed, the vaunted Southern 500 disappeared from NASCAR's schedule in 2005.

The 2004 season also marked the arrival of Toyota as the first foreign nameplate to compete in one of NASCAR's major divisions, rolling out its Tundra to duel alongside Fords F-150s, Chevy Silverados, and Dodge Rams in the truck series.

Finally, NASCAR radically overhauled the formula for crowning its annual champion. In Brian France's view, the sport had to do something to spice up its entertainment value during the season's waning months. TV ratings dipped each fall when the NFL and college football seasons got going in earnest. And the erosion was even more pronounced when there wasn't a down-to-the-wire battle for the championship.

The 2003 season had been one of those anticlimactic years, later characterized by ESPN's Ryan McGee as "more of a mercy killing than a fight." Matt Kenseth, a remarkable racer with an unremarkable public persona, ran away with the championship in his Roush Racing Ford, clinching the title with one race remaining. It was the fifth time in six years that NASCAR's champion had been determined before the final race. Moreover, Kenseth did it by winning only one of the season's thirty-six races.

Part of the problem, Brian France concluded, was that NASCAR's points structure placed too much of a premium on consistent finishes rather than spectacular ones. It also made it too easy for one team to run away with the title, robbing the season of drama down the stretch. So he took a cue from major-league sports and created stock-car racing's first "postseason," in which the top ten drivers after the first twenty-six races would qualify for a shot at the title. To ensure excitement over the ten races that remained, those drivers would have their point totals compressed, with only five points separating each.

It was dubbed the NASCAR Nextel Cup Chase for the Championship. And it rankled many traditional fans, who wanted to be able to stack Dale Earnhardt's seven championships point for point against however many Jeff Gordon might end up winning in his still-young career. Gordon wasn't wild about the changes, either, calling them "too far to the entertainment side."

Brian France acknowledged that the stakes were high in remaking the family business. Speaking to *BusinessWeek* on the eve of the 2004 Daytona 500, he said: "You never want to alienate the core fans, but we are going to take risks."

His risk-taking only got bolder in the years ahead, as NASCAR's new CEO looked abroad for the next generation of fans and drivers. None, though, would have the pleasure of meeting Miss Winston.

Chapter 10

GEARING UP FOR THE GLOBAL ECONOMY

Mexico City's Autodromo Rodriguez Hernandez snakes through the biggest public park in the most populous city in North America. Just over 2.5 miles long, it consists of eight turns, alternately sweeping and precariously tight, that wend around a baseball stadium and soccer fields that stay busy every day of the year. Palm trees line sections of the course. And the prerace rituals are a little different from those in the United States, starting with the blessing of the track by a Catholic priest who sprinkles holy water on the asphalt and offers a prayer in Spanish.

But if you stood on the frontstretch on March 6, 2005, closed your eyes and ignored the smog that shrouded this metropolis perched in the clouds, you might have thought, for a split second, that you were at South Carolina's Darlington Raceway or some other traditional stop on the NASCAR circuit.

Apart from the Mexican flags fluttering above the weather-beaten grandstands and the roving mariachi bands, the aura wasn't that different from other NASCAR races when the forty-three drivers fired up their engines for the start of the inaugural Telcel-Motorola Mexico

200. The deep-throated roar of so many hopped up V-8s was an alien sound to most of the 97,000 spectators, who were accustomed to the high-pitched whine of exotic Formula 1 cars that had graced the track in years past. But to NASCAR fans, that unmistakable sound was the earth-jarring promise that something spectacular was about to happen. In this case, it was the first points race on Mexican soil in NASCAR's fifty-seven-year history.

An unheralded driver named Jorge Goeters—one of ten Mexican entrants in a field that included such NASCAR stars as Rusty Wallace, Jeff Burton, and Kevin Harvick—won the pole the previous day with a blistering lap that moved his family to tears. New Jersey's Martin Truex Jr. roared into Victory Lane after leading forty-five of its eighty laps in a Chevrolet owned by Dale Earnhardt Inc. But neither feat was as significant as the simple fact that a NASCAR Busch race was staged outside the United States.

NASCAR had dabbled in overseas markets before. The sport held an exhibition race in Australia in the mid-1980s that was of little consequence. And in the late 1990s it ran a few so-called demonstration races in Japan. The Japanese races weren't part of the Winston Cup season and were held in late November, after the annual champion was crowned. The trip was costly for the sport's team owners, and drivers didn't understand why NASCAR was racing in Japan in the first place—particularly those whose sponsors didn't do business in Asia. Besides, Japanese sports fans didn't seem too enthralled with the show—at least not enough to trek to the hard-to-reach circuits in Suzuka and Motegi in sell-out numbers. After three years, the experiment was halted.

Yet other major American sports were beginning to make inroads with their overseas development efforts. The National Basketball Association would gain a fervent Asian following with the addition of a single Chinese player, seven-foot-six Yao Ming, in 2002. Major League Baseball, whose talent pool had long benefited from a pipeline to the Dominican Republic, was now importing Japanese heroes as well as gifted Latin prospects. The National Football League created an entire developmental league for export—NFL Europe, which brought American-style football to countries where the word *football* meant something entirely different—and had begun staging preseason games abroad involving its more storied franchises, as well.

In the face of such global initiatives, NASCAR couldn't afford to sit idly by, especially after having worked so hard to establish itself as the country's fourth major-league sport. Stock-car racing needed to grab its slice of the world's sporting pie, too.

Big Bill France had fancied doing just that half a century earlier. The word *international* had been part of NASCAR's original logo, though few recalled as much decades later. Big Bill imported top European drivers to race in his events. He shipped his most charismatic figure, Fireball Roberts, to France to do battle in the famed 24 Hours of Le Mans in 1962. And he courted the international governing body of motorsports, the Federation Internationale de l'Automobile, in hopes it would recognize stock-car racing as part of the competitive landscape. France was ignored; his sport, shunned.

Bill France Jr. didn't care what the rest of the world thought about the family sport when he took charge in 1972. NASCAR's smartest play, he felt, was branding itself as the sport of homegrown drivers, homespun values, and American-made cars.

But by 2001 that attitude had changed. That's when NASCAR got serious about extending the sport's reach worldwide and created a division charged with plotting a global strategy. For expertise in running NASCAR International, the sport turned to a former NFL executive who had helped launch NFL Europe.

The first step was getting NASCAR races on TV overseas. Brokering agreements with networks around the world would have been impossible if NASCAR hadn't recently consolidated its broadcast rights. The owner of Martinsville Speedway, for example, wasn't likely to negotiate a deal to air his two annual races on Brazilian TV any more than the CEO of the new track in Kansas City was going to sell European TV rights to his lone stock-car race.

In five years' time, NASCAR races were aired in 150 countries. And I won a bet with a coworker who said I couldn't find the Daytona 500 on live TV in a remote Italian skiing village during the 2006 Winter Olympics. But in a driving snowstorm I trudged out to Sestriere's town square at around ten p.m. (four p.m. back on the East Coast) and started making the rounds of local bars. My third stop led me down a set of stairs to an underground pub that was run by a British ex-patriot who was crazy about NASCAR. And there, on a wide-screen TV, were Dale Earnhardt Jr. and Ryan Newman battling for the lead in the waning laps at Daytona International Speedway.

The next step for NASCAR International was identifying countries where stock-car racing had the best chance of catching on with fans over the next five or ten years, assuming the sport launched an aggressive marketing campaign. Seven nations were targeted, according to Robbie Weiss, the former NFL executive turned NASCAR strategist: Mexico, Canada, Brazil, the United Kingdom, Germany, Japan, and China. NASCAR started with Mexico.

NASCAR's popularity had never been greater in 2001. Dale Earnhardt's death hadn't spelled its demise but, oddly, sparked even more national interest. TV ratings went up. New speedways opened in Chicago and Kansas City, filling in geographical bare spots on the Winston Cup calendar. NASCAR's top series now raced in every region of the country except the Pacific Northwest. Yet two major segments of the U.S. population were invisible in the grandstands: African Americans and Hispanics.

Roughly forty million native Spanish speakers lived in the United States at the time. Most were from Mexico. And most were clustered in markets that now hosted NASCAR races, including Miami, Dallas–Fort Worth, Phoenix, southern California, Chicago, and, increasingly, North Carolina. But in 1995, market research indicated that just 1 percent of NASCAR fans were Hispanic. NASCAR International set its sights on expanding that percentage and, more important, the total number of Hispanic fans, by making stock-car racing part of the Mexican sports culture. It was an audacious goal, given the magnitude of the country's passion for soccer and open-wheel racing.

Step one involved bringing NASCAR's show to Mexico City. NASCAR found a local ally in Latin America's richest man, billionaire telecommunications scion Carlos Slim, a race fan and friend of NASCAR team owner Felix Sabates. One of Slim's many companies, Telcel, sponsored the inaugural Busch race and bankrolled racecars for several Mexican drivers.

But if NASCAR wanted to truly permeate the Mexican culture, it had to do more than simply stage an annual event. Stock-car racing needed a year-round presence in the country. So it teamed up with Mexico's leading concert promoter, Ocesa, to develop a Mexican racing series that would stage NASCAR-style races throughout the country. Ideally the series, initially called the Corona Challenge and then the NASCAR Mexico Corona Series, would educate Mexican sports fans about the wild, fender-rubbing sport of stock-car racing and develop Mexican racers to someday compete in NASCAR's elite Nextel Cup ranks.

"The end game is we want to be part of the local sports culture," Weiss said. "It's great to have the big event that creates a lot of excitement and buzz, but it really is the other series—the series that is authentic to Mexico, with Mexican drivers and Mexican sponsors—that carries the torch. *That's* what will create fans who follow that and *also* watch the Daytona 500."

It was a tall order. Stock-car racing was unknown in Mexico. Racing heroes such as Carlos Contreras and Adrian Fernandez had raced open-wheel cars exclusively, whether in CART or the Indy Racing League. Other famous Latin racers—such as Colombia's Juan Pablo Montoya and the late Ayrton Senna of Brazil—had made their marks in Formula 1.

It made sense to Fernandez, Mexico's most popular racecar driver, who strapped into a Chevrolet fielded by NASCAR championship car owner Rick Hendrick for Mexico City's inaugural stock-car race. "NASCAR is so huge, sometimes you get so big you can't grow," Fernandez said. "The only way for them to grow now is with Hispanics."

. . .

At the same time NASCAR was trying to integrate stock-car racing into the Mexican sports culture, Japan's largest automaker, Toyota, started wondering what NASCAR's culture could do for its products—specifically its full-sized Tundra pickup.

For decades Toyota had showcased its engineering expertise in open-wheel racing. But with audiences dwindling following the sport's destructive power struggle in the mid-1990s, few seemed to notice that Toyota was routing the field in the country's most sophisticated form of motorsports. Toyota engines were winning races. But except for the Indianapolis 500 (which Toyota won in 2003), only fifteen thousand or so people were in the grandstands to witness its triumphs, while NASCAR was drawing ten times that at many of its events. Moreover, Toyota's on-track success wasn't driving showroom sales. The company's motorsports division, known as Toyota Racing Development (TRD), was costing plenty of money but wasn't generating any profit.

The inescapable conclusion, recounts Lee White, senior vice president of TRD, was that open-wheel racing may have had more cache among the engineering cognoscenti, but NASCAR was a better investment if Toyota wanted to use motorsports to sell vehicles. "We weren't selling product," White said. "And it was self-preservation, if nothing else. We wanted to remain viable—and justifiable—in Toyota's grand scheme."

But Toyota's top brass had to be persuaded about the merits of stock-car racing. In their view, the point of auto racing was to showcase technological superiority. But in NASCAR, technological superiority wasn't allowed. The premium was on competitive balance, and the France family's ever-changing rulebook guaranteed that no automaker dominated the races for long. A racecar that was *too* good, in NASCAR's view, only "stunk up the show." It was White's job to explain to Toyota executives why this peculiar approach to racing would ultimately serve Toyota's interest. "We had to convince them that even though we're an engineering company, this isn't necessarily about engineering," White said. "It's entertainment."

NASCAR, meanwhile, had to finesse a rule that had been a pillar of the sport since the sanctioning body was founded in 1948: Its races were open to "American-made passenger car production sedans" only. Big Bill France had inserted that requirement with both pragmatism and marketing in mind. France knew that his competitors weren't wealthy men. By restricting his races to late-model castoffs that littered southern salvage yards in the 1950s and 1960s, he kept costs low enough that plenty of drivers could enter. France also believed fans could relate to the sport better if the drivers raced cars that resembled their own.

Detroit's Big Three automakers were delighted. As the sport caught on, NASCAR became a powerful advertising vehicle in the South. Whatever make of car won on Sunday, they claimed, sold on Monday.

Bill France Jr. had taken the first step toward relaxing NASCAR's "American made" restriction in welcoming Dodge back to the Winston Cup ranks in 2001. By then, Dodge was owned by Germany's DaimlerChrysler Corporation.

That was among the facts White cited when he met with NASCAR's senior vice president, George Pyne, during the 2002 Brickyard 400 to sell him on the idea of letting Toyota compete. White reminded Pyne that Toyota had been a key player in motorsports for decades. White told him that Toyota had been building cars and trucks in the United States since 1957. Toyota's Tundra pickup, for example, was built in Texas. Its Camry sedan was built in Kentucky. Moreover, Toyota had more than thirty thousand employees working in its nine production plants in the United States.

Finally, White pointed out that Dodge had entered NASCAR without meeting several of the rulebook's long-standing technical requirements. Its production cars didn't have pushrod V-8 engines or rear-wheel drive. Nor was Dodge an American car. White concluded his pitch by saying, "I think Toyota can be as good of a partner to NASCAR as DaimlerChrysler."

NASCAR mulled over the pros and cons. It studied Toyota's financial reports. And it hired an independent research firm to gauge public sentiment about the unlikely partnership. Within months Bill France Jr. met with White in NASCAR's Los Angeles office, housed in the glitzy Century City entertainment complex, to give him an answer.

"Y'all are welcome to come and compete in our series," France said, staring White in the eye across the table. "And you're welcome to win." Then he held his index finger and thumb no more than a centimeter apart and added: "But only by *this* much."

• • •

News of Toyota's impending arrival in NASCAR's truck series upset many longtime fans, who interpreted it as a prelude to the company entering stock-car racing's elite Nextel Cup ranks. And indeed, it would in 2007.

Charles Walker, a columnist for the racing website Catchfence .com, was bombarded by e-mails from impassioned NASCAR fans after writing in spring 2003 that NASCAR should "stay American." Sentiment ran 80 percent in favor of his stance. "You've got Yao Ming in the NBA and Hideo Nomo in baseball, which is fine," Walker wrote. "But leave *one* American pastime an American sport. When you start including Toyota, and now there are rumors of Nissan, where do you stop? . . . Nobody wants to go to work on Monday and say, 'The guy in the Toyota beat Dale Earnhardt Jr. yesterday.' America is the home of the muscle cars. And who wants to say, 'Our American hot-rod got whipped by a rice-rocket'?"

Toyota's entry into NASCAR's truck series raised the thorny question of just what qualified as an American-made vehicle. Was it a vehicle that was built entirely in the United States? A vehicle built with foreign parts but assembled in the United States? A vehicle built in the United States for a company based in Japan? A vehicle built in Canada or Mexico for a company based in Detroit? A vehicle built by a German manufacturer that had bought what once was an American company?

NASCAR's more prominent team owners had no such trouble. Rick Hendrick was the country's biggest Honda dealer; Roger Penske, among the biggest Toyota dealers. Even former NASCAR champion Cale Yarborough owned two car dealerships in Florence, South Carolina—one of which sold Hondas, the other sold Mazdas. "We never would have thought about this in my day," said Yarborough, then sixty-four. "But since Toyota and Honda and other Japanese companies play such an important role in the automobile industry in the United States, I think this day has got to come. I don't think it will hurt the sport. All race fans don't drive Fords and Chevrolets and Pontiacs anymore."

But the issue became more emotionally charged as Toyota prepared to enter the Nextel Cup ranks in 2007 with seven full-time Camry teams. No matter where the Japanese giant had competed, whether in CART, the Indy Racing League, sports cars, or off-road racing, it had developed a reputation for spending whatever it took to win. And several established NASCAR team owners warned that Toyota would do the same in stock-car racing and, in the process, skew the sport's finely tuned competitive balance and drive up the costs for everyone. Jack Roush, NASCAR's leading Ford owner, likened the challenge to "war." To gird for the arms race, he asked

Ford executives for an additional $20 million a year and sold a 50 percent stake in his team to an investor group led by Boston Red Sox principal owner John Henry.

On the eve of the 2007 Daytona 500, NASCAR chairman Brian France was asked about concerns that Toyota's deep pockets would drive up costs. Rather than deny there was any basis for the fear, France saluted it. "That's capitalism!" France told Jeff Greenfield, host of the PBS program *CEO Exchange*. "That's part of how it works!"

Toyota was already winning the race in automotive dealerships across the country. Its Camry had overtaken Ford's Taurus as the country's top-selling sedan. More significantly, Toyota was poised to overtake General Motors as the world's largest carmaker in the second quarter of 2007. Detroit's major automakers were hemorrhaging money while Toyota was reaping record profits, helped by a favorable exchange rate for the Japanese yen. Toyota was also unburdened by costly retirement and health benefits that the U.S. automakers had committed to decades earlier for an aging workforce.

By becoming a player in NASCAR, Toyota hoped to recast its image in the eyes of the American car-buying public. The company had already established that its cars and trucks were reliable and durable. What it wanted *now* was to establish that it wasn't a "foreign" carmaker and, above all, that its cars and trucks didn't represent a threat to American jobs. NASCAR, the thinking went, would give Toyota an American identity. NASCAR, in short, would make Toyota "one of the guys."

NASCAR had something to gain through the association, too. Toyota's participation bolstered NASCAR's argument that stock-car racing had become an emerging, global force. Toyota also was willing to invest millions of its own money to promote the sport. And Toyota represented a valuable safety net. In the unlikely event that one of the financially troubled U.S. automakers was forced to pull out of racing because of a major restructuring or sale, NASCAR would look smart for having diversified its competitive ranks.

Still, disgruntled fans ranted on NASCAR websites, in chat rooms, and over talk-radio airwaves as the contingent of Toyota drivers prepared to qualify their Camrys for the 2007 Daytona 500. One longtime fan and General Motors employee launched a website, FansAgainstRacingToyotas.com, dubbing his cause "FART." The irony was that the Camry was the only competitor in NASCAR's top ranks that was made in the United States. The Ford Fusion was made in Mexico; the Chevy Monte Carlo and Dodge Charger, in Canada. And Toyota's most high-profile driver, three-time Daytona 500 winner Dale Jarrett, pointed this out every chance he got.

Mike Skinner, as the driver of Toyota's top Tundra in NASCAR's truck series, was well acquainted with fans' hostility. "You're always going to have your die-hard people, and that's what has made NASCAR healthy," Skinner said. "But one thing I'd like to bring to people's attention is that the TV you're going to turn on tonight and watch, most likely, wasn't made here. Your microwave and your refrigerators—half the things in your home—were made in China or Japan or somewhere else, for that matter. What we have to do as Americans is enjoy the fact that we live in a free country and *enjoy* the competition of NASCAR. And if Toyota is a part of that competition, then so be it. Let 'em come into our marketplace and *earn* their spot, just like everybody else has."

Mindful of the potential for an icy reception by NASCAR fans, Toyota tiptoed into the Nextel Cup ranks with arguably the most polite ad campaign in automotive history, built around the theme "Thanks for having us!" Said Toyota's White: "It's more an approach of blending in rather than standing out. That's Toyota's philosophy."

General Motors and Ford took a different approach, using the 2007 Daytona 500 as an occasion for trumpeting their companies' deep American roots. GM's ad campaign made no reference to the

232 · LIZ CLARKE

merits of its vehicles. It focused entirely on patriotism and was built around an anthem sung by John Cougar Mellencamp with the catchy refrain "This is *our* country!" and set against a backdrop of little boys playing football, a triumphant Dale Earnhardt raising his fists in Victory Lane, and Chevy trucks rumbling through the mud.

GM also sponsored the American-themed prerace show for that year's Daytona 500, in which each driver, after being introduced to the crowd, climbed into the back of a red, white, or blue Chevrolet Corvette convertible for a lap around the track. The national anthem was performed by the country duo Big & Rich as six red, white, and blue Chevy trucks roared down the frontstretch pulling a massive American flag that fluttered in the breeze behind it.

Ford's prerace ad campaign wasn't as lavish, but it struck a similar theme. It included a radio spot that took a slightly veiled swipe at Toyota's Texas-built Tundra. "Lately, it's been fashionable to talk about trucks made in America," the husky voice in the commercial said. "Our trucks *made* America."

Before the green flag was thrown on the season-opening Daytona 500, Toyota was smarting from a massive black eye. It had been delivered by Michael Waltrip, the glib, charismatic driver with the famous last name who Toyota executives had hoped would give them instant credibility. Instead, Waltrip was exposed as a cheat during a routine inspection of his No. 55 Camry following his qualifying attempt. NASCAR inspectors discovered an illegal substance in the car's gas line, reportedly similar to jet fuel.

• • •

In many ways, Brian France's NASCAR had shaken the stereotypes of being a peculiarly southern institution.

For an eleven-year span that ended in 2006, every driver who won stock-car racing's prestigious Rookie of the Year honor came from outside the South. Indiana had produced Tony Stewart, Ryan Newman, and Kenny Irwin. Mike Skinner and Kevin Harvick were

Californians. They were joined by Ricky Craven of Maine, Johnny Benson of Michigan, Missouri's Jamie McMurray, Kyle Busch from Nevada, Kasey Kahne from Washington, and Matt Kenseth of Wisconsin.

By 2005, the Nextel Cup series held more races in California than in North Carolina. That was the year that Rockingham's North Carolina Motor Speedway was lopped from the NASCAR schedule, just as its neighbor to the west, North Wilkesboro, had been a decade earlier.

And its Busch Series crossed another boundary in 2007, adding a race in Montreal to complement its date in Mexico City.

Yet NASCAR's audience, as well as its competitors, remained overwhelmingly white.

In Brian France's view, diversifying NASCAR's ranks of fans and drivers, and doing a better job in particular with African Americans, was the sport's next critical challenge.

Brian's father, Bill France Jr., had consistently brushed off suggestions that NASCAR needed to do something to attract more minorities. When asked about the sport's all-white grandstands and garages, his stock answer was that the sport had always been open to everyone. His son, however, argued that NASCAR needed to do more than simply fling open its doors, if for no other reason than to sustain its impressive rate of growth.

"The whole mission—after you get the racing right—is to grow the franchise, grow the awareness, grow the participation every way you can grow it because that's when everybody can financially win," Brian France said in a 2007 interview. "We're trying to be good marketers. And you can't miss an entire market and say you're a good marketer. So if we don't get diversity right, in my view, over the long term that will be one big missed opportunity. Socially, of course, it's the right thing to do—to knock barriers down and reach out. We embraced that a long time ago. We're now into just not wanting to miss the market."

. . .

NASCAR's color barrier had been broken forty-six years earlier by a Danville, Virginia, garage owner named Wendell Scott, who entered stock-car racing's elite ranks in 1961.

In Hollywood's glossy treatment of his life, the 1977 movie, *Greased Lightning,* Scott was portrayed to comedic effect by Richard Pryor. The credits claimed the film was based on Scott's "true life story," and it ended with him triumphing over adversity and winning the big race.

It was true that Scott was the first (and, to date, only) African American to win a major NASCAR race. But it's also true that he was initially denied the victory after he lapped second-place finisher Buck Baker two times in his 1962 Chevy Impala to win a 100-mile race in Jacksonville, Florida, on December 1, 1963. Part of the reason, the story went, was that the promoter was nervous about the Victory Lane scene, where the beauty queen traditionally kissed the winner. So Baker was presented the trophy instead. Scott protested. After the photographers left, the promoter apologized and gave Scott his $1,150 winnings. Scott never got the trophy.

In a racing career that spanned 32 years, Scott won 128 lower-level races before moving up to NASCAR's big leagues in 1961. There, he competed alongside greats like Richard Petty and David Pearson in 506 Grand National races. But he died with little to show for his time in racing and a legacy that was all but forgotten.

Scott got his first break in racing at the local racetrack in Danville. The owner was having trouble attracting crowds. So in what may have been auto-racing's first initiative to diversify its audience, he went to the police station looking for names of black residents with speeding records. Police provided them with Scott's name, and a racing career was born. Scott campaigned in a beat-up 1935 Ford and won the third race he entered.

He toured what was known as the Dixie circuit—short tracks in southwestern Virginia—and won the state's late-model title in 1960. The next year he moved up to NASCAR's Grand National ranks, the equivalent of modern-day Nextel Cup. He wrote letters to Detroit automakers seeking financial backing. He wrote the beer companies, too, and a Philadelphia-based trucking company. None offered sponsorship money. So he competed as an independent. Scott never raced new cars, just "junk," as he later described it. Some of the better-funded drivers, such as Ned Jarrett and Junior Johnson, gave him spare parts and used racing tires. Other drivers looked for any opening to put his car into the wall. Scott worked on his cars himself, and he relied on his sons and cousins to service his car during pit stops.

Winston-Salem's Bowman-Gray Stadium refused to let him race in the early 1960s. Locals wouldn't let Scott's sons, who traveled with him, use the restrooms, either. Darlington Raceway also refused his entry blanks for three years but relented in 1965.

His biggest payday came in the 1967 Daytona 500, in which he finished fifteenth and won $2,200. What was billed as his biggest opportunity came in May 1972, when the general manager at Charlotte Motor Speedway announced he would provide Scott with a first-rate Chevrolet built from Junior Johnson's powerhouse stable for the World 600.

"I feel sorry for Wendell," the track's manager, Richard Howard, told the *Charlotte News.* "I took a look at his old car and realized how much trouble he's had. He's never had a chance to win a race. Well, I decided to give him a Chevrolet and a chance to win one."

Scott was thrilled. "I'm $7,000 in the hole," he told the newspaper. "Everybody in Danville who has got any confidence in me, I owe. Maybe I can make that back in one race."

But the car, it turned out, was a third-rate backup, and its engine expired 283 laps into the 400-lap race. Scott was running ninth at the time, and he collected $1,710.

The following year he quit competing full-time after he was involved in a nineteen-car pileup at Talladega. Scott had staked his savings and borrowed another $12,000 to get a car ready to race at the Alabama speedway that day. His car was totaled. It took him eleven years to pay off the debt.

Scott's long struggle to carve out a meaningful place in NASCAR underscored the harsh lesson every driver confronts. To succeed, a racer needs money and opportunity. In Scott's day, most African Americans who loved racecars were short on the former and denied the latter. But the fact that no black driver managed to build on his legacy and become the second African American to win a major NASCAR race suggested that little had changed in the four decades that followed.

Wendell Scott died in 1990, at age sixty-nine, after a six-month battle with spinal cancer. His funeral, held at Danville's North New Hope Baptist Church the day after Christmas, was the first racing story I covered. The modest sanctuary wasn't big enough to hold the seven hundred relatives, friends, and handful of former racers who attended. I remember how proud his children looked, how handsome his sons were, and thinking what a remarkable legacy he had left, though none of the children, unlike so many racers' children, had followed their father into the sport.

The program for the service included a poem that Wendell Jr., one of three sons, had written about his father and his No. 34 racecar when he was twelve years old. It read:

34, 34 Where next do you flee,
North Carolina, South Carolina, maybe even Tennessee.
It's a cute little Chevy with great big thick tires
And the way she roars around those ole dirt tracks,
Seems as though she's soaring to the clouds.
So if you're at home asleep one night and you hear a great big roar,
Have no fear, just lie still,
It's only 34.

A handful of former racers served as honorary pallbearers, including Jarrett, Johnson, Earl Brooks, and Leonard Wood. Jarrett spoke during the service on behalf of the NASCAR racers.

"He helped open many doors in racing, but more important, he helped to open hearts and minds," Jarrett said. "He was not as fortunate as some of us as far as equipment. I don't know any man who worked harder and did better with what he had."

Others paid tribute to Scott's dignity, recalling how he never complained about his second-rate equipment or the knocks he took, both subtle and overt, for no reason other than his skin color. Afterward, Brooks, his old friend and fellow racer from Lynchburg, Virginia, remembered how Scott's brush with fame—the big Hollywood movie purportedly based on his life—also left him short-changed.

"That story was written in my house," Brooks said. "Wendell came up, and we sat in my living room and told stories about everything we'd done, and they ran about five or six tape recorders. We were promised a lot of money. But it was just a promise. A promise you couldn't spend."

• • •

Scott's lone major NASCAR victory stood as an anomaly rather than the advent of a new era for stock-car racing. Much the same could be said for Janet Guthrie, who in 1977 became the first woman to compete in the Daytona 500.

Guthrie's arrival in stock-car racing had been engineered by Charlotte Motor Speedway's Humpy Wheeler, who'd been following the media frenzy surrounding her effort to qualify for the 1976 Indianapolis 500. When Guthrie failed to make the field, Wheeler lined up a car owner, Charlotte banking executive Lynda Ferreri, who was willing to field a stock car for Guthrie in his World 600 NASCAR race, held the same weekend at Indy. Why let all that great publicity go to waste? Wheeler thought.

Guthrie had proven her courage and confidence at speed in nu-merous arenas—as a pilot, flight instructor, aerospace engineer, and accomplished racer in other series. But NASCAR was a world apart, and it was hard to say what was more alien: the culture of the garage, so clearly hostile to her presence; or the heavy, unresponsive stock cars, which weighed 3,700 pounds at the time and had no power steering. In her biography, *Janet Guthrie: A Life at Full Throttle,* she re-counted her struggle to conquer both.

Prevailing sentiment was that a woman wasn't physically strong enough to muscle a stock car around an oval—and particularly not in the sport's longest race, a 600-miler that took more than four hours to complete. The sport's biggest stars, Richard Petty and Cale Yarbor-ough, gave her an icy reception. NASCAR president Bill France Jr. was livid about Wheeler's promotional stunt to put a woman in one of his races. But apart from getting his ears blasted by France over the phone, Wheeler considered it a wild success. ABC clamored for TV rights, and he sold a record 103,000 tickets. While many fans cheered Guthrie as she went out to qualify the car, others heckled, "No tits in the pits! Get the tits out of the pits!"

Guthrie went the distance and finished fifteenth, despite being cut off in traffic by Petty's famed No. 43 in what she considered an unsportsmanlike manner. Asked about it afterward, she said simply, "Racing is an aggressive sport."

NASCAR saw a lot more of Guthrie in 1977. With backing from Kelly Services, which supplied businesses with temporary office help, she campaigned for NASCAR's Rookie of the Year honors in a green Chevrolet Laguna emblazoned with the phrase "Kelly Girl." And despite strained relations with her engine builder, the legendary Ralph Moody, she battled Ricky Rudd closely for top rookie honors, finishing ahead of him at several tracks.

Gradually she earned the grudging respect of some drivers, Don-nie and Bobby Allison, among them. Even Yarborough conceded she could handle herself in a car. Others never came around. Near season's end, the Kelly brass announced it would fund her for only a handful of stock-car races the next year, saying that NASCAR's geographical reach didn't mirror its own market.

Guthrie shifted her attention back to open-wheel racing. And NASCAR's top ranks only saw an occasional woman try to make the field in the three decades that followed. There are hosts of theories why, including a hostile culture toward female racers and the lack of opportunities for young girls to develop racing skills. In Guthrie's view, the one constant barrier women have faced has been money. She writes in the epilogue to her book: "I have said for years that what this sport needs is a woman with all the stuff that it takes, plus her own fortune."

Meanwhile, Tiger Woods and sisters Venus and Serena Williams were converting legions of fans to the predominantly white sports of golf and tennis. TV ratings spiked for each event they entered, and their success inspired youngsters of all backgrounds to pick up a golf club or tennis racket.

NASCAR responded, spurred largely by the automakers and corporate sponsors that wanted to see the sport's fan base more closely mirror the full spectrum of Americans who not only bought cars and trucks, but also bought cereal, beer, cell phones, and power tools.

In 2003, Joe Gibbs Racing joined with former NFL lineman Reggie White, an avid NASCAR fan, to start two grassroots late-model teams for the sole purpose of giving young minorities an opportunity to develop their racing skills. One of its prospects, Aric Almirola, whose father had fled Cuba in the mid-1960s, progressed to NASCAR's Nextel Cup ranks midway through the 2007 season, sharing a ride in the No. 01 Chevy with Mark Martin. NASCAR followed Gibbs's lead in 2004, launching a "Drive for Diversity" program to cultivate a new generation of minority and female drivers and crew members. Other NASCAR team owners, including Richard Childress, Rick Hendrick, and Ray Evernham, also subsidized minorities and young women who dreamed of careers in stock-car racing.

But the driver with the greatest potential of shaking up stock-car racing's traditional demographic wasn't the product of any such initiatives. Colombia's Juan Pablo Montoya, thirty-one, was fully established as one of the brightest racing talents in the world—having won the 1999 CART championship, the 2000 Indianapolis 500, and seven Formula 1 races—when he announced in summer 2006 that he was quitting F1, where his prospects at a front-running ride were dimming, to race in NASCAR's Nextel Cup series.

It was a preposterous story line. So preposterous that it was only a slight variation on the plot of Will Ferrell's latest slapstick comedy, *Talladega Nights,* a lampoon of stock-car racing in which a French Formula 1 driver brings his prissy airs and Perrier sponsorship to Alabama to do battle with NASCAR's dim-witted hero Ricky Bobby. Montoya was, in effect, doing just that, becoming the first F1 driver (as well as the first part-time resident of Monte Carlo) to compete in NASCAR.

NASCAR officials were thrilled. Montoya's improbable career turn promised to deliver much of what they longed for—international validation, more Hispanic fans, and greater exposure among auto-racing sophisticates worldwide.

Montoya's stock-car racing debut in a third-tier ARCA race that fall at Talladega, Alabama, was front-page news in Colombia. Diego Fernando Mejia, a Colombian journalist who had traveled the globe chronicling Montoya's exploits for the previous six years, was suddenly a fixture in the NASCAR press box. Montoya's NASCAR team, Chip Ganassi Racing, unveiled a Spanish-language website. ESPN Deportes, a Spanish-speaking sports radio network, signed a five-year deal to broadcast NASCAR races and news updates. And the following season, NASCAR unveiled a new website, NASCAR .com/espanol.

Montoya made his Nextel Cup debut in the 2006 season finale at the Homestead-Miami Speedway. Track officials had conducted market research in Miami's Latin community well before Montoya considered switching to stock cars and found that its residents weren't attracted to NASCAR because they didn't feel welcome in the sport. The track had been trying to change that sentiment by playing Latin music and selling Latin food in the carnival-like midway behind the grandstands. They also staged the finals of a salsa-dancing competition on race day, called Dancing for the Cup. Montoya promised to be an even bigger draw.

Meanwhile, Montoya couldn't believe how welcome NASCAR drivers were making him feel. Kevin Harvick and Casey Mears gave him tips on getting his racecar to handle on the track. Jimmie Johnson invited him to his motor home to hang out. In six years in F1, Montoya said, not one driver had done that!

But getting comfortable in stock cars took time. Nextel Cup cars weighed more than twice what F1 cars did, yet had skinnier tires and brakes that weren't nearly as effective. To Montoya, stock cars had the responsiveness of an ancient tortoise. He also couldn't believe how close to the concrete wall NASCAR drivers ran. And he was shocked by all the bumping and shoving. If the fenderless F1 cars touched wheels, it was almost sure to cause a wreck, so F1 drivers avoided even slight contact. Not so in NASCAR, where drivers rubbed on each other's cars for all sorts of reason—to give someone a helpful, aerodynamic push through traffic, for example, or to express anger or impatience. It was a huge adjustment for Montoya, who had trouble distinguishing a friendly push from a hostile one.

He was still trying to figure out the difference, in fact, when contact from Ryan Newman sent him into the wall with just sixteen laps remaining in his first Nextel Cup race. Montoya's No. 42 Dodge smacked the concrete with its rear end and exploded in flames. He calmly climbed out, waved to the crowd, and proclaimed himself proud to have proven he could run up front with NASCAR's best.

But it was Montoya who dished out the contact in claiming his first NASCAR victory, the 2007 Busch race at Mexico City's Autodromo Rodriguez Hernandez. After falling to twenty-first because of a botched pit stop, Montoya charged through the field in the waning laps and worked his way up to second, trailing teammate Scott Pruett with eight laps to go. Montoya's Dodge was clearly faster, and he had plenty of time to execute one last pass that would put him in the lead. But he refused to be patient. He knocked Pruett sideways as they entered a turn, then veered across the grass and roared back on the track.

Ganassi, owner of both racecars, winced in dismay over Montoya's roughhousing. Pruett's crew chief, Tony Glover, flung his arms in disgust. Montoya's crew chief, Brad Parrott, hung his head as if his puppy had just soiled the neighbor's carpet. But the crowd cheered, and Colombian flags waved as Montoya hopped on his car's roof and pumped his fists.

"That was just no-good, low, nasty, dirty driving!" Pruett groused, flashing a double–thumbs down for the ESPN cameras.

Aggression was Montoya's strong suit, and his fellow racers would see more of it in the months to come. He was fast, brash, and unburdened by any notion of a stock car's limits. And it rankled several of his new peers. After Montoya was implicated in a pileup during the Nextel Open, a high-stakes feature race that determined which drivers advanced to the sport's all-star race, fellow driver Paul Menard cracked over his radio: "Pedro takes out five cars."

In the next month, in June, Montoya won his first Nextel Cup race, on the road course in Sonoma, California. Montoya's rookie season was successful enough to lure other international open-wheel racers to NASCAR in much the same way that Jeff Gordon had done on a national scale a decade earlier. Former Formula 1 champion Jacques Villeneuve of Canada made his Nextel Cup debut at Talladega in 2007 in preparation for a full-scale campaign in 2008. And the defending Indianapolis 500 champion, Dario Franchitti of Scotland, started his apprenticeship in the ARCA series. Like Villeneuve, Franchitti signed on to compete in NASCAR full-time the following year.

NASCAR officials interpreted the open-wheel defections as a compliment of the highest order: affirmation of the competitiveness of their races, the safety of their cars, and the handsome financial reward for racers who excelled on stock-car racing's high banks. But many of the sport's core fans weren't as enthused. In September 2007, the *Charlotte Observer* conducted an online poll that presented the issue as follows:

Foreign cars and foreign drivers are a hot topic for many NASCAR fans. How do you feel about stock-car racing going global?

More than seven thousand responded. Fewer than one in five (17 percent) checked the response, *It's great. Fresh talent might make for better racing.*

About one-third (32 percent) checked, *"Don't care. Let's race."* And more than half (54 percent) checked, *"It's wrong, and it troubles me."*

Said Richard Petty: "Two or three of those guys sprinkled in is great because it gives us worldwide recognition and international PR. But it does *not* help anything at the turnstile. Guys in Iowa are not going to pull for somebody from Brazil—or from England or France or wherever they're from. It ain't gonna work that way."

What NASCAR was banking on in the push to diversify its audience is that it would gain two new fans for each one it might lose.

THAT'S ENTERTAINMENT

I n the end, despite all the glitzy new speedways, the migration from the Southeast to major markets, and the exposure that came with its billion-dollar TV deals, what drove NASCAR's popularity in the twenty-first century was the same thing that had driven it at the outset. Stock-car racing's chief selling point was the personalities of its drivers—personalities that had never been far removed from the fans.

And more than six years after his death, Dale Earnhardt remained NASCAR's strongest personality. If anyone had overlooked that, they were reminded of it twice during the 2007 season: on April 21, when Jeff Gordon tied Earnhardt's mark of seventy-six career victories, and again the next weekend, on April 29, when Gordon passed Earnhardt by winning his seventy-seventh race on a track that was hallowed ground to Earnhardt fans, Talladega Superspeedway. And he did it on what would have been Earnhardt's fifty-sixth birthday.

Gordon had planned for weeks how to honor the late champion when the time came, mindful of the passions it was likely to stir. So after getting that seventy-sixth victory at Phoenix International

Raceway, taking the lead with a bump of Tony Stewart that surely would have made Earnhardt smile, Gordon grabbed a giant black flag with the Intimidator's famous No. 3 from his crew chief, who had been bringing it to every race for the occasion, and held it out his driver's side window as he circled the track in tribute. A few fans booed, which Gordon had expected. But Dale Earnhardt Jr. was touched by the gesture and went to Victory Lane to thank Gordon on behalf of his family.

The crowd at Talladega, where Earnhardt's command of the high banks had been unrivaled, was a tougher bunch. They hated Gordon simply for showing up. They still blamed Gordon for denying Earnhardt that eighth championship in 1995, and they resented him for hogging Victory Lane ever since. They cheered when Gordon wrecked, and they raged when he won—particularly in 2004, when fans threw beer bottles and trash after Gordon beat Dale Jr. for a victory.

So it was significant that it was Dale Jr., in the days leading up to Talladega's April race in 2007, who spoke out about how dangerous, stupid, and generally uncool it was to throw bottles on a racetrack. He urged fans to throw toilet paper, if they had to throw something, hoping to preempt an ugly scene. But the message didn't get through to everyone. Gordon won the race, and hard-core Earnhardt fans erupted. By day's end, twelve were arrested for pelting the track with bottles and banned from the speedway for life.

On one hand, the scene underscored Dale Earnhardt's enduring hold on NASCAR fans. On another, it highlighted the fact that no current NASCAR driver (Dale Jr. excepted) evoked the same profound passion that the Intimidator inspired.

Drivers' personalities had become more muted as NASCAR's popularity grew. As a rule, twenty-first-century stock-car racers were younger, better mannered, more carefully groomed, and more polished than their predecessors. And it was no accident. NASCAR drivers weren't being paid just to race the car; they were being compensated (and handsomely so) to sell their sponsors' products and sell NASCAR itself.

Richard Petty had done precisely that his whole career, pioneering the art of being a sport's ambassador. But the stakes were far higher now, with major sponsors spending $20 million or more each year to link their corporate image to the performance of champions such as Gordon, Jimmie Johnson, and Tony Stewart. More than a hundred Fortune 500 companies advertised on the hoods of NASCAR's flying billboards, as its racecars were often called. The scrutiny of drivers' behavior was more intense, as the often tempestuous Stewart learned. Stewart not only drew a fine from NASCAR for smacking a tape recorder out of a reporter's hand once, but he also was fined by his sponsor—an unprecedented public reprimand. On the matter of drivers' behavior, NASCAR and its sponsors were of like mind. The sport and its stars needed to appeal to every demographic and alienate none.

To Humpy Wheeler, the veteran promoter charged with filling the 160,000-seat grandstands at Lowe's Motor Speedway, all the polish and perfection was cause for concern. "Perhaps the worst thing, and the most difficult thing, is that the drivers are losing a lot of color—*that,* and us not being able to replace Dale Earnhardt Senior," Wheeler said. "We have lost a lot of fans because he's not here. We lost the last workingman's driver, somebody that the shrimp-boat captain, the mill worker, the common, ordinary man can pull for."

In Wheeler's view, the irony was that if another Earnhardt came along, NASCAR would turn its back. Earnhardt's exterior was just too rough for corporate CEOs to gamble on. NASCAR's new wave of sponsors didn't want a driver who looked as if he'd just crawled out from under a car. They wanted a driver who looked as if he'd just driven that car to the golf course.

"There's just too much homogenization for me," Wheeler continued. "NASCAR has always been built around characters. But the problem is, we don't have any! All these young drivers—they've all been racing since they were seven, and they've been brought up a certain way, and they talk a certain way, or they don't say anything at all! Where is Muhammad Ali when you need him?"

If drivers had gotten bland, NASCAR had only itself to blame. Through monetary fines, probations, and point deductions, the sport had repeatedly sent the message that spontaneity wasn't smiled upon, particularly if it involved coarse language. Its most stinging rebuke came in October 2004 at Talladega, where Dale Earnhardt Jr., who was in the thick of the battle for the championship, made a stirring charge through the field to claim his fifth victory at the daunting speedway. Moments after he climbed from his racecar, delirious with joy, he was asked by an NBC reporter about the significance of winning at Talladega five times.

"It don't mean shit right now!" he blurted out in self-deprecating glee. "Daddy's won here ten times!"

NASCAR officials slapped him with a $10,000 fine and docked him 25 points, which dropped him from first to second in the standings. Almost immediately Earnhardt's team appealed, arguing that an expletive uttered in euphoria didn't offend as much as one blurted in rage. NASCAR fans joined the fray, flooding phone lines at the sport's Daytona Beach headquarters and bombarding websites and Internet chat rooms with diatribes about what they deemed offensive and what they didn't. The vast majority sided with the twenty-nine-year-old Earnhardt Jr., who had bucked convention at almost every turn of his career to the delight of his fan following—the biggest in the sport.

To them, the punishment was too extreme—yet another sign that NASCAR, in its furious race for mass appeal, had lost touch with its southern, blue-collar roots. One fan wrote on NASCAR's official website: "NASCAR has gotten so out of hand with their li'l rulebook that I am threatening a boycott just because of their stupidity. People can say 'hell' and 'damn' and get away with it, but a little 'shit,' and it's boom! You are fined and docked. Hell, I had much rather hear someone say 'shit' than have to watch that morally inept *Will and Grace*."

NASCAR's sensitivity to profanity had been heightened by the uproar earlier that year over Janet Jackson's breast-baring halftime show during the National Football League's Super Bowl broadcast, which resulted in more than half a million complaints and a record $550,000 fine by the Federal Communications Commission against twenty CBS-owned stations. But Dale Jr.'s utterance barely drew notice. NBC received fewer than twenty complaints following the Talladega broadcast, and the FCC got a few dozen telephone and e-mail complaints.

In appealing NASCAR's sanctions, Richie Gilmore, an official with Dale Earnhardt Inc., which owned Dale Jr.'s No. 8 Chevrolet, wrote: "The popularity of this sport is based on colorful personalities and the fact that everyone can relate to the drivers and their emotions. Now, it seems like that's a detriment."

• • •

The demands of being a front-running NASCAR driver are littered with public-relations land mines. Increasingly, drivers turn to media consultants for help, whether with curbing their temper, overcoming shyness, or confronting a phobia of public speaking.

Kasey Kahne was among them. A native of the tiny farming community of Enumclaw, Washington, Kahne had never wanted to do anything but race. And he had mastered every rung on the open-wheel ladder, just as Gordon and Stewart had before him, when he got the chance to try stock cars, driving for car owner Robert Yates in NASCAR's Grand National Series in 2002. Kahne was wicked fast behind the wheel. But there was nothing that terrified him quite like public speaking. Nearly a decade later, he was still haunted by the hour-long history report that he had to give in front of his class in high school.

Until he got to NASCAR, Kahne had no idea that racecar drivers had to do anything but drive the car. He quickly learned that stock-car racers were always selling, whether selling themselves to prospective sponsors or selling a sponsor's product to the public. Those demands increased even more after he jumped to the Nextel Cup ranks in 2004. Kahne was twenty-three by then but easily could have passed for sixteen, with his slight build, soft-spoken voice, and aw-shucks manner. In street clothes—typically baggy jeans, sneakers, and a baseball cap—he looked more like an awestruck fan than a racer. But suddenly, he was the guy in the spotlight, with corporate executives, sales representatives, and hordes of reporters eager to hear what he had to say.

Kahne's race day often started with a trackside meet-and-greet with guests of his various sponsors. That was a challenge. But it wasn't nearly as difficult as the speech he had to make at NASCAR's awards banquet at the Waldorf-Astoria after winning the 2004 Rookie of the Year honors. He was out of his element just being in New York. Wearing a tuxedo only made him feel more out of place. He looked out from the stage that night, bright spotlights in his eyes, and saw all the drivers he had raced with, all the team owners and the sponsors dressed in tuxedos, too. There were wives and girlfriends in ball gowns. And he felt as if he belonged anywhere but at that spot.

"It was just so far from what I was used to," Kahne recalled. "It's very easy to do an interview in a driving suit; I'm perfectly fine with that. But when I get into that stuff, my knees start shaking a bit."

Enter Kathleen Hessert, founder of Charlotte-based Sports Media Challenge. Her office is in Charlotte's Carmel Executive Park—the sort of place you might go to get your investment portfolio reviewed, hire a website designer, or book a European vacation. Once past the fountain out front and the marble foyer in the lobby, you enter an office that's a sports-fan's dream. There's an impossibly oversized sneaker in a glass case that belonged to Shaquille O'Neal, an autographed football from Peyton Manning, and framed magazine covers of Hessert's protégés in golf, tennis, and gymnastics. A flat-screen, high-definition TV is mounted on the wall and tuned to ESPN. A grease board enumerates each employee's list of clients, with a marketing goal beside each name. Hessert's list reads, in part:

PEYTON—MORE

EVERNHAM—BUZZ

KASEY KAHNE—MORE

SHAQ—MORE

"One of the most fearful situations for Americans today, identified over and over again, is fear of public speaking," Hessert says. "It's number one in the Gallup Poll. The fear of dying is number seven."

She's a striking woman who resembles a young Phyllis George—perfectly accessorized, with a comforting, clearly enunciated voice. A former corporate communications specialist, Hessert started working with racecar drivers after her brother, a successful sports-car racer, asked for help with his interviewing skills. From that she launched a business that works strictly with sports figures. In 2006, Hessert took on a new client: NASCAR's 2004 Rookie of the Year, Kasey Kahne.

In Kahne's case, Hessert started with the basics. She studied his interviews in newspapers, magazines, and on TV and talked with him about which comments were effective and which weren't. The goal wasn't to quash a personality or to create one, she said. It was simply to analyze whether Kahne was getting his point across.

She explained what she calls the "Success Pie." For modern-day athletes, it's the key to maximizing their "personal brand." The pie has three equal pieces: performance, image, and exposure. If any piece is lacking, the athlete has failed to exploit his brand to its fullest.

Hessert identified Kahne's strength—his blue eyes—and explained how to use that more effectively. That meant not wearing sunglasses during TV interviews, not pulling his baseball cap so low it obscured his eyes, and concentrating on making eye contact with his audience. She also talked about how young he looked and suggested not shaving for a few days. The stubble gave him the credibility that comes with age. But the idea was short-lived. Soon afterward, Kahne signed a sponsorship deal with Gillette, and he had to start shaving again.

Then she moved to a more substantive analysis of Kahne's effectiveness in the media: the Buzz Manager.

In NASCAR's early days it was easy to figure out how fans felt about a certain driver. They either cheered when he roared into Victory Lane or threw chicken bones and beer cans. But now the Internet teemed with more detailed information. So Hessert developed a web-based search engine, which she dubbed "Buzz Manager," to collect all the chatter, which she would sift through and analyze so her clients could tell at a glance what fans thought about them. Her Buzz Manager also helped corporate sponsors get a grassroots feel for the return on their stock-car racing investment. If NASCAR's notoriously brand-loyal fans hated a driver, his sponsor wouldn't sell as much cereal or beer. If they liked him, fans were probably buying in bulk.

Hessert developed an algorithm to come up with a specific number—based on the frequency of mentions on the Internet, the volume of chatter, and the influence of the source—that conveyed at a glance what the "buzz" was about an athlete. She called it the Buzz Rating. And Kahne's was particularly high—seven on a ten-point scale—during the week he was named to the President's Council on Volunteerism in 2006. Fans looked favorably on his charitable work. Conversely, Michael Waltrip's Buzz Rating was low the week after NASCAR officials found the illegal substance in his Toyota's fuel line earlier that year at Daytona.

Finally, Hessert helped Kahne learn to deftly mention a sponsor's name in interviews and do what NASCAR's Miss Winston had done so well: get a sponsor's logo on TV. Hawking the sponsor's product had been an obligatory chore for NASCAR drivers for decades. But simply blurting out thanks to a laundry-list of companies was no longer considered effective communication. There was an art to dropping a sponsor's name, and it took multiple forms.

First was finding a way to weave the sponsor's name or product in conversation, as if it naturally arose. Kahne learned this particular lesson well. While being interviewed during a rain delay at one NASCAR race, Kahne told the TV audience that he was thinking about hopping in his car and running out to get his crew members some of that great McDonald's coffee. The fast-food giant, one of Kahne's secondary sponsors, had just launched a line of flavored coffees that week.

Another method was product placement. Tony Stewart won't be interviewed after a race without an Old Spice towel draped over his shoulder. The towel serves no purpose other than to display the logo.

The well-timed gesture is another. Jeff Gordon delays his replies to TV reporters' questions so he can take a swig from a Pepsi, carefully turning the bottle's logo toward the camera first. The ritual is aped by all drivers with a beverage sponsorship. Then there is Scott Pruett, whose Busch car is sponsored by Juicy Fruit gum. During one ESPN broadcast, Pruett actually paused during his postrace remarks to pull a wad of gum from his mouth.

"Juicy Fruit!" he announced.

• • •

To Brian France, it wasn't enough for the sport's drivers to be known simply for hawking sponsors' products at racetracks. He wanted them to become as recognizable *out* of their racing suits as they were in them. Well before he became NASCAR's CEO in 2003, France opened a NASCAR office in Hollywood to cultivate the entertainment industry's help in making stock-car racers crossover stars.

France hired Dick Glover, a former ESPN and Disney executive, to run the office. He then met with the head of every major studio to introduce stock-car racing to the uninitiated and dispel stereotypes that it was strictly a down-scale, red-state phenomenon. France's sales pitch was direct: NASCAR had 75 million brand-loyal fans who were three times as likely to buy products associated with the sport than rival brands. He also stressed NASCAR's openness to corporate tie-ins—whether that meant splashing ads for movies on its racecars' hoods; inviting movie stars to wave the green flag or give the famous command, "Gentlemen, start your engines!"; or collaborating on actual movie productions by supplying NASCAR footage, opening its speedways for the filming of racing sequences, or consulting on dialog and story lines.

The stance stood in sharp contrast to the posture of Major League Baseball, which beat a frantic retreat on a promotional campaign for *Spider-Man 2* in 2004 after baseball fans balked at the idea of putting movie logos on the bases during interleague play. "You'd have thought heaven and earth were going to fall," Glover recalled. "There was a big negative reaction, whereas in our sport, we're just the opposite. We have always embraced sponsorship."

Within six years of the launch of NASCAR's Entertainment Division, the initiative blossomed. Hollywood latched on to NASCAR's bumper to promote its latest movies, TV projects, and music. Racecar hoods advertised major studio releases from *Pirates of the Caribbean III: Dead Man's Chest* to *The Last Temptation of Christ*. Celebrities such as Ashton Kutcher, Jessica Alba, and Ben Affleck suddenly popped up in the NASCAR garage to get their pictures taken with Dale Earnhardt Jr. And NASCAR personalities and story lines turned up in almost every form of entertainment imaginable: from cartoons for the prekindergarten set to soap operas; from reality TV to made-for-TV dramas; from hip-hop videos to MTV Cribs; from Harlequin romance novels to major studio releases.

In 2006, NASCAR sashayed down the red carpet in two of the year's top-ten-grossing films: *Cars,* the second highest grossing (at $244.1 million), the Disney/Pixar tale of a brash young stock-car racer named Lightning McQueen who learns that life is about more than trophies; and *Talladega Nights: The Ballad of Ricky Bobby,* the tenth biggest earner ($148.2 million), which NASCAR's Hollywood office collaborated on. *Talladega Nights* was reportedly sold to Sony Pictures on nothing more than a six-word pitch: "Will Ferrell as a NASCAR driver." NASCAR officials got wind of the project when someone phoned their Los Angeles office and asked how to spell "Talladega." They jumped on the chance to get involved, offering racetracks, drivers, and expertise. NASCAR had a representative on the movie set every day of shooting, and two of its executives ended up with production credits.

NASCAR didn't collaborate on the jokes, which roundly mocked stock-car racing's quirky culture. "Certainly we didn't want to be anywhere near the creative process," Brian France said. But when the movie was finished, France said he found it "gut-wrenchingly funny" and viewed its potshots at the sport "no different than the stereotypes about journalism" in Ferrell's previous hit, *Anchorman.*

Added France: "Everybody said it couldn't be done: that a sports league would not be able to mesh from A to Z with a theatrical release. That from script to production to marketing to distribution to final product, they wouldn't let us have a role in that. We changed all that."

NASCAR drivers started appearing on unlikely TV shows, too. Carl Edwards, whose signature move at the track was doing celebratory back flips off his car-door ledge before heading to Victory Lane, had a bit part as a Homeland Security officer on an episode of the Fox drama *24.* David Stremme was singled out as a member of the audience during a taping of *American Idol.* Jamie McMurray had a cameo on *The West Wing,* playing a NASCAR driver who riled the president's wife by kissing her in Victory Lane. And Dale Earnhardt Jr. appeared in a music video with Jay-Z.

NASCAR's estimated thirty million female fans weren't overlooked in the campaign. NASCAR's book-licensing division forged a partnership with Harlequin Romance, which published three NASCAR-themed novels in 2006 and sixteen more the next year. Edwards, among NASCAR's single drivers, appeared as a character in one of the books, *Speed Dating,* by Nancy Warren. To the dismay of Edwards's sizable female following, he wasn't involved in a torrid, illicit liaison in the novel. NASCAR retained approval over content, insisting that nothing be more racy than PG-13. So Warren kept Edwards out of any compromising positions in the book, characterizing him as an all-around good guy who offered advice to the fictional lovelorn protagonists.

To celebrate the book's launch, Harlequin held a "speed-dating" event at Daytona International Speedway the week of the 500. Edwards made an appearance, though he didn't take part in the frenzied courtship ritual, in which available men plop down on one side of a long banquet table across from an equal number of available women and chat for a few minutes before sliding down one seat at the sound of a buzzer. Instead, Edwards sat in a director's chair on the stage and fielded fans' questions about racing and love. He wore jeans, boots, and a navy polo shirt with a Harlequin logo on it. He talked about how his mother read Harlequin books. And he blushed a lot, especially when Warren discussed how the genre had changed. "The romance novel's hero . . . it's not that bare-chested pirate anymore. It's more contemporary. Like Carl!" she said, turning to Edwards and looking him over approvingly. "A little larger than life. Could he be any *more* gorgeous? And he's just a general nice guy!"

Edwards then waved a green flag, which signaled that the time for "speed dating" had begun.

According to NASCAR figures, its fans devour eight hours of programming about the sport each week. They watch races on TV, monitor garage news and rumors online, argue about caution flags in Internet chat rooms, and play NASCAR video games, pretending they are Tony Stewart and Dale Jr. "We are a sports brand, but we are also an entertainment brand and lifestyle brand," said Mark Dyer, then NASCAR's vice president of licensing. "The wonderful thing about our sport is, it seems like there is no end to the avenues we can create to follow this sport."

. . .

There was no mistaking NASCAR's most successful crossover star in the charge for mainstream appeal. It was Dale Earnhardt Jr., who had written a *New York Times* best seller, promoted Drakkar cologne, hung out with rock stars, voiced the No. 8 Chevy in *Cars,* and appeared in music videos by a range of artists. But the extent of his offtrack pursuits apparently rankled his car owner and stepmother, Teresa Earnhardt. And their disagreement over his priorities erupted in the biggest NASCAR story of 2007. It started when Teresa aired her grievances in the *Wall Street Journal,* telling the newspaper in December 2006 that Dale Jr., the sport's biggest star, needed to decide whether he wanted to be an entertainer or a racecar driver.

The comments lifted a veil on what had been a strained relationship for years. Dale Jr.'s parents divorced when he and his sister, Kelley, were two and four. It was Dale Earnhardt's second failed marriage; the first had produced a son, Kerry, who lived with his mother following his parents' split. Dale Jr. and Kelley did the same, moving in with their mother in Kannapolis while their dad chased his racing dreams. Dale Jr. was a typical little boy, for the most part. He was smaller than most his age and a little more shy. But he loved toys, hated chores, watched as much TV as he could, and dressed up as a devil for Halloween.

In the summer of 1981, when he and Kelley were six and eight, their mother's house burned down, and they were sent to live with their father—a man they didn't know well because he traveled so much, raising hell as the latest hard-charger to storm into NASCAR's top ranks.

Relatives and nannies took turns looking after the children. And Kelley filled in where they couldn't, making sure Dale Jr. had his lunch money and reminding him to do his chores. Earnhardt married a third time, in 1982, to Teresa Houston of Hickory, North Carolina, who came from a racing family, too. Within a few years, at age twelve, Dale Jr. was sent to military school. Kelley went with him, worried that he was too young to leave home.

"At the time I thought it was the worst possible thing that could ever happen to me," Dale Jr. said later. "Turns out, it was probably the best. It gave me the proper discipline and motivation that I carry with me to this day."

Growing up, Dale Jr. treasured nothing more than time with his dad. But there was so little of it. When there was, the boy seemed to tiptoe in his presence, as if worried he'd get in the way or say something wrong. A favorite photo taken in the infield of Bristol Motor Speedway in 1981, when Dale Jr. was six, tells the story. His father had crashed just thirty-one laps into the race and found himself stuck inside the track and forced to watch everyone else continue racing, because there wasn't a tunnel or bridge out. He looks slightly dazed in the picture, his eyes staring off in the distance. He wears a Wrangler cap, short-sleeved shirt with Western-style snaps, a hand-tooled leather belt, Wrangler jeans, and boots. And a blond-headed little boy dressed almost identically, in jeans, sneakers, and a Goodyear jacket, is huddled right beside him with a smile so big you'd think the Easter Bunny had just arrived with a giant basket of candy.

A poster-sized print of the photograph hangs in the lobby of JR Motorsports, the race shop Dale Jr. started as a hobby in 1999. Beside it is an explanation of why it means so much. "My dad was just as much an iconic figure to me as he was to his fans," Dale Jr. writes. "He was rugged, tough, always wore boots and never backed down from a challenge. I looked up to him, and no amount of time with him was ever enough. . . . We watched the rest of the race from the infield, where it became exceedingly hard to hide the fact that I was more excited that I got to spend 469 laps with him than disappointed that he only completed 31."

After Dale Jr. finished high school, all three grown Earnhardt children tried their hand at stock-car racing, competing in late-model cars they had to build and repair themselves. But he didn't think it would amount to anything, so he got a two-year automotive degree from Mitchell Community College, not far from home, and was on his way to a career as an auto mechanic when his father agreed to give him a chance in a NASCAR Grand National car. In just a few years, he went from being the fastest oil-change man at his father's Chevrolet dealership to a two-time Busch Grand National champion.

Budweiser signed on to underwrite his move to the Winston Cup ranks. Dale Jr. was edged for NASCAR's 2000 Rookie of the Year honors by Matt Kenseth. And he was racing toward a second-place finish in the 2001 Daytona 500 when his father was killed.

A copy of Dale Earnhardt's will and related documents, more than a hundred pages' worth, is on file in Iredell County's Superior Court. The clerk keeps the original documents in a safe, fearing it would otherwise be stolen and end up on the online auction site eBay. But its essence can be reduced to a few sentences. The seven-time champion bequeathed 100 percent of Dale Earnhardt Inc., the company that fielded his three NASCAR teams, to his wife, Teresa. He also left her the rights to his name and "Intimidator" persona, his Chevrolet dealership, all household possessions, numerous boats and vehicles, and his seats on the New York and Amex stock exchanges. A separate trust of undisclosed value was set up for other family members.

After his death, all of his children rallied to Teresa's side, particularly during her public battle to keep his autopsy photos private. She immediately took over the NASCAR race teams as well, and Dale Jr. professed his confidence that she could run the three-car operation without a hitch.

Things got off to an impressive start. A Dale Earnhardt Inc. car won the Daytona 500 twice (2003 and 2004). And Dale Jr. finished third in the points standings in 2003. But after that, the teams struggled. On the eve of the 2005 season, Teresa approved a swap of crew chiefs and cars between Dale Jr. and Michael Waltrip, a move neither driver had sought. It proved disastrous, with Dale Jr. failing to qualify for NASCAR's postseason. In the three years that followed, in fact, he would win only two races. Business associates complained privately about the lumbering pace of decision making, and the company lost the competitive edge it had enjoyed, particularly in building motors for NASCAR's two tracks that required the use of restrictor plates.

The high-stakes drama that unfolded trumped all other NASCAR story lines from the moment Dale Jr. answered Teresa's public criticism. First, he said he didn't appreciate it. Then, he disclosed that he had been seeking an ownership stake in Dale Earnhardt Inc. for some time but had been refused. During preseason testing at Daytona in January 2007, he revealed that he wanted a controlling interest in the company.

It was a multimillion-dollar power struggle, made more compelling by the family tension that simmered underneath. *Forbes* magazine had recently estimated the value of Dale Earnhardt Inc. at $57 million. Without Dale Jr., and the sponsorship money he brought to the table, the company's worth was projected to plunge more than 50 percent.

No NASCAR driver attracted more attention. Dale Jr. represented NASCAR's past, present, and future. He was stock-car racing's link to its most compelling figure. He was its runaway most popular driver, eliciting such thunderous applause that you could attend a race blindfolded and know the instant the No. 8 Chevy took the lead. NASCAR fans love to put black and white hats on the sport's leading figures. And if Internet chatter, trackside sentiment, and online polls were a gauge, Teresa was wearing the black hat in the eyes of more than 90 percent of fans, and Dale Jr., the white.

Other NASCAR drivers weighed in as negotiations dragged on. Kevin Harvick called Teresa a "deadbeat" owner for not coming to the racetrack to support her drivers and teams in the same way that his own car owner, Richard Childress, did, along with Rick Hendrick, Robert Yates, Chip Ganassi, Jack Roush, Bill Davis, and others. Tony Stewart questioned Teresa's judgment in not doing whatever it took to keep Dale Jr. with the team. "What is DEI without Junior?" Stewart said. "Nothing but a museum."

After yet another proposal to buy a majority stake in the company was rejected, Dale Jr. made the split official on May 10. In most major-league sports, career moves by high-profile athletes no longer shocked fans, generating fleeting interest only for their staggering dollar figures. But the abdication of Earnhardt Jr. from his father's team stunned many NASCAR insiders and fans, including Rusty Wallace, who felt sure the two would work things out given the sweat equity that Dale Earnhardt had invested in the company. "I was wrong about everything," Wallace said. "I told everybody, 'Don't worry! They'll work it out. He's not going to leave.' I thought he cared that much. But when you're not blood, that's huge. And Teresa and him aren't blood."

Dale Jr. took pains to say that his decision was made strictly for competitive reasons rather than personal ones. At thirty-two, he was growing impatient to win a NASCAR championship. (He didn't note the fact, but Jeff Gordon had won four NASCAR championships by that age.) And he had grown weary of his erratic results in recent years. "It is time for me to compete on a consistent basis and contend for championships," he told a capacity crowd of reporters and TV cameras during a press conference at the Mooresville, North Carolina, race shop he owned. "What team I'll drive for next season, I don't know. We'll see who wants to hire me."

No prospective signing in NASCAR history generated as much publicity. In most major newspapers, analysis of Dale Jr.'s decision dwarfed coverage of pole qualifying for the 2007 Indianapolis 500, which was held the following day. Two decades earlier, Indy's qualifying day had been regarded as the second most important day of the year in American motorsports.

• • •

From the outset, Dale Jr. made clear he wanted to continuing racing Chevrolets. He didn't care about the money he said; all he wanted was a chance to win. Eager suitors lined up, including Childress, who had fielded the Chevys that won six of his father's seven championships; and Washington Redskins coach Joe Gibbs, who had won three championships with drivers Tony Stewart and Bobby Labonte.

In June, Dale Jr. announced he was joining Hendrick Motorsports, NASCAR's most dominant team, in 2008. It was a brilliant deal for both. To make room in his four-car stable, car owner Rick Hendrick fired the gifted but abrasive Kyle Busch, who had disappointed the team repeatedly—most inexcusably by stalking away from the track after wrecking during a race that spring, despite the fact that his team was frantically repairing the damage so he could return to the track. Dale Jr., who had also crashed, hopped in and finished the race for him—a gesture whose irony became clear months later.

Many longtime Earnhardt fans choked on the notion that the Intimidator's son would now be a teammate of Jeff Gordon. But as Dale Jr. and Rick Hendrick sat beside each other on the stage that day in June to unveil their new partnership, it seemed right. They filled an unspoken void in each other's lives. Hendrick had lost his one son, Ricky, in a plane crash that killed ten team members a few years earlier. Dale Jr. had lost a father.

And a new round of speculation began: What would Dale Earnhardt have thought about Dale Jr.'s decision?

It was unknowable, of course, just as it had been impossible to know what Earnhardt was thinking as he rounded that last turn before his fatal crash at Daytona in 2001. Was he blocking to protect a third-place finish for himself? Or was he blocking to protect his son and his front-running driver Michael Waltrip?

I thought back to the ride I'd taken with Earnhardt to North Wilkesboro that day in 1993. At one point he got a call on his mobile phone from Dale Jr., who had forgotten a gear that he needed to qualify his late-model car that afternoon. Could his dad bring it?

Earnhardt hung up and started griping about his kids. But without a second's hesitation, he spun the big Chevy truck around and headed back to the shop to get what his son needed.

"They've got a long way to go to become real racers," Earnhardt groused that day, implicating all his grown children in the rant. "Real racers work hard! They don't sit around the house waiting for somebody to give 'em what they need. They don't sit around the garage. If they ain't got it, they figure out a way to get it."

Dale Earnhardt embodied the essence of NASCAR: the romantic notion that a man could improve his lot in life strictly on merit, grit, and courage. He was the original self-made man who believed not only in *being* a man, but also in being his *own* man. He also knew, as all racers did, that a racer's life is short, and that the most committed racers will do whatever it takes to get in a faster car, with a stronger engine and better crew. Real racers would do anything for a better shot at winning. Earnhardt had done it himself several times. Then he rejoined car owner Richard Childress in 1984, and they built a dynasty.

Some viewed what Dale Jr. did as turning his back on his father's legacy. To me, he had taken that first step toward becoming a real racer.

As his dad said, "If they ain't got it, they figure out a way to get it."

CONCLUSION

Humpy Wheeler, who has promoted NASCAR races for decades, likes to joke about what archaeologists of the future will think when they unearth Lowe's Motor Speedway, the massive oval just north of Charlotte, a few millennia from now. They'll find so many chicken bones strewn across the acreage that they'll have to call in cultural anthropologists to piece together just what went on there. Did they race chickens? Or were the people no bigger than chickens?

It's Wheeler's way of acknowledging that all things come to an end after they've served their purpose—including the speedway, which will be plowed under one day—so there's no point getting too attached.

I suspect a similar thing will happen after I'm gone, too. Whoever inherits the task of sorting through my possessions will come across a cardboard box in the basement, look inside, and wonder just what I was thinking in keeping this stuff. Among its contents:

An old yellow lug nut that came from Richard Petty's No. 43 Pontiac.

An unopened jar of Folgers coffee, which was a gift from Harry

Hyde, the old crew chief for Tim Richmond and the No. 25 Folgers Chevrolet.

A garage pass from the inaugural Brickyard 400 at Indianapolis Motor Speedway in 1994.

A factory-sealed box of forty-two Action Packed trading cards labeled "The Champ and the Challenger: Honoring Dale Earnhardt and Jeff Gordon."

A white, plastic ashtray with a red NASCAR Winston Cup Series logo.

A small vial of sand scooped from Daytona Beach.

And a black satin ribbon fashioned in a loop, fastened by a stick pin, worn by those at Earnhardt's memorial service on February 22, 2001.

I was an unlikely person to end up at the NASCAR races in 1991. But you learn what you need to know with every newspaper assignment. And along the way, you learn things you never planned on. I certainly never planned on caring about stock-car racing.

NASCAR was unlike other sports in so many obvious ways—the Technicolor explosion of cars, the bone-rattling noise, the singular smell, the thousands of fans screaming their vocal cords raw. But it differed in other respects, too. It wasn't a sport to the drivers and mechanics who worked so hard. It was an all-consuming calling, with all the joy and sorrow of life itself. NASCAR drivers helped one another in hard times. They fought over trophies whether winning paid a lot or a little. If they felt wronged, they cussed each other or threw a punch. The next day they made up and moved on. And when the time came, they attended one another's funerals.

They say Earnhardt's death made NASCAR better because it made racing safer. It did indeed. But for me, it left a sadness I could never explain. For months, I felt numb to everything around me. And inside, there was an emptiness as black as the car he drove.

Like NASCAR, Earnhardt's hometown of Kannapolis is trying to create something good from his legacy. Not long after losing its famous son, the town lost its textile mill and, with it, five thousand jobs. But a sprawling biotechnology research center is rising where the old brick smokestack stood. And the Kannapolis Convention and Visitors Bureau is courting tourists through what it's calling "The Dale Trail"—a self-guided tour along the town's main thoroughfare, which has been renamed Highway 3/Dale Earnhardt Boulevard. The trail passes Center Grove Lutheran Cemetery, where Ralph Earnhardt is buried, and leads to a nine-foot, nine-hundred-pound bronze statue of the seven-time champion in Dale Earnhardt Plaza.

In Randolph County, Petty Enterprises still struggles to stay competitive. Its teams have won only three races in the last twenty-four years. To catch up, Richard and Kyle Petty plan to move the race shop from Level Cross, its home for more than fifty years, closer to Charlotte, where the sport's top engineers and mechanics are based. They're also considering selling an ownership stake to a private investor. But the Petty's most lasting monument may be the one Kyle and his wife, Pattie, built in honor of their son Adam. It's the Victory Junction Gang Camp for disabled children, an idea Adam had before his death in 2000—a vibrant, joyful retreat in nearby Randleman for children whose hardships make the Pettys forget their own.

Farther west, the residents of North Wilkesboro still follow NASCAR even though their racetrack has been shuttered for more than a decade. Stock-car racing gave the town an identity. Now, the city fathers are trying to rebrand North Wilkesboro as the Homeplace of Americana Music—a tribute to the local bluegrass pioneer Doc Watson and his late son Merle. But it hasn't caught on like NASCAR. Losing the stock-car races destroyed the local economy worse than any tornado ever could.

The caretaker of the track lives in a double-wide trailer on the property, overlooking Highway 421. I knocked on his door one November day and told him Junior Johnson said I could take a look around. He grabbed a set of keys and trudged to the sagging gate and opened the padlock. "Don't step on anything wooden," he said. "It's rotten. And lock it behind you when you leave."

I'd been there many times, but seeing it again, I couldn't believe the track had ever hosted a major NASCAR race.

The frontstretch held only twenty rows of seats—seats that were nothing but rusted metal chairbacks welded to concrete bleachers. The wooden bleachers along the backstretch were falling in. Trees were growing between the rows, and the sign that read "Junior Johnson Grandstand" was in tatters.

I walked the track's asphalt, rutted with fissures. Weeds sprouted from the cracks. I closed my eyes and imagined all the grandstands and concession stands covered in a fresh coat of paint. The place still didn't rise above pitiful. Yet in its day, it hosted the wildest, most electrifying show in western North Carolina.

Suddenly I had an urge to steal something—a small keepsake I could put in my cardboard box in the basement. No one would know. And even if they found out, I'd be no worse than the county's own famous outlaws—Tom Dula, Otto Wood, and Junior Johnson himself. I scoured the grandstands, the track, and the infield, but there wasn't a thing to put in my pocket or pry off a wall. There were just paint chips and weeds. The track had been picked to the bone, a carcass in the sun.

I locked the gate behind me.

During the long drive home I thought about the country's love affair with the automobile. Did cars have such a hold on Americans because they symbolized running away from someplace? Or did they symbolize running *to* a place everyone dreamed of going? I tried thinking of as many songs about cars as I could, and I decided you could argue the case either way.

Still, NASCAR fit neither category. It was like baseball—a sport that ended up where it began, whether that place was home plate or the start–finish line.

So the point of racing, it seemed, wasn't the destination. It was the ride itself. It was the sheer exhilaration of hurtling into a corner with total commitment, as Mark Martin had shown me that day at Road Atlanta. Racing was the ultimate leap of faith, trusting the machine beneath you and every instinct inside you, even when you didn't know what was around the next turn.

NASCAR'S ALL-TIME
CHAMPIONS
1949–2007

YEAR	DRIVER	MAKE	WINNINGS
1949	Red Byron	Olds	$5,800
1950	Bill Rexford	Olds	6,175
1951	Herb Thomas	Hudson	18,200
1952	Tim Flock	Hudson	20,210
1953	Herb Thomas	Hudson	27,300
1954	Lee Petty	Chrysler	26,706
1955	Tim Flock	Chrysler	33,750
1956	Buck Baker	Chrysler	29,790
1957	Buck Baker	Chevrolet	24,712
1958	Lee Petty	Olds	20,600
1959	Lee Petty	Plymouth	45,570
1960	Rex White	Chevy	45,260
1961	Ned Jarrett	Chevy	27,285
1962	Joe Weatherly	Pontiac	56,110
1963	Joe Weatherly	Pontiac	58,110
1964	Richard Petty	Plymouth	98,810

YEAR	DRIVER	MAKE	WINNINGS
1965	Ned Jarrett	Ford	77,966
1966	David Pearson	Dodge	59,205
1967	Richard Petty	Plymouth	130,275
1968	David Pearson	Ford	118,842
1969	David Pearson	Ford	183,700
1970	Bobby Isaac	Dodge	121,470
1971	Richard Petty	Plymouth	309,225
1972	Richard Petty	Plymouth	227,015
1973	Benny Parsons	Chevrolet	114,345
1974	Richard Petty	Dodge	299,175
1975	Richard Petty	Dodge	378,865
1976	Cale Yarborough	Chevrolet	387,173
1977	Cale Yarborough	Chevrolet	477,499
1978	Cale Yarborough	Oldsmobile	530,751
1979	Richard Petty	Chevrolet	531,292
1980	Dale Earnhardt	Chevrolet	588,926
1981	Darrell Waltrip	Buick	693,342
1982	Darrell Waltrip	Buick	873,118
1983	Bobby Allison	Buick	828,355
1984	Terry Labonte	Chevrolet	713,010
1985	Darrell Waltrip	Chevrolet	1,318,735
1986	Dale Earnhardt	Chevrolet	1,783,880
1987	Dale Earnhardt	Chevrolet	2,099,243
1988	Bill Elliott	Ford	1,574,639
1989	Rusty Wallace	Pontiac	2,247,950
1990	Dale Earnhardt	Chevrolet	3,083,056
1991	Dale Earnhardt	Chevrolet	2,416,685
1992	Alan Kulwicki	Ford	2,322,561
1993	Dale Earnhardt	Chevrolet	3,353,789
1994	Dale Earnhardt	Chevrolet	3,300,733
1995	Jeff Gordon	Chevrolet	4,347,343

YEAR	DRIVER	MAKE	WINNINGS
1996	Terry Labonte	Chevrolet	3,991,348
1997	Jeff Gordon	Chevrolet	6,375,658
1998	Jeff Gordon	Chevrolet	9,306,584
1999	Dale Jarrett	Ford	6,649,596
2000	Bobby Labonte	Pontiac	7,361,386
2001	Jeff Gordon	Chevrolet	10,879,757
2002	Tony Stewart	Pontiac	9,163,761
2003	Matt Kenseth	Ford	9,422,764
2004	Kurt Busch	Ford	9,661,513
2005	Tony Stewart	Chevrolet	13,578,168
2006	Jimmie Johnson	Chevrolet	15,952,125
2007	Jimmie Johnson	Chevrolet	15,313,920

"ONE HELLUVA RIDE"

Key Events in NASCAR's Development

1947

DECEMBER 14: The National Association for Stock Car Auto Racing is conceived at a meeting convened by Bill France Sr. at the Streamline Hotel in Daytona Beach, Florida.

1948

FEBRUARY 15: Red Byron wins NASCAR's first race, on the beach-and-road course in Daytona.

1950

SEPTEMBER 4: Darlington (South Carolina) Raceway, NASCAR's first paved speedway, hosts the inaugural Southern 500, NASCAR's first 500-mile race. It lasts more than six hours.

1959

FEBRUARY 22: Daytona (Florida) International Speedway hosts the inaugural Daytona 500. Lee Petty is declared the winner by a two-foot margin sixty-one hours after the finish, following a review of news-reel footage by Bill France Sr.

1963

December 1: Wendell Scott of Danville, Virginia, becomes the first African American to win a race in NASCAR's top series, at Jacksonville (Florida) Speedway.

1964

July 2: Fireball Roberts dies thirty-nine days after a fiery crash in the World 600 at Charlotte Motor Speedway.

November 8: Richard Petty wins the first of his seven championships.

1965

Firestone introduces the fuel cell in response to fire-related deaths the previous year.

1966

October 2: Junior Johnson retires as a driver after running his last race at North Wilkesboro (North Carolina) Speedway.

1969

September 14: Alabama International Speedway (later renamed Talladega Superspeedway) opens as the largest oval on the NASCAR circuit, at 2.66 miles. Top drivers boycott the inaugural race over safety concerns.

1971

R.J. Reynolds becomes title sponsor of NASCAR's top series, which is renamed the NASCAR Winston Cup Grand National Division.

1972

JANUARY 10: Bill France Jr. takes NASCAR's reins from his father, founder Big Bill France. The sport's schedule is trimmed from forty-eight to thirty-one races, marking advent of the "modern era."

1977

FEBRUARY 20: Janet Guthrie, thirty-eight, becomes the first woman to compete in the Daytona 500. She finishes twelfth in the Kelly Girl Chevrolet.

1979

FEBRUARY 18: CBS airs the first flag-to-flag coverage of a NASCAR race, the Daytona 500. Richard Petty sails past for the victory as Cale Yarborough and Donnie Allison tangle on the last lap, then brawl in the infield, joined by Bobby Allison.

NOVEMBER 18: Richard Petty wins his record seventh championship.

1983

NOVEMBER 20: After more than twenty years of trying, Bobby Allison, forty-five, wins a NASCAR championship.

1985

SEPTEMBER 1: Bill Elliott claims R.J. Reynolds's $1 million bonus for winning three of the season's four major races: the Daytona 500, Talladega's Winston 500, and Darlington's Southern 500.

1987

APRIL 30: Bill Elliott runs the fastest lap in NASCAR history, 212.809 miles per hour, at Talladega Superspeedway.

MAY 3: Bobby Allison's Buick gets airborne and crashes into the frontstretch fence at Talladega. NASCAR responds by mandating carburetor restrictor plates to keep speeds below 200 miles per hour at its two biggest tracks, Daytona and Talladega.

1988

FEBRUARY 14: Bobby Allison and son Davey finish first and second, respectively, in the Daytona 500.

JUNE 19: Bobby Allison suffers career-ending injuries in a crash at Pocono Raceway.

1992

MAY 16: Charlotte Motor Speedway becomes the first 1.5-mile oval to stage a night race under the lights, The Winston, which ends with Davey Allison taking the checkered flag as he loses control of his Ford battling with Kyle Petty.

JUNE 7: NASCAR founder Bill France Sr. dies at eighty-two.

NOVEMBER 15: In the season finale at Atlanta Motor Speedway, Richard Petty retires after thirty-five years and two hundred victories, Wisconsin's Alan Kulwicki wins the championship in a Ford he owns himself, and twenty-one-year-old Jeff Gordon makes his Winston Cup debut.

1993

APRIL 1: 1992 NASCAR champion Alan Kulwicki, thirty-eight, is killed in a plane crash en route to Bristol (Tennessee) Motor Speedway.

JULY 13: Second-generation driver Davey Allison, thirty-two, dies of injuries suffered when the helicopter he is piloting crashes in the infield of Talladega (Alabama) Superspeedway.

1994

AUGUST 6: NASCAR holds its first race at Indianapolis Motor Speedway. Jeff Gordon wins the inaugural Brickyard 400.

OCTOBER 23: Dale Earnhardt clinches his seventh championship to match Richard Petty's record, at North Carolina Motor Speedway in Rockingham with three weeks left in the season.

1995

FEBRUARY 24: Speedway Motorsports Inc. goes public and sets off a trend of racetrack expansion, construction, and acquisition.

NOVEMBER 12: Jeff Gordon edges Earnhardt by 34 points for his first championship after squandering a 205-point lead.

1996

SEPTEMBER 29: North Wilkesboro (North Carolina) Speedway hosts its final Winston Cup race. Jeff Gordon wins.

NOVEMBER 24: NASCAR holds the first of three demonstration races in Japan. Rusty Wallace wins.

1997

FEBRUARY 16: Jeff Gordon leads a 1-2-3 Hendrick Motorsports finish in the Daytona 500. Two new tracks in major TV markets join the Winston Cup schedule: Texas Motor Speedway (April 6) and California Speedway (June 22). Jeff Burton and Jeff Gordon, respectively, win the inaugural races.

NOVEMBER 16: Jeff Gordon, twenty-six, clinches his second championship, becoming NASCAR's youngest two-time champion.

1998

FEBRUARY 15: Dale Earnhardt wins the Daytona 500 on his twentieth attempt.

NOVEMBER 8: Jeff Gordon finishes the season with thirteen victories, $9.3 million in winnings, and his third Winston Cup championship.

1999

FEBRUARY 9: Charlotte Motor Speedway becomes the first NASCAR track to sell its naming rights, to Lowe's home-improvements chain, for a reported $35 million over ten years.

FEBRUARY 10: Bill France hands NASCAR's day-to-day operations to Mike Helton, marking the first time someone outside the France family has controlled the sport.

NOVEMBER 11: NASCAR announces the signing of its first national TV deal. The six-year pact with Fox, NBC, and Turner Sports is reportedly worth $2.4 billion and takes effect in 2001.

2000

APRIL 2: Fourth-generation racer Adam Petty makes his Winston Cup debut and Dale Earnhardt Jr. wins his first Winston Cup race, at Texas Motor Speedway.

MAY 12: Adam Petty, nineteen, is killed in a crash during practice at New Hampshire International Speedway.

JULY 7: Kenny Irwin, thirty, NASCAR's 1998 Rookie of the Year, is killed in a crash during practice in the same turn at New Hampshire where Adam Petty died.

OCTOBER 14: Tony Roper, thirty-five, dies of injuries suffered the previous day in a crash during a NASCAR truck race at Texas Motor Speedway.

NOVEMBER 28: Mike Helton becomes NASCAR's third president.

2001

FEBRUARY 18: Dale Earnhardt, forty-nine, is killed in a last-lap crash in the Daytona 500. He is the fourth NASCAR driver to die in ten months, and his death prompts widespread mourning and an unprecedented examination of safety measures in the sport.

OCTOBER 4: Blaise Alexander, twenty-five, is killed during an ARCA race at Lowe's Motor Speedway. His death convinces NASCAR to mandate the use of head-and-neck restraints by its drivers.

2003

JANUARY 21: NASCAR's Research and Development Center, a $10-million facility dedicated to safety initiatives, is unveiled in Concord, North Carolina.

JUNE 19: NASCAR announces that Nextel will replace R.J. Reynolds as sponsor of its top series, under a ten-year deal worth a reported $750 million, beginning in 2004.

SEPTEMBER 13: Brian Z. France becomes NASCAR's new chairman of the board and CEO, succeeding his father, Bill France Jr.

NOVEMBER 16: Matt Kenseth gives Roush Racing its first Winston Cup championship. The fact that he clinches the title by winning only one race plays a role in the decision to revamp NASCAR championship formula.

2004

Stock-car racing's top division is renamed the NASCAR Nextel Cup Series.

JANUARY 20: Brian France unveils a new format for crowning the season's champion, based on a ten-race postseason and known as the Chase for the NASCAR Nextel Cup.

FEBRUARY 13: Toyota debuts NASCAR's Truck series, fielding the Tundra.

FEBRUARY 22: North Carolina Motor Speedway hosts its final NASCAR race.

JUNE 16: Kyle and Pattie Petty open Victory Junction Gang Camp in Randleman, North Carolina, in honor of their son Adam.

NOVEMBER 14: Darlington (South Carolina) Raceway hosts its final NASCAR event. Jimmie Johnson wins the last Southern 500.

2005

MARCH 6: NASCAR's Busch Series holds its first points race on foreign soil, at the Autodromo Rodriguez Hernandez road course in Mexico City.

NOVEMBER 20: Tony Stewart clinches his second NASCAR championship and collects record winnings of $13.6 million for the season.

2006

NOVEMBER 19: Colombia's Juan Pablo Montoya makes his Nextel Cup debut at Homestead-Miami Speedway. He finishes thirty-fourth after his Dodge hits the wall and bursts into flames.

2007

FEBRUARY 14: Michael Waltrip cheating scandal on the eve of the Daytona 500 mars the debut of Toyota's Camry as the first foreign nameplate to compete full-time in NASCAR's top series.

MARCH 25: NASCAR's redesigned, winged car, the so-called Car of Tomorrow, makes its competitive debut at Bristol (Tennessee) Motor Speedway. Kyle Busch wins the race and says the car "sucks."

APRIL 29: On what would have been Dale Earnhardt's fifty-sixth birthday, Jeff Gordon passes him for career wins at Talladega Superspeedway by winning his seventy-seventh race.

JUNE 4: Bill France Jr., seventy-four, dies after a long battle with cancer.

JUNE 13: One month after announcing he would leave Dale Earnhardt Inc., the team founded by his late father, at season's end, Dale Jr. announces he has signed a five-year deal to race for Hendrick Motorsports.

JUNE 24: Rookie Juan Pablo Montoya wins his first Nextel Cup race in his seventeenth start, at Infineon Raceway in Sonoma, California.

AUGUST 4: NASCAR's Busch Series holds its first points race in Canada, at the Circuit Gilles Villeneuve road course in Montreal.

NOVEMBER 18: Jimmie Johnson wins the final Nextel Cup championship; NASCAR's top series will be renamed the Sprint Cup in 2008.

ACKNOWLEDGMENTS

So many professional athletes and sports executives regard their playing fields as exclusive domains, and they telegraph the fact that outsiders—particularly reporters—aren't welcome in innumerable ways. But in seventeen years prowling NASCAR's speedways and garages, I can name only one instance in which someone in racing made me feel that way.

That attitude, as well as the uncommon accessibility of NASCAR drivers, is gradually disappearing from auto racing, as it has from so many sports. But I am fortunate to have arrived when it was the norm, and I am indebted to those who still see merit in explaining the sport, shedding light on issues of the day, and lifting a veil on the personalities at play.

This book isn't so much a product of a barrage of interviews as it is the result of years spent watching, listening, asking, and musing about stock-car racing. As a result, a proper list of those who had a hand in its pages would be longer than the book itself.

But I must begin with Jill Schwartzman, my editor at Random

House, whose e-mail set the idea in motion and whose diligence and enthusiasm carried it to completion.

I am profoundly grateful to Sally Jenkins, the *Washington Post's* wonderful columnist, whose generosity helped me begin. And I am especially thankful to Esther Newberg at ICM for taking a chance on a first-time author.

My colleague Bill Gildea, whose keen ear for language is eclipsed only by his kind heart, told me at the outset that any story about NASCAR had to "start in the dirt." It was my good fortune that so many racers whose careers started precisely there, Junior Johnson chief among them, are uncommonly insightful about the sport's past and willing to share it.

And on that count, my regard and appreciation for Richard and Kyle Petty are immeasurable. Their family history is inextricable from NASCAR's, yet neither regards the sport as his own but rather something that belongs to everyone.

From the first day I went to a racetrack, Humpy Wheeler, president of what's now Lowe's Motor Speedway, was there to decode stock-car racing's idiosyncratic rulebook and singular culture. Max Muhleman, a distinguished journalist before launching a sports-marketing career that transformed Charlotte, North Carolina, broadened my understanding of stock-car racing in similar fashion. And numerous promoters filled in blanks along the way, including Eddie Gossage of Texas Motor Speedway, Jeff Byrd and Wayne Estes of Bristol Motor Speedway, and Chris Powell of Las Vegas Motor Speedway.

The same is true of stock-car racing's public relations and marketing people, who I consider the most capable in sports. I owe a special debt to the late Ray Cooper, and to Kevin Triplett, Dan Zacharias, Nancy Wager, Marc Spiegel, Denny Darnell, George McNeilly, Andy Hall, Mike Zizzo, Andrew Booth, and Scott Cooper.

Among the sages in the NASCAR garage who consistently found time for my questions are Kirk Shelmerdine and Ray Evernham. I also owe thanks to the late Harry Hyde, and to Rick Hendrick, Felix

Sabates, Rusty Wallace, Don Miller, Ken Schrader, Kasey Kahne, Bobby and Judy Allison, Mike and Angie Skinner, John Bickford, Kathleen Hessert, Ken Barbee, Ken Welbourn, Wanda Goddard, Myra Faulkenbury, Sheila Coleman, and Ann Eaton.

In NASCAR's corporate offices I am grateful to Brian France, Jim Hunter, Robin Pemberton, Ramsey Poston, Dick Glover, Herb Branham, Brett Bodine, Tracey Judd, and Laz Benitez.

That said, there is no more lively place to gain insight into NASCAR than the press box, alternately caustic and uproarious. I count myself lucky to have plugged in my laptop and soaked up the wisdom of countless colleagues over the years, including Tom Higgins, Steve Waid, Deb Williams, Chris Economaki, Ben White, Mike Hembree, Larry Woody, Sandy McKee, David Poole, Monte Dutton, Ed Hinton, Mike Harris, Dustin Long, and Claire B. Lang.

Since 1998 I've had the great privilege of working at the *Washington Post*. The *Post's* Emilio Garcia-Ruiz allowed me to pursue this book, and editors Matt Rennie and Tracee Hamilton graciously adjusted their schedules and mine to make it possible. I am also grateful to former bosses George Solomon, Dave Smith, Monte Lorell, and Steve Ballard.

At Villard/Random House, I owe thanks to Libby McGuire, Jack Perry, Tom Nevins, Brian McLendon, Sarina Evan, Penny Haynes, Sarajane Herman, Rachel Bernstein, and Becca Shapiro.

This book never would have been written without Gary Schwab, projects editor of the *Charlotte Observer*, who supplied guidance and courage at every turn; researcher Julie Tate, for her resourcefulness and good humor; Bill Gildea, who read and improved each page; and photographer Mark Sluder, who taught me many years ago to get my nose out of a notebook and watch the sport around me. Finally, I extend warm thanks to my friends Kathleen McClain, Kathy Orton, and Chris Stacey. And to my parents, Bill Clarke and Martha Stephenson, and my brother, Bill, boundless gratitude for their support and patience throughout.

INDEX

About the Author

A sportswriter for the *Washington Post,* Liz Clarke has covered NASCAR for the *Charlotte Observer, Dallas Morning News, USA Today,* and the *Post,* and was twice honored with the Russ Catlin Award for Excellence in Motorsports Journalism (1996 and 2003). She spent four seasons as a *Post* beat writer on the Washington Redskins and has written extensively about the Olympics, tennis, and college sports.

A graduate of Barnard College, she lives in Washington, D.C., with her beloved Lab, Rusty.

About the Type

This book was set in Bembo, a typeface based on an old-style Roman face that was used for Cardinal Bembo's tract *De Aetna* in 1495. Bembo was cut by Francisco Griffo in the early sixteenth century. The Lanston Monotype Company of Philadelphia brought the well-proportioned letterforms of Bembo to the United States in the 1930s.